*AMERICAN
INTELLECTUAL
HISTORIES AND
HISTORIANS*

AMERICAN INTELLECTUAL HISTORIES AND HISTORIANS

ROBERT ALLEN SKOTHEIM

PRINCETON, NEW JERSEY

PRINCETON UNIVERSITY PRESS

1966

TO NADINE

Preface

WHAT follows is not intended to be a definitive investigation of all the problems and achievements of Americans who have dealt with their country's intellectual past. Such a definitive work would treat all those American historical works which have been concerned with thought; it would discuss them with respect to the methods and uses of evidence by a developing craft of writing specialized histories of ideas, and it would assess their strengths and weaknesses from a standpoint of present day knowledge; finally, it would relate the histories to the "climates of opinion" in which they were written, viewing the histories themselves as documents of the history of ideas. A book done in this complete fashion might need no prefatory statement of limitations.

This slender volume, however, does not do the things indicated above definitively, but only selectively. I have attempted to sketch the nature of American historians' interest in ideas in America, insofar as this interest has been expressed in their published writings. Most attention is directed to scholars of this century, and in particular, to academic historians, since it is they who have most often written intellectual histories or, what I generally refer to for the sake of clarity as histories of ideas. The writings of the last 100 years which have been selected for treatment are viewed partly from the perspective of an emerging specialty—the writing of histories of ideas. Certain recurrent problems of method and characteristic themes of interpretation are selected for discussion, but no attempt is made to assess the accuracy or inaccuracy of the histories. There is no intention to construct the "Compleat Guide to Writing Histories of Ideas." Such a purpose is beyond the book's scope and exceeds the author's knowledge.

There is, however, analysis of certain problems in the writing of histories of ideas as a separate specialty, and there is considerable treatment of the ideological positions, or the social thought, of the various historians of ideas discussed. Carl Becker's conception of written histories as themselves documents in the history of ideas, because of their expression of the climates of opinion in which they were composed, is to this extent accepted.

Because a good deal is said in the book concerning the climates of opinion in which modern histories have been written, it may be worthwhile suggesting the perspective from which this study was made. I am a young (born in 1933) member of a university history department, holding attitudes toward ideological questions and problems of historical method which are not greatly different from those of most of the younger and middle-aged academic historians discussed in the concluding chapter. This means that the ideological and methodological disputes of the first half of the twentieth century were those of my elders rather than of my own generation. I therefore take it for granted, as do most members of younger generations, that it is more important to make a viable synthesis of formerly opposing intellectual views than to perpetuate the differences intact. The most basic problem of method for historians of ideas today seems to me, as it seems to most historians who came of age after the pioneering classics from Beard to Curti, to be that of taking ideas seriously and describing them precisely without losing sight of their environmental relationships. The most elementary ideological or public policy problem, and again I think

I am quite typical in saying this, appears to be the articulation of ethical standards in a world increasingly governed by cold war considerations. Like most younger and middle-aged professional historians in the United States, my conception of the public good is derived in large part from American reform traditions, and to that extent I am a child of progressivism. But, like most who matured in the era of totalitarianism, my progressivism has been modified by reactions to totalitarianism which have ramifications for our views of human nature and of social progress through planning. All this, of course, is only to indicate that, like any other historian young or old, I have a relationship to the subject investigated in the book.

Throughout, the perspective is that of a member of the history guild, even if a young one, rather than the perspective of, say, a philosopher or sociologist. For better or worse, therefore, the book perpetuates many of the characteristics of the writings which are discussed. A philosopher, for instance, might insist upon greater analysis of definitions and ideas, and a sociologist might show more impatience with the failure of historians to quantify and to provide evidence for statements concerning the holding of opinions. This book about historians, then, is written by an insider rather than by an outsider. Nevertheless, I do conclude, as can be seen in the book's final paragraphs, by questioning whether the characteristic approach of American historians of ideas might not result in their disappearance and their replacement by topic specialists. These specialists will write about ideas as one part of their field, be it the ante-bellum South, patterns of urbanization, or political reform movements. In other words, American historians today seem to attach more importance to ideas in history than to histories of ideas. But, despite some present questioning of the history of ideas as a separate scholarly entity, there was in the past and there remains today the belief that histories of ideas can justifiably be written. That belief is the subject of this book.

I gratefully acknowledge the intellectual guidance and personal encouragement of several teachers, colleagues, and friends, including especially: W. Stull Holt, who suggested and supervised the study in its original form as a doctoral dissertation; Thomas J. Pressly, whose *Americans Interpret Their Civil War* was a model for my study; John Higham, who graciously extended help to a novice in a field Higham knew so well; Lee Benson, who stimulated my historiographical interest through conversations; and Kermit Vanderbilt, who generously contributed to my analysis of Vernon Louis Parrington. I also wish to thank Alfred H. Kelly, chairman of the History Department, Wayne State University, for providing me sufficient freedom from teaching duties to facilitate completion of the manuscript. Finally, I would like to thank Eve Hanle and Marjorie Putney of the Princeton University Press.

The first section of Chapter Three appeared in a somewhat different form as "Vernon Louis Parrington: The Mind and Art of a Historian of Ideas," in the *Pacific Northwest Quarterly*, LIII (July 1962), 100-113. I thank the editor of that journal for permission to incorporate the article.

Detroit, Michigan R.A.S.
June 1965

Contents

AMERICAN
INTELLECTUAL
HISTORIES AND
HISTORIANS

TREATMENT OF IDEAS IN
THE EARLY WRITINGS

THERE is probably no aspect of historical writing which concerns such vague and elusive subject matter as histories of men's thoughts. "Writing intellectual history," the political historian William Hesseltine once grumbled, "is like trying to nail jelly to the wall." There is more than a little truth to the charge. For how exactly is the historian to approach the gelatinous part of man's past which we call his ideas? There is no agreement in historians' answers to the difficult question. Intellectual histories, or what this study will often call histories of ideas, have investigated all kinds of intellectual activities, from formal philosophies to works of art, to short-lived opinions on transitory public issues. Some ideas described by historians therefore are the rarefied creations of isolated genius, working apart from the surrounding society. But other ideas, devoid of intellectual abstraction, are so obviously part of the everyday pressures of life that they almost merge into general behavior. Is the historian then to be a chronicler of the abstract thought of great men? Or is he to be a George Gallup of past opinion on public issues?

As this already suggests, it is not only a question of the historian's source material, but also of his methods of analysis. Does he study his chosen ideas intensively as if they had intrinsic importance and interest? If so, the historian might analyze the internal structure, the tensions, the intellectual progenitors, and the legacies of the thought. Or does the significance of the ideas stem only from their relation to other and less cerebral aspects of man's behavior? In this case, perhaps the historian will be most interested in the extent to which ideas "mirror" society.

To mention different relationships between ideas and the societies in which they exist is to suggest the most serious question facing the intellectual historian. Do ideas play a causal role in human affairs? Are they mere reflections of a more "real" economic, political, and social world? Or does thought itself create that world? Our common sense may say that in this case, as in the others, truth lies somewhere in between the extremes—but where? And is the blend of environmental influence and the independent power of thought always the same, or does that blend vary? As the questions mount, one hears in the background Hesseltine's reply that the jelly will not survive our attempts to nail it to the wall.

Despite the criticisms expressed, or, more frequently left unsaid, by American historians who are not altogether convinced of the worth of histories of ideas, students of thought have made their specialty an increasingly popular one. The popularity is not to be found in essays giving theoretical answers to the problems and criticisms raised by the new specialty. Such essays until recently hardly existed. This increasing popularity is evidenced by the countless books, articles, and university courses which in general ignore the theoretical problems and proceed to recount the history of ideas in the United States.[1] To write and teach history, rather than to discourse upon the difficulties of doing so, has been the

[1] For evidence pertaining to the increased popularity of the history of ideas, see Appendix A.

American historian's motto. Americans have not been completely oblivious to the problems of studying ideas in their country's past, but neither in this area nor in other areas of their historical writings have they expressed particular interest in what they have regarded as "theoretical" or "analytical" matters.

From the time of the earliest American chronicles, an active desire to tell what happened has prevailed over a more philosophical perusal of the theoretical problems of historical analysis. The traditional conception of the meaning of history has not been significantly different from the common sense of the community at large, or at least that part of the community which writers have represented. This has been true from the beginning. The voice of everyday judgment never spoke more loudly than in Puritan New England chronicles. Writers of these seventeenth century accounts were usually leading citizens of their colonies, acting as record keepers and defenders of the faith. They reflected the concerns of their colonies and dealt primarily with the hazards of hunger, Indians, religious heresy, and political disorganization.

The conception of the role of ideas in human affairs which was expressed in Puritan histories mirrored what the colonists took to be the common sense of the matter. New England was developed in accordance with righteous ideas, and in opposition to ideas born in evil. God directed the entire drama between the holy and the unholy, to be sure, but nonetheless the players were attempting to adhere to good and to shun evil. It was in this sense that New Englanders, as Richard Dunn has said, saw their history "as an idea in action."[2] Thus, regardless of the fact that Puritan writers were more

[2] "Seventeenth Century Historians of America," in James Morton Smith, ed., *Seventeenth Century America: Essays in Colonial History*, Chapel Hill, 1959, p. 196.

like local annalists than later specialists in the history of thought, it should be noted that these seventeenth century writers paid special attention to certain ideas.

To these religious ideas which they singled out, the chroniclers attributed great causal power. The beliefs comprising Puritanism were assumed to affect human behavior decisively. Original emigration from Europe to New England, for example, was interpreted by seventeenth century chroniclers at Plymouth and Massachusetts Bay as a direct result of conflicts over religious views. The Pilgrims, who went eventually to Plymouth colony, left England, William Bradford (1590-1657) wrote, because of a "bitter warr of contention and persecution about the ceremonies, and servise-book, and other popish and antichristian stuffe."[3] Future Massachusetts Bay colony Puritans too, according to Edward Johnson (1598-1672), were opposed to the doctrines of the "irreligious, lascivious and popish affected persons" in England who participated "in vaine Idolatrous Ceremonies," and who thought heaven could be reached by good works alone.[4] The assumption in these two statements explaining why emigration occurred is that certain religious beliefs in the minds of men caused historical events to occur. The same assumption is reflected in histories written later in the 1600's. William Hubbard (1621-1703), giving the reasons for emigration to Massachusetts Bay, asserted that "the chiefest intentions and aims of those that managed the business were to promote religion, and if it might be, to propagate the Gospel, in this dark corner of the world."[5] At the end

[3] William T. Davis, ed., *Bradford's History of Plymouth Plantation 1606-1646*, New York, 1952, p. 25.

[4] J. Franklin Jameson, ed., *Edward Johnson's Wonder-working Providence of Sions Saviour in New England, 1628-1651*, New York, 1959, p. 23.

[5] William Hubbard, *A General History of New England from the Discovery to MDCLXXX*, Massachusetts Historical Society

of the century, Cotton Mather (1663-1728) repeated the declaration that "the sole end" of settling the Plymouth and Bay colonies was to "plant the gospel in these dark regions of America."[6] The attitude which these quotations express is a familiar one, as most later historians have followed the chroniclers in emphasizing the influence of religious opinions in early New England settlement. What needs to be stressed is that the familiar attitude implies a crucial temporal role for at least some ideas in history, irrespective of the role of ultimate responsibility accorded God.

Original emigration from the Old World to the New was not the only result of beliefs associated with Puritanism, according to seventeenth century chronicles of New England. The development of the colonial communities after initial settlement also was interpreted as being largely dependent upon religious ideas. The reason that heresy in the Bay colony had to be located and expelled, the chroniclers said, was that bad religious beliefs would lead to a colony which behaved badly. It was assumed that actions followed thoughts. Therefore, John Winthrop (1588-1649) characterized Anne Hutchinson's religious opinions as dangerous not merely because they were theologically unorthodox, but because he took for granted that unorthodox theology threatened the social order of the Bay colony in the early 1600's. As Winthrop told it, Anne Hutchinson unleashed an anarchy of emotional individualism by holding that "the person of the Holy Ghost dwells in a justified person," and she encouraged social upheaval against the ruling saints by holding that "no sanctifica-

---

Collections, Second Series, Vols. 5, 6, Boston, 1848, Vol. 5, pp. 115-116.

[6] Cotton Mather, *Magnalia Christi Americana*, 2 vols., Hartford, 1855, Vol. 1, p. 45.

tion can help to evidence to us our justification."[7] Winthrop detected a threat to the community's stability in her minimization of the importance of worldly status, hierarchy, and government. Because he assumed that ideas had consequences, he was convinced that heresy had to be uprooted.

The same assumption appeared in the other chroniclers' accounts of Hutchinsonian doctrines. Edward Johnson declared that they threatened the social order by denigrating good works so far as to deny "the Morral Law to be the Rule of Christ."[8] William Hubbard echoed Johnson and Winthrop, asserting that the assault on earthly status and works challenged communal authority and stability:

> These erroneous notions [Hubbard wrote of Anne Hutchinson's ideas] inspired many of the place also with a strange kind of seditious and turbulent spirit, and that upon every occasion they were ready to challenge all, that did not run with them, to be legal Christians, and under a covenant of works. Under the veil of this pretence men of corrupt minds and haughty spirits secretly sowed seeds of division and schism in the country, and were ready to mutiny against the civil authority.[9]

Cotton Mather too assumed that heretical ideas such as those propagated by Anne Hutchinson seriously threatened the texture of the Bay colony. Hutchinsonians argued, according to Mather, that the most important evidence of an individual's justification was " 'the spirit of God by a powerful application of a promise,' begetting in us, and revealing to us a powerful *assurance* of

[7] James Kendall Hosmer, ed., *Winthrop's Journal 1630-1649*, 2 vols., New York, 1908, Vol. 1, p. 195.

[8] *Edward Johnson's Wonder-working Providence*, p. 31.

[9] Hubbard, *General History of New England*, pp. 281-282.

our being *justified*."[10] Mather agreed with the Orthodox that this heresy opened the door "for new *enthu-
siastical revelations*," for the "neglect" of worldly virtues, and for "subversion to all the peaceable order in
the colonies."[11]

Musty theological quarrels such as this may seem
to the modern reader to offer the choice of Tweedle-
dum and Tweedledee, but the importance of the disputes
to seventeenth century writers reflected the chroniclers'
assumption that certain ideas made history. It is this
assumption which makes their writings relevant to the
later appearance of intellectual histories in the United
States. Mather, like Hubbard, Johnson, and Winthrop,
viewed religious beliefs as crucial factors in determining the development of colonial society after original
settlement, just as all seventeenth century chroniclers
interpreted emigration from England as a direct result
of religious ideas. And though Providence was held ultimately responsible even for the ideas men held, the
ideas themselves were crucial determinants on earth.
Ordinarily God did not appear in the pages of the chronicles as an immediate, temporal causal force. Instead,
as a rule, men acted independently upon their beliefs.

The attention paid Puritanism in seventeenth century
writings was repeated in the following century's histories. Puritan ideas continued to be held responsible
for original European emigration to New England, and
for the early development of society there. But a new
idea, or group of ideas, which appeared in the colonies
during and after the 1600's began to receive joint emphasis along with Puritanism in eighteenth century historical writings—religious toleration. The growing belief
in toleration was added to Puritanism as another idea
which influenced American history. The eighteenth cen-

[10] Mather, *Magnalia*, Vol. 1, p. 508.
[11] *Ibid.*, pp. 508-509.

tury writers who first described the development of tolerance did not deny the earlier causal significance of Puritan doctrines, but rather moved chronologically from the original importance of Puritanism to the later rise of toleration.

Religious toleration provided the foundation for Rhode Island, according to John Callender (1706-1748), just as religious Puritanism was the basis for first New England settlement. "Liberty of conscience was the basis of this Colony," wrote Callender of Rhode Island: "Our fathers thought it just and necessary to allow each other mutually to worship God as their consciences were respectively persuaded. They thought no man had power over the spirit of God, and that the duty of the magistrate was to leave every one to follow the light of his conscience."[12] Rhode Island's dedication to the principle of toleration was also emphasized by Isaac Backus (1724-1806), in his account of New England and the Baptists, whose growth he equated with the success of tolerance.[13] These eighteenth century allegations of the influence of belief in toleration extended to a new idea the same assumption customarily made earlier concerning belief in Puritanism. Certain ideas made history. Writers during the 1700's, however, went no further than did their predecessors in making general statements concerning the influence of thought. They did not indicate, for example, whether they thought that the power of religious ideas in the 1600's was indicative of the pervasive significance of human

[12] John Callender, *An Historical Discourse on the Civil and Religious Affairs of the Colony of Rhode-Island*, Collections of the Rhode Island Historical Society, Vol. 4, Providence, 1838, p. 159.

[13] Isaac Backus, *A History of New England with Particular References to the . . . Baptists*, Backus Historical Society, 2 vols., Newton, Mass., 1871, originally published in three volumes in 1777, 1784, 1796.

opinions in history. Nor did they indicate whether special circumstances were responsible for the successes of Puritanism and toleration, circumstances which controlled the power of the ideas. Nor, again, did the eighteenth century writers any more than the seventeenth century writers, analyze in detail the components of the ideas to which they ascribed such strength. American colonists simply made the common-sense assumption that certain ideas had had important consequences in the history of the colonies.

The two triumphs of human thought—New England's Zion in the Wilderness and the rise of toleration —were brought together by Benjamin Trumbull (1735-1820) in his history of New England which featured Connecticut. "The settlement of New-England, purely for the purposes of Religion, and the propagation of civil and religious liberty," he wrote, "is an event which has no parallel in the history of modern ages." He continued: "The happy and extensive consequences of the settlements which they made, and of the sentiments which they were careful to propagate, to their posterity, to the church and to the world, admit of no description." Enthusiastically, he concluded that "they are still increasing, spreading wider and wider, and appear more and more important."[14]

Few chronicles were written outside of New England during the seventeenth century. During the eighteenth century, however, other authors on occasion contributed to the celebration of the power of ideas. Robert Proud (1728-1813), writing of Pennsylvania and the Quakers, told of the "oppression, persecution and big-

[14] Benjamin Trumbull, *A Complete History of Connecticut: Civil and Ecclesiastical from the Emigration of its First Planters, from England in the Year 1630, to the Year 1764: and to the Close of the Indian Wars*, 2 vols., New London, Conn., 1898, Vol. 1, p. 1. Vol. 1 was originally published in 1797, Vols. 1 and 2, in 1818.

otry," which the Quaker views provoked in England and in the original colonies. It was for the "restoration and enjoyment of those natural and civil rights and privileges," Proud explained, that "the predecessors of the present inhabitants of *Pennsylvania*, at first, peaceably withdrew into this retirement."[15] Proud, the Quaker, Callender and Backus, the Baptists, and Trumbull, the Congregationalist, were all in agreement that religious ideas caused the settlement of the New World, and that the idea of religious diversity was crucial to the development of the colonies in the late 1600's and 1700's.

As soon as the American Revolution worked its way into historical narratives, the great causal influence attributed to ideas associated with Puritanism and with the rise of freedom of conscience came to be attributed to a third allegedly powerful idea, or group of ideas, namely, those beliefs declared to be responsible for American independence.

Isaac Backus, who had not finished his last volume on New England and the Baptists until the Revolution was over, added the newly powerful idea of American political liberty to the older idea of religious liberty which he had discussed earlier in his narrative. Just as New World immigrants originally sought freedom from English tyranny in the seventeenth century, just as the principles of tolerance rose to combat intolerance in the colonies after settlement, so the idea of independence grew to throw off English secular control.[16]

The merging of the allegations concerning the power of human ideas in the three events—colonial settlement, rise of toleration, and Revolution—was also expressed

[15] Robert Proud, *The History of Pennsylvania in North America*, 2 vols., Philadelphia, 1797, 1798, Vol. 1, pp. 15, 5.
[16] Isaac Backus, *A History of New England with Particular Reference to the . . . Baptists*, Chapters 23-24.

by Jeremy Belknap (1744-1789), in his history of New Hampshire. Belknap, like all previous commentators on the founding of New England, accepted the immigrants' profession that "their principal design was to erect churches on the primitive model."[17] His assumption as to the power of ideas was implicit as he traced the rise of toleration:

> It is melancholy to observe what mischiefs were caused by the want of a just distinction between civil and ecclesiastical powers, and by that absurd zeal for uniformity, which kept the nation in a long ferment, and at length burst out into a blaze, the fury of which was never thoroughly quelled till the happy genius of the revolution gave birth to a free and equitable toleration, whereby every man was restored to the natural right of judging and acting for himself in matters of religion.[18]

To understand the Revolution, Belknap insisted upon the necessity of understanding "the ideas" the colonists had of "their political connexion with the parent state."[19] It was these ideas, which included the belief that "no part of the empire could be taxed, but by its own Representatives in Assembly," which caused the colonists to revolt.[20]

Belknap was a patriot, but loyalist affiliation during the Revolution did not prevent Thomas Hutchinson (1711-1780), when he wrote his history of Massachusetts, from making similar implications concerning the influential role of thought in the conflict with England, as well as in colonial settlement and in the growth of toleration. Massachusetts assumed its original political, legal, and ecclesiastical form because of "one great de-

[17] Jeremy Belknap, *History of New Hampshire*, 3 vols., Philadelphia, 1784, 1791, 1792, Vol. 1, p. 61.
[18] *Ibid.*, p. 58.   [19] *Ibid.*, p. 95.
[20] *Ibid.*, Vol. 2, p. 256.

sign" of the founders to have a society "as appeared to them to be most agreeable to the sacred scriptures."[21] Hutchinson also took for granted the power of ideas in his discussion of the Salem witchcraft episode, although he regretted the bigotry which preceded the rise of toleration. "In all ages of the world," he wrote, "superstitious credulity has produced greater cruelty than is practised among the Hottentots, or other nations, whose belief of a deity is called in question."[22] Behind Hutchinson's detailed political narrative of the coming of the Revolution, was the assumption that opposing principles, rival conceptions of empire, were at issue. He asserted that by 1767 "the colonies, in general" had "acquired a new set of ideas of the relation they stood in to the parliament of Great Britain. The constitutional authority of parliament to impose taxes on America was admitted in none." Hutchinson concluded, "From admitting a principle of partial independency, gradual advances were made until a total independency was asserted."[23] Thus a Tory, while differing in his evaluation of the rebellion, joined with patriots in viewing it as originating in a conflict between rival ideas.

Even this brief glance into seventeenth and eighteenth century writing reveals that these histories attributed causal significance to certain ideas. Twentieth century historians of ideas in the United States are to this extent only carrying on an old native tradition when they take ideas seriously. But these early writers of the seventeenth and eighteenth centuries did not analyze at length the ideas which they stressed—nor did they ex-

---

[21] Lawrence Mayo, ed., Thomas Hutchinson's *The History of the Colony and Province of Massachusetts Bay*, 3 vols., Cambridge, 1936, Vol. 1, p. 352. Vol. 1 was originally published in 1764, Vol. 2 in 1767, Vol. 3 in 1828.

[22] *Ibid.*, Vol. 2, pp. 44-45. Discussion of witchcraft appears on pp. 12-47.

[23] *Ibid.*, Vol. 3, p. 119.

plore the environmental contexts from which the ideas emerged. Further, they left unsaid what conception, if any, they held concerning the role of thought generally in history. Finally, they did not expand their interest in certain ideas into a suggestion that historians might write histories focused exclusively upon ideas.

To sketch these characteristics of the treatments of ideas by colonial historians is not to ridicule the primitive state of their scholarship. On the contrary, the characteristics of colonial histories have been remarkably enduring. There is probably no field of learning in the United States in which there are so many similarities between the colonial and the modern as in written histories. Modern historians can and, compared with their fellow scholars in other disciplines, do read their predecessors with relative understanding and sympathy. The traditional goal of a well-told story on a subject important to the community, interpreted with manly good sense, has largely survived the centuries.

An approach to ideas similar to that of the colonial historians was expressed in the works of the nineteenth century scholar whose books are customarily said to mark the coming-of-age of the writing of American history. George Bancroft (1800-1891) was the first American historian who had been exposed to the new seminars in German universities, and his research for his multi-volume *History of the United States* was unprecedented. But his treatment of ideas was almost identical with that of his colonial predecessors. Like them, he attributed great causal significance to Puritanism, to religious toleration, and to Revolutionary thought. And like them too, he did not depict the ideas in detail nor investigate the environments from which they emerged. Further like his predecessors, Bancroft's attribution of grandiose power to human thought was only one part of his history which was largely concerned with other matters. Bancroft's volumes, composed and revised during the half century after 1830, focused almost exclusively upon military and political events, but behind the events and decisively influencing them were ideas.[24]

He synthesized the traditionally emphasized ideas of Puritanism, toleration, and national independence into a progressive development toward democracy. "From Protestantism," according to Bancroft, "there came forth a principle of all-pervading energy," which was "the right of private judgment."[25] European emigration to New England was consequently an attempt to realize freedom of conscience for the colonists. "The enfranchisement of the mind from religious despotism," he wrote,

> led directly to inquiries into the nature of civil government; and the doctrines of popular liberty, which sheltered their infancy in the wildernesses of the newly-discovered continent, within the short space of two centuries, have infused themselves into the life-blood of every rising state from Labrador to Chili, have erected outposts on the Oregon [*sic*] and in Liberia, and, making a proselyte of enlightened France, have disturbed all the ancient governments of Europe, by awakening the public mind to resistless

[24] One of Bancroft's contemporaries, Richard Hildreth, devoted even less space to ideas in his history than had his predecessors. Hildreth's indifference to thought in *The History of the United States of America* was particularly striking in view of his exceedingly great involvement with the social and philosophical ideas of his time. He wrote two works of social philosophy, *Theory of Morals* and *Theory of Politics*, and the abolitionist novel, *Archy Moore*. For Hildreth's biography, see Donald Emerson, *Richard Hildreth*, The Johns Hopkins University Studies in Historical and Political Science, Series LXIV, No. 2, Baltimore, 1946.

[25] Bancroft, *History of the United States*, 10 vols., 1834-1874 (25 edns.), 15th edn., 1852, Vol. 5, p. 4. All quotations will be from this edition.

action, from the shores of Portugal to the palaces of the czars.[26]

Following successful settlement and later toleration in the colonies, the eventual political effect of the idea of liberty was the movement for independence from Great Britain. "Principles grow into life by informing the public mind," he said, "and in their maturity gain the mastery over events." In the mid-eighteenth century, "the hour of revolution was at hand," according to Bancroft, and it promised "dominion to intelligence" as well as "freedom of conscience."[27] American democracy during Bancroft's day, which had enthroned the opinions of the people, was thus the culmination of the earlier ideas of individual freedom. As liberty for individuals had formerly been achieved in certain areas, American democracy had extended liberty more widely throughout all areas of life. The result was, in Bancroft's view, that the beliefs of the people ruled. "Public opinion," he declared, "knows itself to be the spirit of the world, in its movement on the tide of thought from generation to generation."[28] It was in this sense that Bancroft was a "democratic historian," as von Ranke called him, glorifying the ideas of the common man, though he devoted

[26] *Ibid.*, Vol. 1, pp. 266, 267. Bancroft treated Puritan ideas approximately as had his predecessors. He devoted eight pages to the "character of Puritanism," and adopted a similar tone. He avowed the desire to refrain from defense of Puritan "excesses," but argued vigorously that the Puritans were only trying "to protect themselves" from Roger Williams, Wheelright, the Quakers, and the Anabaptists, who were threats to the civil state and so had to be expelled. See *ibid.*, pp. 461-468.

[27] *Ibid.*, Vol. 4, p. 4.

[28] *Ibid.*, p. 11. The quotation suggests Bancroft's transcendentalism, which I have not discussed in the text. It is not clear in such cases to what extent Bancroft's attribution of causal power to ideas is an attribution to a Hegelian world-spirit. Insofar as Bancroft expressed a transcendental interpretation of the power of ideas over and through worldly events, he had no followers among later American historians of ideas.

few pages either to ideas or to the common man.[29] Despite Bancroft's celebration of the democratic mind, his approach to ideas was essentially that of his colonial predecessors.

During the later years of George Bancroft's long lifetime, after the Civil War, there were two developments in American historical scholarship which contributed to a new interest in the history of ideas. These late nineteenth century developments do not in themselves fully explain why the first consciously conceived histories of ideas were written. But the new scholarly tendencies in the writing of history did suggest a definition of subject matter which prominently featured ideas.

One of these developments, anticipated by Bancroft himself, was a democraticizing of the subject matter of written histories. There was increased talk of studying "the life of the people" rather than solely the public acts of the leaders.[30] Because of the breadth of activities in the lives of the people, intellectual activity had at least a chance to be included. John Bach McMaster (1852-1932) opened *A History of the People of the United States from the Revolution to the Civil War* (1883-1913) by declaring:

> it shall be my purpose to describe the dress, the occupations, the amusements, the literary canons of the times; to note the changes of manners *and morals*:

[29] David Levin, in *History as Romantic Art*, Palo Alto, 1959, in a chapter entitled "Representative Men," discusses the manner in which Bancroft kept the traditional focus upon the "leaders" while glorifying the "followers." Heroic leaders were assumed to be representative of common men.

[30] It is a curious fact that despite the many pleas during the last century for allegedly unprecedented "histories of the people" rather than "political and military histories," there is an old American tradition of "social histories." Virtually all the colonial chroniclers, for instance, were concerned with what most scholars would today call social history.

to trace the growth of *that humane spirit which abol-
ished punishment for debt, which reformed the discipline of prisons and of jails, and which has, in our
own time, destroyed slavery and lessened the miseries
of dumb brutes.* Nor shall it be less my aim to recount the manifold improvements which, in a thousand ways, have multiplied the conveniences of life
and ministered to the happiness of our race; to describe the rise and progress of that long series of
mechanical inventions and discoveries which is now
the admiration of the world, and our just pride and
boast; to tell how, under the benign influence of liberty and peace, there sprang up, in the course of a
single century, a prosperity unparalleled in the an-
nals of human affairs; how, from a state of great poverty and feebleness, our country grew rapidly to one
of opulence and power; how her agriculture and her
manufactures flourished together; how, by *a wise
system of free education and a free press, knowledge
was disseminated, and the arts and sciences advanced.*[31]

As the added italics indicate, McMaster's statement
of intention included ideas, or opinion, within the com-
prehensive scope. But even as announced, the interest in
beliefs was merely part of a wide-ranging interest in
social history. In McMaster's history, as it was actually
written, thought received much less attention than the
prefatory announcement suggested. (McMaster's volumes were not even social histories except for occa-

[31] McMaster, *A History of the People of the United States
from the Revolution to the Civil War*, 7 vols., New York, 1907,
Vol. 1, pp. 2-3. McMaster first vowed to write a history of the
people of the United States, according to his biographer, when
he read Thomas Macaulay's famous third chapter "The State
of England in 1685," in *History of England from the Accession
of James II*. See Eric Goldman, *John Bach McMaster*, Philadelphia, 1943, p. 13.

sional sections.) From the standpoint of the development of the writing of histories of ideas, John Bach
McMaster was a publicist for writing about thought by
the accident of his plea for a proposed history of the
people. But, finally, as in the case of Bancroft, thought
was celebrated, rather than described, in the course of
writing conventional political history.

McMaster admitted Thomas Macaulay's influence in
originally directing him to social history, but apparently
McMaster was not influenced by the other Englishman
who wrote an early history of the English people, John
Richard Green.[32] It was, however, Green's history
which led John Fiske (1842-1901) to consider writing a parallel history of the American people, according
to Fiske. He invidiously compared "old-fashioned history, still retaining the marks of its barbaric origin,"
which "dealt with little save kings and battles and court
intrigues," with the newly broadened histories best exemplified by Green's, which paid attention, among other
things, "to changes in beliefs."[33] But Fiske, while as
willing as McMaster to speak favorably of a "new history," was no more successful in writing one, and his
historical writings and public lectures of the 1880's
and 1890's were narrowly political and military in
context.[34]

Despite the fact that early supporters of a broadened
social history which would include ideas, such as Mc-
Master and Fiske, did not themselves write histories

[32] William Hutchinson, "John Bach McMaster," in *The Marcus W. Jernegan Essays in American Historiography*, Chicago,
1937, p. 125; Goldman, *McMaster*, p. 15.

[33] On Fiske, see Milton Berman, *John Fiske*, Cambridge,
1961, pp. 145-146. Quotation is from John Fiske, *Essays Historical and Literary*, 2 vols., New York, 1902, Vol. 2, p. 23.

[34] Fiske's choice not to write the history of thought is particularly striking in view of his intense involvement in philosophical questions of his own day. See his *Outlines of Cosmic
Philosophy*, 2 vols., Boston, 1874.

according to these new precepts, nevertheless the variety and breadth of social history did presumably encourage the growth of the history of ideas. One cannot read, for instance, the following plea from Frederick Jackson Turner in 1891 for broadened studies of history which would investigate "all the spheres of man's activity," without thinking that it explains how a teacher of the westward movement could produce a student of the history of ideas such as Carl Becker:

> The economic life and the political life touch, modify, and condition one another. Even the religious life needs to be studied in conjunction with the political and economic life, and vice versa. Therefore all kinds of history are essential—history as politics, history as art, history as economics, history as religion—all are truly parts of society's endeavor to understand itself by understanding its past.[35]

Turner's enthusiasm for broadly conceived histories happened to be one part of his conscious desire to investigate the past more "scientifically" than was usual. Turner's implicit admiration for science was common; this constituted the second development in American historical scholarship in the late nineteenth century which contributed to the new interest in the study of the history of ideas.[36] The apotheosis of science yielded

[35] "The Significance of History," in Fulmer Mood, ed., *The Early Writings of Frederick Jackson Turner*, Madison, 1938, pp. 53-54. The article was originally published in the *Wisconsin Journal of Education*, October and November, 1891.

[36] There were of course other developments important to historical scholarship, such as the emergence of the professional historian through graduate training, the growth of universities, the founding of the American Historical Association in 1884, and the publication of the *American Historical Review*. Such developments, however, did not affect the study of the history of ideas differently than it affected historical scholarship generally.

both a "scientific history" and an interest in "scientific" ideas in history.

The concept of "scientific history" which contributed to the history of ideas was, to employ W. Stull Holt's distinction, grandly interpretative rather than fact-finding.[37] The grand-interpreters valued exact knowledge but they cherished imaginative hypotheses even more, and their writings encouraged the study of the history of ideas. Specifically, these scientific historians raised the question of the causal relationship between thought and its environment. They sought an answer which could be expressed in scientific terms.

Henry Adams (1838-1918), for example, raised the possibility of ascertaining the causal influence of ideas while he sketched the intellectual life of early nineteenth century Americans. More than eight volumes of the nine comprising Adams' *History of the United States During the Administrations of Thomas Jefferson and James Madison* were political narrative, but he appended introductory and concluding sections which discussed ideas.

He opened with a 150-page survey of the "intellect" of various sections of the United States in 1800, and he concluded with a shorter assessment of ideas in politics, religion, and the arts in 1815. These first and last sections were utterly disconnected from the body of his history, yet he avowed great interest in them. "The movement of thought," Adams wrote, was "more interesting than the movement of population or of wealth."[38]

[37] W. Stull Holt, "The Idea of Scientific History," *Journal of the History of Ideas*, I (June 1940), 352-362. Fact-finding scientific history, which emulated science by its careful, detailed, seemingly objective investigation of evidence, probably diminished interest in the history of ideas by preferring the more concrete source material of political history.

[38] Adams, *History of the United States During the Administrations of Thomas Jefferson and James Madison*, 9 vols.,

He suggested that there was genuine significance to be found in pursuing the popular mind: "A few customs, more or less local; a few prejudices, more or less popular; a few traits of thought, suggesting habits of mind, —must form the entire material for a study more important than that of politics or economics."[39] Adams went on to indicate the popular mind which he thought would be discovered if such a study were made: progressive, democratic, secular, libertarian. "European travellers who passed through America noticed," according to Adams, "that everywhere, except for a few Federalists, every American, from Jefferson and Gallatin down to the poorest squatter, seemed to nourish an idea that he was doing what he could to overthrow the tyranny which the past had fastened on the human mind."[40]

To the popular mind Adams gave the name "national character," and he explicitly raised the question of the impact of national character, by which he meant opinion and belief, upon other human behavior. "Of all historical problems," he wrote, "the nature of a national character is the most difficult and the most important." He posed the problem with specific reference to his own political narrative: "Readers will be troubled, at almost every chapter of the coming narrative, by the want of some formula to explain what share the popular imagination bore in the system pursued by government."[41] Whether or not troubled, the reader in fact received no suggested answers throughout the following eight volumes to the question of the relationship between beliefs and actions.

New York, 1889-1891, Vol. 9, p. 175. The political narrative which comprised the bulk of Adams' *History* exemplified W. Stull Holt's fact-finding scientific history, in contrast to the exceptional pages concerning the history of thought.

[39] *Ibid.*, Vol. 1, p. 42.   [40] *Ibid.*, p. 175.

[41] *Ibid.*, p. 176.

But Adams was himself troubled, at least troubled enough to return in his last chapter to the subject of the emergent democratic national character of the early 1800's. As if to admit the hopelessness of finding a "formula" by which to determine the impact of opinion, or national character, upon political events, but as if to hold out still the hope of some kind of scientific history, Adams suggested that perhaps the focus of American historical researches should be the national character itself. In a democratic society, he argued, individuals were more important as types than as unique heroes, and the concept of national character would allow a direct avenue to types of individuals.[42] Thus, even though he turned to European history when he chose to write at length about man's "inner life," in *Mont Saint Michel and Chartres*, Adams expressed interest in the history of the American mind which he characterized as remarkably democratic, and which he suggested could be approached scientifically.

Another American who urged scientific histories of thought, but who preferred to deal with the ideas of Europe and the politics and wars of the United States, was John William Draper (1811-1882). Draper was born and raised in England, and wrote his *Intellectual Development of Europe* (1862) after he made a reputation as an American scientist. Draper conceived of the science of history as an exploration into the laws of human development. "The equilibrium and movement of humanity are altogether physiological phenomena," he wrote.[43] When Draper spoke in this vein, he minimized the causal power of thought and emphasized the determining influence of the material environment:

If from its original seats a whole nation were trans-

42 *Ibid.*, Vol. 9, p. 222.
43 Draper, *History of Intellectual Development of Europe*, 2 vols., 1862, rev. edn., 1876, Vol. 1, p. 2.

posed to some new abode, in which the climate, the seasons, the aspect of nature were altogether different, it would appear spontaneously in all its parts to commence a movement to come into harmony with the new conditions—a movement of a secular nature, and implying the consumption of many generations for its accomplishment.[44]

But Draper was a reforming man of science whose belief in human progress included a celebration of certain ideas which he did not relate to their physical environment. "I come to the conclusion," he said, "that in the unanimous consent of the entire human race lies the human criterion of truth—a criterion, in its turn, capable of increased precision with the diffusion of enlightenment and knowledge":

> In the intellectual collisions that must ensue, in the melting down of opinions, in the examinations and analyses of nations, truth will come forth. Whatever can not stand that ordeal must submit to its fate. Lies and imposture, no matter how powerfully sustained, must prepare to depart. In that supreme tribunal man may place implicit confidence.[45]

The truth which Draper had in mind was above all scientific knowledge as opposed to historic religious superstition. Thus the *History of the Intellectual Development of Europe* traced mainly the conflict between science and religion, and it was the story of emergent truth. In this way the scientific historian's zeal to locate the environmental or physiological influences upon ideas gave way to enthusiasm for the ideas of modern science.

But whether European thought was a cause or a result of its environment, American thought was left

[44] *Ibid.*, p. 14.   [45] *Ibid.*, p. 236.

unexplored by Draper. For when he chose to write American history, rather than European, a three-volume military and political narrative was the product.[46] The same relative lack of interest in American thought was revealed by others who, like Draper and Adams, wrote of European thought.

Andrew Dickson White (1832-1918) attempted to show, as did John William Draper, the importance of scientific thought through his argument that science had liberated the modern mind from the ignorance of traditional theology. This interest in modern scientific thought joined with the interest in scientific history to stimulate the study of the history of ideas. For White studied the past to expose the evils of religious ideas and the glories of science. Although White's *A History of the Warfare of Science with Theology in Christendom* (1896) was not a "scientific history" in Draper's and Adams' sense of exploring the relation between ideas and their environments, or in their sense of establishing laws, it did argue for the importance of the history of ideas.[47]

White's and Draper's interest in showing the superiority of modern science over medieval religion, as well as Draper's and Adams' interest in finding the relationship between ideas and their environments, were American expressions of currents in European historical scholarship during the last half of the nineteenth century. The history of European ideas, rather than American thought was, of course, the focus of these European studies.

Draper's mid-century and Adams' late-century pleas

[46] *History of the American Civil War*, 3 vols., New York, 1867, 1868, 1870.

[47] See also Henry Charles Lea, *An Historical Sketch of Sacerdotal Celibacy in the Christian Church*, Boston, 1867, and *A History of the Inquisition of the Middle Ages*, 3 vols., New York, 1887-1888.

for scientific investigation of the relationship between ideas and their environments were paralleled by the Englishman Henry Thomas Buckle's (1822-1862) *History of Civilization in England*, published in two volumes in 1857 and 1861. "I hope to accomplish for the history of man," Buckle wrote, "something equivalent, or at all events analogous, to what has been effected by other inquirers for the different branches of natural science."[48]

His plea for scientific history featured the role of thought, because man's history was "the fruit of a double action; an action of external phenomena upon the mind, and another action of the mind upon the phenomena." According to Buckle, "we have man modifying nature, and nature modifying man," and "out of this reciprocal modification all events must necessarily spring." Buckle's dream was to make written history a science which would discover "the laws of this double modification," and so find out "whether the thoughts and desires of men are more influenced by physical phenomena, or whether the physical phenomena are more influenced by them."[49]

Buckle's own conclusion, like John William Draper's, was one which suggested his faith in progress and education: that ideas have been increasingly more influential than the physical environment as man has moved away from barbarism toward civilization. The enlightened modern man of science and democracy could control the environment, even though the environment controlled early man. Buckle's enthusiasm for making a

---

[48] Buckle, *History of Civilization in England*, 3 vols., New York, 1913, Vol. 1, p. 5. Draper's biographer concludes that "it seems fairly certain that Draper had arrived at his conclusions independently" of Buckle. Draper announced his projected history of European thought in 1856, prior to publication of Buckle's first volume. See Donald Fleming, *John William Draper*, Philadelphia, 1950, p. 74.

[49] *Ibid.*, p. 15.

science of history extended to both situations. Thus, he wrote, "the advance of European civilization is characterized by a diminishing influence of physical laws, and an increasing influence of mental laws."[50] Buckle made it clear that physical laws would define the impact of the environment upon human thought. It was not so clear what mental laws would define, for he was mainly occupied in indicating the grandeur of ideas which governed their environments instead of being governed by them. Human progress was due to the triumph of those ideas which were not conditioned by the physical environment. "I pledge myself to show," wrote Buckle, "that the progress Europe has made from barbarism to civilization is entirely due to its intellectual activity; that the leading countries have now, for some centuries, advanced sufficiently far to shake off the influence of those physical agencies by which in an earlier state their career might have been troubled." When he discussed these ideas to which man owed his progress, Buckle did not relate them to environmental factors but instead celebrated them for their autonomy:

> it is to them we owe all that we now have, they are for all ages and all times; never young, and never old, they bear the seeds of their own life; they flow on in a perennial and undying stream; they are essentially cumulative, and giving birth to the additions which they subsequently receive, they thus influence the most distant posterity, and after the lapse of centuries produce more effect than they were able to do even at the moment of their promulgation.[51]

Buckle thus placed stress upon the autonomous quality of thought even as he argued for a science of the environmental influences upon ideas. He was as enthusiastic about the unchallenged power of ideas in the

[50] *Ibid.*, p. 112.   [51] *Ibid.*, pp. 162-163.

modern age as he was concerning the possibility of showing the environment's power over ideas in ages past. In its entirety then, Buckle's theoretical outline for scientific history proposed a system which would study the relative power of the physical environment and of thought. And if determinism received support in his conclusion that "lower" civilizations were largely controlled by nature, free will seemed to be endorsed by the celebration of human thought in "higher" societies.

Buckle's plea for a scientific history of thought, like the Frenchman Hippolyte Taine's (1828-1893) argument for scientific literary history (*History of English Literature*),[52] was rooted in his confidence concerning the superiority of modern scientific ideas. Traditional theological wisdom was relegated to an ignorant past. This championing of skeptical scientific thought was the foundation for other pioneer European historians of ideas too, even if they did not join in Buckle's and Taine's search for hidden laws of history.

William Edward Hartpole Lecky (1838-1908), whose first notable work, *History of the Rise and Influence of the Spirit of Rationalism in Europe*, was published in 1865, shared his contemporaries' faith in human progress. Like Buckle and Taine, Lecky spoke of "the great laws of eternal development which preside over and direct the progress of belief."[53] And, like them too, Lecky mentioned the nonintellectual environment as one of the factors influencing the course of thought. "It is impossible to lay down a railway without creating intellectual influences," he wrote, just as to create a commercial society "is to encourage the opinions that

[52] Taine's *History of English Literature* was published in three volumes in the late 1860's in French, and translated into English by the next decade.

[53] *History of the Rise and Influence of the Spirit of Rationalism in Europe*, 2 vols., rev. edn., New York, 1890, Vol. 1, p. 113.

are most congenial to it."[54] Unlike Buckle and Taine, however, Lecky spent almost all his time describing the beliefs with which he was concerned, and he devoted only slight space to their environmental relationships.

Leslie Stephen's (1832-1904) *History of English Thought in the Eighteenth Century* (1876) analyzed ideas at even greater length and in more depth than did Lecky's writings. Stephen's plan of approach to the history of ideas was "to deal chiefly with the logical condition," that is, to analyze thought without regard to influences other than ideas.[55] He articulated the concept of an intellectual "spirit of the age," which he attempted to describe, indicating how this "spirit" was transformed into a new intellectual temper. But Stephen, as well as Lecky, shared Buckle's and Taine's evolutionary viewpoint and belief in human progress through modern knowledge. "The history of thought is in great part a history of the gradual emancipation of the mind from the errors spontaneously generated by its first childlike attempts at speculation," Stephen wrote. "Doctrines which once appeared to be simply expressions of immediate observation have contained a hypothetical element, gradually dissolved by contact with facts."[56]

Thus Leslie Stephen and W. E. H. Lecky, who were more interested in ideas than in their environmental relationships, shared the progressive faith of rationalism expressed by the scientific historians Henry Thomas Buckle and Hippolyte Taine. It was in this

[54] *Ibid.*, p. 8.

[55] Stephen, *History of English Thought in the Eighteenth Century*, 2 vols., 3rd edn., New York, 1902, reprinted 1949, Vol. 1, p. 19.

[56] *Ibid.*, Vol. 1, p. 5. See also Vol. 2, p. 91: "A scheme of morality deduced from self-evident and necessary truths must produce a code as rigid as its fundamental axioms, and, therefore, incapable of varying with the development of the race."

sense that most of the pioneer writings on the history of thought, whether by Europeans or Americans, were rooted in an admiration for secular knowledge and the rational, scientific outlook of the modern western mind. The idea of modern science joined with the idea of modern scientific history to argue for the importance of the study of the history of ideas.

The history of European ideas received the most benefit from these new currents in scholarship during the late 1800's, but the currents were present in the United States and they comprised part of the background from which the first conscious American histories of ideas emerged. Much of the scholarly background, of course, was not new and scientific, but was old and originally Puritan.

MOSES COIT TYLER

From Bradford to Bancroft, American chroniclers and historians expressed the conviction that ideas were important in history. Early writers, however, did not single out ideas for exclusive treatment in their histories, nor did they analyze the relationship between ideas and their environments. After the Civil War, enthusiasm for social histories which would cover all of man's activities, including intellectual ones, gave indirect support at least to the study of the history of ideas. Enthusiasm for modern science, too, stimulated new interest, on the one hand through scholars who spoke of writing a "scientific" history of ideas and, on the other hand, through scholars who wrote histories of the "enlightened" scientific thought which they championed. But these currents of scholarship during the late nineteenth century were reflected primarily in histories of European ideas rather than in histories of American ideas. European historians of ideas did not turn to American thought, and even in the United States scholars preferred to study European ideas.

The two Americans who did pioneer significantly during the late 1800's in the treatment of their own country's past, Moses Coit Tyler and Edward Eggleston, had similar backgrounds in several respects. Both were raised in the Midwest among Calvinist protestants, after which they were pastors for a time, both turned to the writing of history only in middle-age, and both focused upon intellectual life in the colonies. In their writings, they both emphasized the causal importance of ideas in history. They differed, however, on the ideas and the periods in history which they found admirable: they did not agree in their estimates of the colonial period. And they agreed neither in their assessments of modern currents of thought nor on the theoretical desirability of scientific history that would investigate the influence of the environment upon ideas.

Moses Coit Tyler (1835-1900), who wrote in the 1870's the first history of American ideas, was born in Connecticut of long New England ancestry and was raised in the Midwest. He graduated from Yale and then attended schools of theology in Connecticut and Massachusetts. Throughout his life he retained the religious concern of his forebears. After theological school he became a Congregational pastor; he frequently gave guest sermons after he left the ministry and became a college professor. In middle life, a religious re-examination provoked Tyler to become an Episcopalian; he was ordained a priest and thereafter conducted regular Episcopal services.[57] Both his identification with

[57] All the facts concerning Tyler's life are taken from Howard Mumford Jones and Thomas Edgar Casady, *The Life of Moses Coit Tyler*, Ann Arbor, 1933. This study was based upon a dissertation by Casady, who died before he was able to prepare it for publication. The usefulness of this study is due partly to the fact that Jones was particularly interested in the

New England and his continuous religious sympathy were clearly expressed in his studies of colonial literature.

Tyler was a professor of English literature at the University of Michigan from the late 1860's until he went to Cornell in 1881 as the nation's first professor of American history. While originating courses in American literature for the Michigan curriculum, Tyler was asked by the publisher George Haven Putnam to compile a manual of American literature. As Tyler worked upon the proposed literary manual, it slowly became not only historical but also concerned with the ideas expressed in the literature. Because of the broadened scope of Tyler's topic, his first two volumes, *A History of American Literature, 1607-1765* (1878), dealt with only the colonial years.[58] He carried his subject forward two decades when he added his final two volumes, *The Literary History of the American Revolution, 1763-1785*, in 1897.[59]

"There is but one thing more interesting than the intellectual history of a man," Tyler wrote in his opening sentence of his first volume, "and that is the intellectual history of a nation."[60] Twenty years later, as he began his Revolutionary history, he declared that the "Revolution was pre-eminently a revolution caused by ideas, and pivoted on ideas."[61] Such an enthusiastic con-

---

development of the writing of history of ideas. See also Jessica Tyler Austen, ed., *Moses Coit Tyler, 1835-1900: Selections from His Letters and Diaries*, New York, 1911.

[58] Originally published by Putnam in two volumes. Quotations cited here refer to the revised two-volume edition, New York, 1897. There is also a one-volume edition published in 1949 by Cornell University Press.

[59] 2 vols., New York, 1897. Quotations cited here refer to the 1941 two-volume edition, Facsimile Library, New York.

[60] *A History of American Literature*, Vol. 1, p. 5.

[61] *The Literary History of the American Revolution*, Vol. 1, p. 8.

viction concerning the fascination and significance of thought in history marked all Tyler's writings. Symptomatically, when Tyler once praised Buckle, there was no reference to the latter's scientism, but instead to his "recognition of a spirit of the age as ruling the evolution of the events of the age, and using kings, presidents, statesmen, warriors, as the tide uses the chips that are carried upon its top."[62] Tyler was impressed, in other words, by that strain in Buckle's work which argued the power of ideas, rather than by the strain which placed emphasis upon environmental control over thought.

Tyler's attribution of great influence to ideas was perhaps less a theoretical statement about thought generally than an affirmation of the importance of the particular ideas which he described in his books. These ideas which Tyler treated, usually expressions of New England Puritanism or the making of an American nationality, comprised the center of his work—insofar as it was, as he announced it, an "intellectual history." In Tyler's colonial volumes, his focus was most clearly upon ideas in the sections discussing New England writings, which took up more than two-thirds of the pages. Chapters were devoted to "New England Traits in the Seventeenth Century," "Topics of Popular Discussion," and "The Dynasty of the Mathers."

Tyler's prose, always full-bodied and alive, became enthusiastic when he wrote of early New England Puritans. His chronicle of their intellectual achievement was a labor of admiration. He respected the intellectuality of the Puritans, and he interpreted their theological interests as basically intellectual. He attributed the considerable Puritan literary output to the fact that they were the only "thinkers" among the New World colonists:

[62] Jones and Casady, *Tyler*, p. 141.

Primarily, then, these first New-Englanders were thinkers in some fashion; they assumed the right to think, the utility of thinking, and the duty of standing by the fair conclusions of their thinking, even at very considerable cost . . . the one grand distinction between the English colonists in New England and nearly all other English colonists in America was this, that while the latter came here chiefly for some material benefit, the former came chiefly for an ideal benefit. In its inception New England was not an agricultural community, nor a manufacturing community, nor a trading community: it was a thinking community; an arena and mart for ideas; its characteristic organ being not the hand, nor the heart, nor the pocket, but the brain.[63]

Tyler noted with pride that "probably no other community ever so honored study. . . . Theirs was a social structure with its corner-stone resting on a book."[64]

The specific theological doctrines of the Puritans were not championed by Tyler, but he treated them with respect, emphasized their achievements, and stressed the intellectuality of the Puritan religious quest.

Above all, it was toward religion, as the one supreme thing in life and in this universe, that all this intellectuality of theirs and all this earnestness, were directed. The result was tremendous. Perhaps not since the time of the apostles had there been in the world a faith so literal, a zeal so passionate: not even in the time of the apostles was there connected with these an intelligence so keen and so robust. For the first time, it may be, in the history of the world, these people brought together the subtle brain of the metaphysician and the glowing heart of the fanatic;

[63] *A History of American Literature, 1607-1765*, Vol. 1, p. 98.
[64] *Ibid.*

and they flung both vehemently into the service of religion. Never were men more logical or self-consistent in theory and in practice. Religion, they said was the chief thing; they meant it; they acted upon it.[65]

Tyler's respect for the Puritan mind, and some of his lack of respect for his own late nineteenth century period—"a grinning and flabby age"—were indicated in his remarks on Puritan sermons.

Without doubt, the sermons produced in New England during the colonial times, and especially during the seventeenth century, are the most authentic and characteristic revelations of the mind of New England for all that wonderful epoch. They are commonly spoken of mirthfully by an age that lacks the faith of that period, its earnestness, its grip, its mental robustness; a grinning and flabby age, an age hating effort, and requiring to be amused. The theological and religious writings of early New England may not now be readable; but they are certainly not despicable. They represent an enormous amount of subtile, sustained, and sturdy brain-power.[66]

This Puritan mind—earnest and learned—Tyler depicted sympathetically as it appeared in Puritan writings.

Tyler's entrance to the Puritan mind was through biographical sketches, whether in chapters where the figures were grouped together because of ideas ("Topics of Popular Discussion"), or family and ideas ("The Dynasty of the Mathers"), or genre of writing and ideas ("Verse-Writers," "History"). Common Puritan ideas were indicated in many of these sketches, despite the fact that the sections were not organized principally according to ideas. For example, Tyler's description of William Bradford, "Historical Writer," emphasized the

[65] *Ibid.*, p. 10.   [66] *Ibid.*, p. 192.

Pilgrim's dedication to the Plymouth Zion as he composed his chronicles; John Cotton, "Theological and Religious Writer," was treated in relation to Puritan spirituality; and Anne Bradstreet, "Verse-Writer," was discussed in part, at least, with reference to the Puritan mind. "Literature, for her," according to Tyler, "was not a republic of letters, hospitable to all forms of human thought, but a strict Puritan commonwealth."[67]

Thus, to a considerable extent, Tyler fulfilled his declaration of writing a history of thought. Puritanism supplied a body of ideas which so permeated early New England writings that any study of the literature necessarily involved a study of the ideas. In addition to Puritanism, he also looked for literary manifestation of the idea of a separate American identity—"genuine American talk." He noted writings which expressed "that new note of hope and help for humanity in distress, and of a rugged personal independence":

> this single word America blossomed into a whole vocabulary of words, all testifying plainly to them of a better time coming, of a reasonable chance, somewhere, in this world, of getting a fresh start in life, and of winning the victory over poverty, nastiness, and fear; nourishing within them a manly might and pride, a resolute discontent with failure, a rightful ambition to get on in the race, a healthy disdain of doing in this life anything less than one's best.[68]

The delineation of the American dream, a combination of belief and hope, idea and faith, was one of Tyler's purposes. Perhaps the nationalism implicit in his desire to locate a peculiarly American dream was what provoked Tyler to study his own country's intellectual life, instead of Europe's, as was more commonly done.

This search for an American credo blurred the dis-

[67] *Ibid.*, p. 281.   [68] *Ibid.*, pp. 56-57.

tinction beween "high" and "low" thought insofar as "American" characteristics were not restricted to any single stratum of ideas. Although Tyler's survey, which was confined to written works, necessarily constituted a study of an "elite" group in the population, early American writings offered few examples of intellectual works which were remote from the immediate "popular" concerns of the community. The attempt to locate an American identity also blurred to some extent the distinction between an environmental approach to ideas and one which analyzed thought irrespective of environmental factors. For Tyler assumed that the new wilderness environment, that is, the lack of an Old World environment, had contributed to the formulation of the American dream.

Despite Tyler's interest in depicting attitudes characteristically American, and in describing Puritanism, his first colonial volumes did not comprise an unalloyed history of ideas. Tyler was writing of literature as well as of ideas; his book, *A History of American Literature, 1607-1765*, pioneered equally in each area. As extraordinary as his dual achievement was, it necessitated a dual focus, which meant that Tyler's history of ideas was not consistently or exclusively a history of ideas. He faced the problem of writing the history of thought from sources which had esthetic, as well as intellectual, relevance to the historian. Literature, like painting or architecture, presents the historian with a question of esthetic judgment as well as the customary ones of historical description and explanation. Although it is theoretically possible to ask only historical questions of esthetic works, historians have seldom refrained from making esthetic evaluations when studying art. The failure stems not so much from weaknesses of historians (for historians have not really tried to refrain from making those judgments), as from the very nature of art itself. To discuss art is to imply standards of judgment. Works of art survive and are discussed by mankind on the basis of esthetic criteria, which is not the case with other historical source material. Thus as soon as a historian selects for historical treatment a work of "art," as contrasted with a work too esthetically deficient to be considered "art," he has allowed esthetic rather than purely historical criteria to enter.

Apart from the problem of evaluation, esthetic source material presents a second problem to the historian of ideas. Art forms have their own special histories, and these are not necessarily relevant to anything outside the art form. Literature has its internal development of genre and style, for example, and a historian of literature almost by definition is interested in those developments. But the relationship between the history of genre and style on the one hand, and the history of ideas on the other, may be nonexistent. Tyler's history exemplified the extent to which the history of literature and the history of ideas, though not mutually exclusive, are not really focused in the same direction.

That the volumes would be concerned with the history of literature as well as with the history of ideas was clearly indicated in Tyler's prefatory remarks. For at the same time that he said he was interested in the history of ideas, he also said that the history of literary form was of concern to him, and he noted that he would use a criterion of esthetic value for the inclusion of certain writings. Tyler wrote in the Preface that he had attempted to give a history of writings "which have some noteworthy value as literature," in addition to "some real significance in the literary unfolding of the American mind." He said that he had "aimed in these volumes to make an appropriate mention of every one of our early authors whose writings, whether many or few, have any appreciable literary merit, or throw any helpful light upon the evolution of thought and of style in America, during those flourishing and indispensable days."[69]

Tyler's volumes themselves reflected the dual focus of his prefatory comments. The organization, as noted above, was not ordinarily by ideas, but by writers— usually lumped together by time and region, and sometimes by subject matter and genre of their writings. With the exception of such a chapter as "New England Traits in the Seventeenth Century," ideas were discussed within a chapter organization which was basically literary.

Within this fundamentally literary organization, Tyler's individual sketches discussed both the literary and the intellectual characteristics of the figures treated. Sometimes, as in the chapters on "Verse-Writers," the sketches were predominantly or wholly literary; at other times, as in the chapters on theologians, the sketches were mainly concerned with ideas. This inconsistency was exemplified in Tyler's discussion of Puritan poet Michael Wigglesworth and his verse-writing son Samuel Wigglesworth. In his sketch of Michael Wigglesworth, Tyler placed stress upon the ideas embodied in Wigglesworth's verse and devoted several pages to the discussion. Tyler wrote, for example, that "Michael Wigglesworth stands for New England Puritanism confronting with steady gaze the sublime and hideous dogmas of its creed, and trying to use those dogmas for the admonition and the consolation of mankind by putting them into song. . . . He chants, with utter frankness, the chant of Christian fatalism, the moan of earthly vanity and sorrow, the physical bliss of the saved, the physical tortures of the damned."[70] Here Tyler was clearly using verse as a source for the history of ideas. Yet in his next sketch of Samuel Wigglesworth, Tyler

[69] *Ibid.*, p. v.   [70] *Ibid.*, Vol. 2, pp. 24-25.

said nothing about the ideas expressed in his verse, but remarked that his poems showed esthetic potentiality. Similarly, the following sketch of the poet Nicholas Noyes was almost wholly occupied with Noyes' poetic techniques and included an evaluation of his verse. These three poets, the two Wigglesworths and Noyes, were treated in succession because they all wrote verse in colonial New England, not because their ideas were strikingly similar or significantly dissimilar. In fact, the ideas of the elder Wigglesworth only were discussed at any length. *A History of American Literature, 1607-1765* was indeed a history of literature as well as a history of ideas.

The role of ideas was made more consistently important in Tyler's second two-volume work, *The Literary History of the American Revolution, 1763-1785*, which was not published until almost two decades later in 1897.[71] Ideas played a somewhat different part in the Revolutionary volumes than they had in *A History of American Literature, 1607-1765*, because in the earlier volumes Tyler had attempted to discuss large numbers of different types of writings and writers. In the Revolutionary volumes, the somewhat heterogeneous minds of all the colonials, North and South, were crystallized into two opposing minds poised for intellectual combat; similarly, almost all literature was drawn into the same combat. The result was that there was much more in common between Tyler's history of ideas and his history of literature in the Revolutionary volumes than there had been earlier in his work on the colonies. The two channels, intellectual and literary, flowed into one and he had an opportunity to investigate both currents at the same time.

Tyler in his second work focused quite consistently

[71] Quotations cited refer to a 1941 two-volume edition, New York.

on the intellectual conflicts of the Revolutionary era as expressed in literature, which he defined to include almost all writings. He wrote that whereas the earlier colonial period had no single issue around which ideas were magnetically drawn, the Revolutionary period, by contrast, witnessed a virtually complete attraction to the issue culminating in independence. Imaginative literature and all other writings were drawn into intellectual combat and therefore became best understood in terms of ideas. American writing of all types, wrote Tyler, was characterized during the years 1763-1785 by

> its concern with the problems of American society, and of American society in a peculiar condition— aroused, inflammable, in a state of alarm for its own existence, but also in a state of resolute combat for it. The literature which we are thus to inspect is not, then, a literature of tranquillity, but chiefly a literature of strife, or, as the Greeks would have said, of agony; and, of course, it must take those forms in which intellectual and impassioned debate can be most effectually carried on. The literature of our Revolution has almost everywhere the combative note; its habitual method is argumentive, persuasive, appealing, rasping, retaliatory; the very brain of man seems to be in armor; his wit is in the gladiator's attitude of offense and defense. It is a literature indulging itself in grimaces, in mockery, in scowls: a literature accented by earnest gestures meant to convince people, or by fierce blows meant to smite them down.[72]

In these Revolutionary volumes, consequently, Tyler's concern for significant literature was little different from his concern for significant ideas.

[72] *Ibid.*, Vol. 1, p. 6.

In this literature we must not expect to find art used for art's sake. Nay, art itself, so far as it is here at all, is swept into the universal conscription, and enrolled for the service of the one party or of the other in the imperilled young Republic. No man is likely to be in the mood for aesthetics who has an assassin's pistol at his head. Even the passion for the beautiful has been known to yield to the instinct for self-preservation.[73]

Not only did the Revolutionary conflict shake disparate intellects and poets into a single battle, in Tyler's view, but it was a battle of ideas and determined by ideas. He stated that the "Revolution was pre-eminently a revolution caused by ideas, and pivoted on ideas."[74] He argued that this was true of all revolutions, but it was especially true that

an epoch like this, therefore,—an epoch in which nearly all that is great and dear in man's life on earth has to be argued for, as well as to be fought for, and in which ideas have a work to do quite as pertinent and quite as effective as that of bullets,—can hardly fail to be an epoch teeming with literature, with literature, of course, in the particular forms suited to the purposes of political co-operation and conflict.[75]

Tyler here expressed a view of the Revolutionary period totally involved in ideological combat, similar to the in-

[73] *Ibid.* Only rarely did Tyler, in these volumes, discuss literature without reference to revolutionary intellectual conflicts. For these exceptions, see Vol. 1, Chapter 7, "Descriptions of Nature and Man in the American Wilderness: 1763-1775"; Chapter 8, "Beginnings of New Life in Verse and Prose: Philadelphia, Princeton, and New York, 1763-1775"; Chapter 9, "Beginnings of New Life in Verse and Prose: New England, 1763-1775."

[74] *Ibid.*, p. 8.   [75] *Ibid.*, p. 9.

volvement of many Americans in battle with totalitarianism during and after the 1940's. As many interpreted the contemporary conflict with totalitarianism, so Tyler saw the Revolutionary turmoil: ideas were not only viewed as interesting expressions of differences of opinion, but also as causally important historical forces.

Tyler's conviction that ideas were crucial led him, in the Preface to *The Literary History of the American Revolution*, to discuss the originality of his written history of the American Revolution, focused as it was on ideas:

> There would, perhaps, be no injustice in describing this book as the product of a new method, at least of a method never before so fully applied, in the critical treatment of the American Revolution. . . . In the present work, for the first time in a systematic and a fairly complete way, is set forth the inward history of our Revolution—the history of its ideas, its spiritual moods, its motives, its passions, even of its sportive caprices and its whims, as these uttered themselves at the time, whether consciously or not, in the various writings of the two parties of Americans who promoted or resisted that great movement.[76]

Since there was little literature except that drawn into the Revolutionary conflict and therefore dominated by the ideas of that conflict, literature in an esthetic sense as well as all other writings were equally well studied by a historian of ideas.

Tyler went on to say, in words which were reminiscent of his enthusiasm over Buckle nearly thirty years before, that his interest in ideas required a history different from that of the narrowly political historians.

The proceedings of legislative bodies, the doings of

[76] *Ibid.*, p. vii.

cabinet ministers and of colonial politicians, the movements of armies, are not altogether disregarded, but they are here subordinated: they are mentioned, when mentioned at all, as mere external incidents in connection with the ideas and the emotions which lay back of them or in front of them, which caused them or were caused by them. . . . Instead of fixing our eyes almost exclusively, as is commonly done, upon statesmen and generals, upon party leaders, upon armies and navies, upon Congress, upon parliament, upon the ministerial agents of a brain-sick king, or even upon that brain-sick king himself, and instead of viewing all these people as the sole or the principal movers and doers of the things that made the American Revolution, we here for the most part turn our eyes toward certain persons hitherto much neglected, in many cases wholly forgotten—toward persons who, as mere writers, and whether otherwise prominent or not, nourished the springs of great historic events by creating and shaping and directing public opinion during all that robust time; who, so far as we here regard them, wielded only spiritual weapons; who still illustrate, for us and for all who choose to see, the majestic operation of ideas, the creative and decisive play of spiritual forces, in the development of history, in the rise and fall of nations, in the aggregation and the division of races.[77]

Tyler's view that ideas were important causal agents in influencing attitudes and behavior found expression in his sketches of individuals. In his description of James Otis' speech protesting writs of assistance, before the Massachusetts superior court in 1761, Tyler concluded with John Adams' contemporary remark that "American Independence was then and there born; the

[77] *Ibid.*, p. viii.

seeds of patriots and heroes were then and there sown.
. . . Every man of a crowded audience appeared to me
to go away, as I did, ready to take up arms against
writs of assistance."[78]

Another example of attributing significant causal
power to ideas occurred in Tyler's discussion of Stephen
Hopkins. After discussing Hopkins' pamphlet arguing
that American colonists deserved the full rights of British subjects, Tyler noted that "the impression made by
this strong and sober-minded pamphlet was very great
throughout the colonies," and that it "carried conviction
to many minds."[79] A Loyalist letter written against Hopkins' pamphlet was also thought by Tyler to have "genuine power" among colonists, evidenced by "the instant
and angry" opposition it engendered.[80] Similarly, after
an analysis of Daniel Dulany's pamphlet in 1765 denying the propriety of parliamentary taxation, Tyler
concluded that Dulany's thought not only "made a deep
impression upon a vast number of his fellow colonists,"
but that it also had "no small effect upon the leaders
of liberal politics in England."[81] John Dickinson's "letters" were second only to Tom Paine's writings "in direct power upon events,"[82] and Tyler discussed both
Dickinson's and Paine's ideas at length. Paine's writings, according to Tyler, had "astonishing effects" and
"precipitated the popular debate" upon the question of
independence.[83] Thus, Tyler's volumes were infused
with the conviction that ideas played a crucial part in
determining men's actions.

Because of the nature of the Revolutionary era, as
he interpreted it, Tyler the literary historian went un-
obtrusively along with Tyler the historian of ideas. In
other words there was little literary history during the

[78] *Ibid.*, p. 36.
[80] *Ibid.*, p. 74.
[82] *Ibid.*, p. 236.
[79] *Ibid.*, p. 69.
[81] *Ibid.*, p. 110.
[83] *Ibid.*, pp. 475, 476.

period distinct from the history of ideas, in Tyler's view, and so he was free to write two volumes of history fairly consistently focused on ideas. This may have been an accident of Tyler's subject matter, however, as much as any conscious decision on Tyler's part to separate the history of literature from the history of ideas and to concentrate on the latter. In 1897, as in 1878, Tyler was pioneering in literary history at the same time that he was pioneering in the history of ideas.

Tyler's pioneering was recognized at the time. His inclusion and discussion of so many colonial writings of theology, history and other narratives, verse, and public affairs surprised and pleased commentators. One reviewer expressed astonishment that Tyler had made such apparently dead source material live for the late nineteenth century reader. Political historians praised the contribution Tyler made to the study of the American Revolution by telling the history of the ideas of that revolt. All reviewers were impressed by the original way Tyler used colonial writings—many of them not used previously by any historians—to get at ideas.[84]

Tyler was recognized after 1878 as one of the outstanding students both of literature and of history in the United States. He was asked to fill the first chair of American history in 1881; he was one of the founders of the American Historical Association in 1884; he was vice-president of the Association and would nor-

[84] See the following reviews and comments upon Tyler's work: *Atlantic Monthly* review of the colonial volumes (March 1879), p. 405; Paul Leicester Ford's review of the Revolutionary history in *American Historical Review* (July 1897), pp. 738-740 and (January 1898), pp. 375-377; Herbert Osgood's review of the last work in *Political Science Quarterly* (March 1898), pp. 41-59; William Peterfield Trent, "Moses Coit Tyler," *Forum* (August 1901), pp. 750-758; George Lincoln Burr, "Moses Coit Tyler," *Annual Report of the American Historical Association*, 1901, Vol. 1, pp. 189-195.

mally have been elected president had he not died in 1900.

Moses Coit Tyler's reputation as a distinguished pioneer was deserved (and, it may be added, his failure to attract followers immediately was not). He was the first to announce his work as a history of American thought, he presented a vast body of previously undigested seventeenth and eighteenth century writings, and he expressed an attitude toward America's intellectual past which would be repeated by several historians long after his death. Tyler's celebration of Puritan and Revolutionary thought, his sympathy for American religious traditions, and his view of the virtual autonomy of ideas over events were all characteristic of one approach to the writing of American histories of ideas which was followed later.

EDWARD EGGLESTON

Tyler's only scholarly contemporary to join in an investigation of the history of American ideas, Edward Eggleston (1837-1902), made an approach to their common subject which was in several respects different from Tyler's. Eggleston's ideological position contrasted with Tyler's, as did his conception of the role of ideas in history, and the interpretations of history made by the two men were dissimilar.[85]

Eggleston, who wrote novels before he turned to histories, spoke of his fiction in a way which echoed the scientific histories of Draper, Buckle, and Taine. Eggleston remarked that the characters in his novels

[85] For Eggleston's life, see William Peirce Randel's published dissertation, *Edward Eggleston*, New York, 1946, or virtually the identical volume in the Twayne series on American authors, New York, 1963. See also George Cary Eggleston, *The First of the Hoosiers: Reminiscences of Edward Eggleston*, Philadelphia, 1903.

"were all treated in their relations to social conditions."[86] The people in his stories, he wrote on another occasion, were "the logical results of the environment."[87] Because of this perspective, he concluded that his novels had been, however unintentionally, "forerunners of my historic studies."[88] In the preface to one of his early novels, Eggleston wrote that "I have wished to make my stories of value as a contribution to the history of civilization in America":

> A novel should be the truest of books. It partakes in a certain sense of the nature of both history and art. It needs to be true to human nature in its permanent and essential qualities, and it should truthfully represent some specific and temporary manifestation of human nature: that is, some form of society.[89]

He again sounded like Draper, Buckle, and Taine when he said of himself, that as novelist and as historian, "I am mainly interested in the evolution of society; that in either sort of writing this interest in the history of life, this tendency to what the Germans call 'culture-history,' is the one distinguishing trait of almost all that I have attempted."[90]

Eggleston came to a Darwinian interpretation, and to a serious study of society, hesitantly and only in middle-age. Born and raised in Indiana, he was a Methodist preacher throughout his twenties, a writer for Christian denominational publications as well as other periodicals during his thirties, and as late as his forties

[86] "Edward Eggleston: An Interview," *Outlook*, LV (1897), 433.

[87] Eggleston, "Formative Influences," *Forum*, X (November 1890), 286.

[88] "Edward Eggleston: An Interview," p. 433.

[89] Eggleston, *The Mystery of Metropolisville*, New York, 1873, p. 7.

[90] Eggleston, "Formative Influences," p. 287.

he returned to a pastorate. In these respects, his background was like Tyler's. But, unlike Tyler, Eggleston wrote of himself that the "long and painful struggle for emancipation from theological dogma" started when, as a young man, he could not reconcile evolutionary geology with dogmatic Methodism. Finally, "there came a time, later in life than crises usually come," Eggleston recollected in 1887, "when my intellectual conscience insisted that sentiment of every sort ought to be put aside in the search for truth." He had read Thomas à Kempis while riding circuit as a youth, Eggleston recalled, but no more:

> the true way is to "look upward and not downward, outward and not inward, forward and not backward." À Kempis may rest where he is; I would rather walk in wide fields with Charles Darwin; and, above all, I would rather, if it were possible, get one peep into the epoch-making book of the next century, whatever it may be, than to go back to the best of the crypt-worshippers. Perhaps it is but a reaction from the subjective training of my youth, but the objective life seems the better. I doubt whether one can be greatly benefited by a too constant dia-monologue with his own soul such as à Kempis is given to.[91]

By 1880, Eggleston called himself an unbeliever, but the passage quoted above suggests that as one belief was lost another was gained.[92]

[91] Eggleston, "Books That Have Helped Me," *Forum*, III (1887), 584, 586.

[92] In a letter to his daughter, Mrs. Elizabeth Eggleston Seelye, July 5, 1880. The letter, now among the Eggleston papers in the Collection of Regional History at Cornell University Library, is cited by Charles Hirschfeld, "Edward Eggleston: Pioneer in Social History," *Historiography and Urbanization*, Eric Goldman, ed., Baltimore, 1941, p. 199. Eggleston's faith in the progressive accumulation of knowledge allowed him to minimize the significance of changing answers to spe-

Belief in progress through modern science provoked Eggleston to speak of history in scientific terms. History could be made "a reasonable science" by studying "the action of cause and effect and the continuity of institutions and usages."[93] Prefacing the first of two colonial studies in what was intended to be a multivolume series on American life, he wrote that it was "a history in which the succession of cause and effect is the main topic—a history of the dynamics of colony-planting in the first half of the seventeenth century."[94]

At this point, as Eggleston was preparing to begin his first colonial volume, he might easily have been likened by a contemporary observer to Draper, Buckle, and Taine. Faith in progress through science, hostility toward man's religious past, and criticism of traditional histories were positions shared by all four writers. Further, Eggleston's two future books on the 1600's were to be histories of ideas. But despite these important similarities, Eggleston's colonial histories of American thought turned out to be significantly different from Draper's, Buckle's, and Taine's writings. Eggleston's histories were less theoretical, less grandiose, less daring. They kept close to the more limited piece of

---

cific questions: "What conclusions the detached mind reaches on grave questions is a matter of secondary importance. Such conclusions may well be inconstant quantities, for the sphere of the universe is large and that of a human brain very small." ("Books That Have Helped Me," p. 586.)

[93] Eggleston, *A History of the United States and Its People for the Use of Schools*, New York, 1888, p. iv; "A Full Length Portrait of the United States," *Century Magazine*, XXXVII (1889), 791. I am indebted to Charles Hirschfeld for these citations and for first making me aware of Eggleston's scientism. See Charles Hirschfeld, "Edward Eggleston: Pioneer in Social History," in Eric Goldman, ed., *Historiography and Urbanization*, pp. 189-210.

[94] Eggleston, *The Beginners of a Nation*, New York, 1896. Quotations cited refer to fourth edition, 1899, p. viii.

ground they attempted to cover, and they were based upon new research in the primary source materials rather than upon philosophic interpretations of history. Finally, Eggleston in his histories expressed only a common sense approach to the role of ideas despite the frequent statements he had made previously concerning the desirability of ascertaining the influence of the environment in human affairs. What was left in Eggleston's histories to link him with the more ambitious attempts of the more thoroughgoing scientific historians was an ideological predisposition in favor of progress, democracy, skepticism, rationality, and science.

The lack of theory in Eggleston's approach to ideas in his colonial volumes was revealed in part by the fact that he was not altogether conscious of the extent to which he was writing a history of ideas. *The Beginners of a Nation* was in fact ostensibly a pioneering work in the field of social history—hence, "A History of Life in the United States"—even though it actually pioneered in the history of ideas as well. Subtitled *A History of the Source and Rise of the Earliest English Settlements in America with Special Reference to the Life and Character of the People*, there was perhaps a hint of concern with ideas in the word "Character," and the hint was elaborated in the Preface:

> It has been my aim to make these pages reflect the character of the age in which the English colonies were begun, and the traits of the colonists, and to bring into relief the social, political, intellectual, and religious forces that promoted emigration. This does not pretend to be the usual account of all the events attending early colonization. . . . Who were the beginners of English life in America? What propulsions sent them for refuge to a wilderness? What visions

beckoned them to undertake the founding of new states? What manner of men were their leaders?[95]

These comments seemed to announce a history which was to be both social and intellectual in its emphases, at a time when to execute either emphasis successfully would have been unusual.

Eggleston's *The Beginners of a Nation* described in part "the life of the people," and it also narrated the history of ideas associated with early seventeenth century colonization. In most chapters the ideas were treated together with the social history, as many of the chapter titles suggest: "The Procession of Motives"; "Rise and Development of Puritanism"; "Separation and the Scrooby Church"; "The Pilgrim Migrations"; "The Great Puritan Exodus"; and "The Catholic Migration." The ideas Eggleston described were mainly religious in character, and he related them to seventeenth century behavior, that is, emigration and re-settlement in the New World. For example, Eggleston's opening chapter on Renaissance explorations was titled in terms of ideas, "English Knowledge and Notion of America at the Period of Settlement," and he implied that he included the chapter because

> these erratic notions regarding America give one an insight into the character of the English people at the period of discovery and colony-planting. Credulity and the romantic spirit dwell together. . . . Like every other romantic age the period of Elizabeth and James was prodigal of daring adventure; every notable man aspired to be the hero of a tale.

If one knew this, one better understood that "English beginnings in America were thus made in a time abounding in bold enterprises—enterprises brilliant in

[95] *Ibid.*, p. vii.

conception, but in the execution of which there was often a lack of foresight and practical wisdom."[96] Eggleston had turned a discussion on Renaissance exploration into an example of the mentality of the age. Under Eggleston's scrutiny past ages usually revealed a lack of mentality. The insight which "erratic notions" of the 1600's revealed was just how unenlightened the early colonists were.

Commentators on Eggleston's *Beginners*, at the time and since, have differed as to whether the volume seemed orthodox or unorthodox in content. Those who have failed to see the unorthodox implications of Eggleston's search for ideas as a part of the "life of the people" have probably been deceived by the fact that *The Beginners* was restricted to that early colonization which American historians have always depicted with unusual regard for ideas and for the "life of the people."[97] No previous account had ever denied, for instance, that seventeenth century religious ideas were crucial to the story of New England settlement. Similarly traditional were the source materials Eggleston cited: chronicles, letters, official colony records, diaries, and other familiar writings of the settlers. Because Eggleston was repeating what historians of early colonization had in part already emphasized—its social and intellectual aspects—it was easy to overlook the fact that Eggleston had left out everything else.

If it was difficult to perceive how original were the

[96] *Ibid.*, p. 20.

[97] Commentators who have stressed the orthodox nature of Eggleston's *Beginners*: review in *Outlook*, LV (February 6, 1897), 462-463; Herbert Osgood's review in *American Historical Review*, II (April 1897), 528-530; Arthur M. Schlesinger, introduction to *The Transit of Civilization*, Beacon paperbound edition, 1959, p. xvi. Commentators who have emphasized the unorthodoxy: W. P. Trent's review in *Forum*, XXII (November 1897), 590-599; Charles Hirschfeld, "Edward Eggleston: Pioneer in Social History," pp. 201-204.

innovations of Eggleston in *The Beginners*, it was not hard to see his personal point of view. Reviewers noted Eggleston's unsympathetic account of the Puritans;[98] Eggleston had even warned readers of his intention to debunk, stating in the Preface that he "had not been able to treat" the founding fathers "otherwise than un-reverently." He warned that he had "disregarded that convention which makes it obligatory for a writer of American history to explain that intolerance in the first settlers was not just like other intolerance, and that their cruelty and injustice were justifiable under the circumstances."[99] The intolerance of the first settlers was identified with Puritanism in Eggleston's pages, and Puritanism was vigorously criticized: "When, how-ever, it comes to judging the age itself, and especially to judging the Puritanism of the age, these false and harsh ideals are its sufficient condemnation. Its govern-ment and its very religion were barbarous."[100]

Complementing Eggleston's condemnation of the Puritan establishment was praise for such individuals as Roger Williams or John Robinson, whom Eggleston pictured as forerunners of modern thought. He praised Roger Williams as a forward-looking man of the future who believed in free thought rather than tyranny, and who believed in uncertainty rather than adherence to doctrine:

Here at the very outset of his American life we find that Williams had already embraced the broad prin-ciple that involved the separation of church and state and the most complete religious freedom, and had characteristically pushed this principle to its logical

[98] See *Outlook* (February 6, 1897), pp. 462-463; W. P. Trent's review in *Forum* (November 1897), pp. 590-599.
[99] *The Beginners*, pp. vii-viii.
[100] *Ibid.*, pp. 300-301.

result some centuries in advance of the practice of his age.[101]

And again, he wrote:

> It is interesting to know that Williams, the most romantic figure of the whole Puritan movement, at last found a sort of relief from the austere externalism and ceaseless dogmatism of his age by traveling the road of literalism until he had passed out on the other side into the region of devout and contented uncertainty.[102]

Eggleston's criticism of Puritanism contrasted dramatically with the traditional accounts, but in particular it differed strikingly from Moses Coit Tyler's admiring treatment of the early New Englanders. Even what Eggleston did find to praise suggested his different intellectual outlook. Eggleston complimented the Pilgrim leader John Robinson for his "modern" ideas which contrasted with those of his contemporaries, just as Eggleston had praised Williams. "Robinson understood the progressive nature of truth as apprehended by the human mind in a way that makes him seem singularly modern . . . he declared it 'not possible that . . . full perfection of knowledge should break forth at once.' "[103] Eggleston thought he saw in this seventeenth century divine the same attitude toward truth which Eggleston himself had avowed. It was a conception of truth as both relativistic and progressive; truth was apprehended differently in different periods, but became progressively more true. This conception of truth seemed compatible with the contemporary evolutionary and pragmatic thought of Eggleston's day. Eggleston's own concern with scientific ideas, and his belief in the progress of science and skepticism in making a pro-

[101] *Ibid.*, p. 272.　　[102] *Ibid.*, p. 304.　　[103] *Ibid.*, p. 176.

gressively better world, were distinctive characteristics of his second volume, *The Transit of Civilization*.

Although there was considerable concern for ideas in *The Beginners of a Nation*, it was Eggleston's second and last volume, published in 1900, which was a startlingly original contribution to the history of ideas in America: *The Transit of Civilization: From England to America in the Seventeenth Century*.[104] Eggleston pioneered to such an extent, in fact, that some commentators, in 1900 and afterwards, felt that the book deviated so far from conventional written history as to be pointless and without any comprehensible organization.[105]

The Transit of Civilization was published as the second volume in what was expected to be Eggleston's multivolumed "History of American Life." *The Transit* was not announced as a history of ideas, any more than *The Beginners* had been so announced, but the Preface to the 1900 volume clearly implied that ideas would be featured, and that the ideas would be drawn from previously unexplored areas of colonial intellectual activity. "The complex states of knowing and thinking, of feeling and passion, must be explained," announced Eggleston. "The little world as seen by the man of the seventeenth century must be understood." When Eggleston

[104] Originally published in New York by Appleton and Co. Quotations cited here refer to the 1959 Beacon edition, Boston.

[105] For examples of those who did not know quite what to make of *The Transit*, at the time of publication and since, see Charles Andrews' review in *Political Science Quarterly*, XVII (March 1902), 162-166; Charles Hirschfeld, "Edward Eggleston: Pioneer in Social History," 207-208. Defenders of the volume, on the other hand, have praised its nonpolitical focus, but they have not pointed out explicitly that it was mainly a history of ideas—featuring previously unstudied areas of ideas. An exception is Bernard Bailyn, *Education in the Forming of American Society*, Chapel Hill, 1960, pp. 5-6, who praises it highly.

illustrated briefly what this seventeenth century world was, it turned out to be a world of ideas.

> Its sun, moon, and planets were flames of fire without gravity, revolved about the earth by countless angels; its God governed this one little world with mock majesty. Its heaven, its horrible hell of material fire blown by the mouth of God, its chained demons whose fetters might be loosed, its damnation of infants were to be appreciated and expounded. The inhumanity of punishments and of sport in that day, the mixture made of religion and revenge—these and a hundred other things went to make up the traits of the century.[106]

As Eggleston continued his prefatory remarks, he implied a specific interest in seventeenth century sources of knowledge.

> Eclipses, parhelia, comets, were danger signals hung out in the heavens as warnings. Logic was the only implement for the discovery of truth. Observation was in its birth throes. . . . Right and wrong were thought of only as the result of direct revelation; they had not yet found standing room in the great theater of natural knowledge. Until we understand these things we write the history of the seventeenth century in vain. It is the last age which sought knowledge of physical things by deduction.[107]

Unlike Moses Coit Tyler, Eggleston nowhere actually said he was writing "intellectual history" or a "history of ideas," but he made it clear that he was in effect doing exactly that. Further, Eggleston's prefatory comments implied an interest in a wide variety of areas which had heretofore been untouched.

The variety of the areas is quickly revealed by a sur-

[106] *Ibid.*, p. xxi.   [107] *Ibid.*, p. xxii.

vey of the chapters. The first chapter, "Mental Outfit of the Early Colonists," discussed scientific ideas, particularly astronomical ones. Chapter Two, "Digression Concerning Medical Notions at the Period of Settlement," treated early colonial medical thought. Chapter Three, "Mother English, Folk-Speech, Folk-Lore, and Literature," covered these areas of intellectual activity. Chapter Four, "Weights and Measures of Conduct," treated religious ideas in relation to conduct. Chapter Five, "The Tradition of Education," discussed educational ideas and practices. The concluding section, "Land and Labor in the Early Colonies," described laws and customs of real estate and enforced labor in the colonies. In sum, early seventeenth century ideas of astronomy or astrology, medicine, language, subliterature, religion, education, and property were for the first time in American historical writing discussed in relation to each other and in relation to colonial life generally.

The first chapter exemplified the breadth of Eggleston's scope and yet at the same time his focus on the history of ideas. Entitled "Mental Outfit of the Early Colonists," he argued the importance of understanding colonial ideas:

> Seminal ideas received in childhood, standards of feeling and thinking and living handed down from one overlapping generation to another, make the man English or French or German in the rudimentary outfit of his mind. A gradual change in fundamental notions produces the difference between the character of a nation at an early epoch and that of the same people at a later age.[108]

In the first two pages of this opening chapter, Eggleston mentioned in addition to all the synonyms for ideas

[108] *Ibid.*, p. 1.

already quoted, "controlling traditions," "mental furni-
ture," "opinions," "prejudices," "modes of thinking," "intellectual life," "folk-lore," "superstitions," "beliefs,"
"binding traditions," and "mental outfit." Specifically
Eggleston thought ideas about the astronomical world
crucial to "the popular imagination in the seventeenth
century."[109] Views on astronomy revealed, for example,
the relation of scientific to religious thought:

> When modern light began to dawn and science tried
> to observe, it was not mainly the ordinary and the
> regular that were noted; members of the new Royal
> Society and others thought to learn from the mon-
> strosities and marvels; New England ministers acted
> as soothsayers and expounded the hidden meaning
> of monstrous births, and even played showmen to
> exhibit these ghastly messages from the Almighty.

Scientific and religious ideas were related as well to
everyday life.

> The world invisible as conceived in every age is a
> reflection of the familiar material world; the image
> is often inverted: it may be exaggerated, glorified,
> distorted, but it is still their own old world mirrored
> in the clouds of heaven. Even the love of rank and
> ostentation in the seventeenth century—the snobbery
> of the age—projected itself into heavenly arrange-
> ments.[110]

Eggleston devoted attention to the effect of the New
World environment on the imported ideas:

> The American settlers lived in a different world from
> that which they had left in England, and their con-
> ceptions of the invisible could not escape modification.
> Far removed from the ostentatious conventions of the

[109] *Ibid.*, p. 3.   [110] *Ibid.*, p. 16.

old civilization, the minds of the colonists could no
longer form vivid pictures of heavenly retinues.[111]

Eggleston's opening chapter illustrated also his personal ideology. He repeatedly denigrated the minds of
the seventeenth century and earlier, contrasting them
unfavorably with later minds. References to "that procession of philosophers who with pedantic learning
copied incredibilities from one Latin book to another
down the ages,"[112] to the "never-to-be-questioned authority" of earlier periods, and repeated references to
witchcraft in New England set the tone of Eggleston's
volume. Even the organization of *The Transit* may have
been an expression of Eggleston's unsympathetic attitude toward the past he was describing. The sections
dealing with the scientific ideas of the colonists—those
sections which seemed most absurd to a twentieth century reader—comprised the first one-third of the book
and set the stage for the appearance of the perhaps less
odious remainder of the book. It was a stage set for
unenlightened ideas.

Eggleston's attitude toward the ideas he chronicled
was strikingly different from that of Tyler. Tyler leaned
toward celebrating the ideas he depicted, whereas
Eggleston inclined toward deprecation. In a real sense,
while both focused on the colonial period, Eggleston
wrote a history of "foolish ideas," and Tyler, a history
of "splendid ideas."

The Transit of Civilization, published in 1900, was
Eggleston's last historical writing, and his presidential
address to the American Historical Association, presented in December of 1900, was his last statement
concerning historical scholarship. Eggleston's address,
prepared when he was extremely ill and read for him
because he was unable to attend the meeting, is signifi-

[111] *Ibid.*, p. 18.   [112] *Ibid.*, pp. 12-13.

cant both for the subject matter which he sought to include in written history and for the ideological position which the address revealed.

Eggleston's paper was entitled, "The New History," and this New History was to be largely the "history of culture." When Eggleston spoke for a broadened history which would tell the life of the people, "the real history of men and women," he spoke for historians who, irrespective of their particular social outlooks, objected to history which was primarily political and military in scope. In this vein, Eggleston asked for "the history of culture," history which was "literary," "religious," "cultur-geschichte" [sic]:

> Never was a falser thing said than that history is dead politics and politics living history. Some things are false and some things are perniciously false. This is one of the latter kind. In this saying Freeman expressed his whole theory of history writing, and one understands the point of Green's remark to him: "Freeman, you are neither social, literary, nor religious." A worse condemnation of a historian could hardly be made.[113]

This was not a plea for a separate discipline of intellectual history, but for any broadened history in which the history of ideas would play a large part.

Eggleston predicted that this New History would capture future scholarship, for "when the American Historical Association shall assemble in the closing week a hundred years hence, there will be, do not doubt

[113] *Annual Report of the American Historical Association, 1900*, published in 1901, pp. 39-40. Edward Augustus Freeman (1823-1892) wrote a maxim to the effect that politics constituted the only proper subject matter of history. His friend and fellow English historian, John Richard Green (1837-1883) wrote the pioneering social history, *Short History of the English People* (1874).

it, gifted writers of the history of the people . . . the history of culture, the real history of men and women."[114] The New History ought to replace the old-fashioned, narrow political and military history which, he argued, was as old as Thucydides. Scientists had constantly changed their approach with good results, whereas history was unfortunately always written in the same way. After all, "it would be strange if we had not learned anything of the art of writing history in a cycle of nearly twenty-four hundred years. Let us brush aside once for all the domination of the classic tradition."[115]

The classical histories, which featured politics and wars, were criticized by Eggleston because of the view of man and of the human condition which these histories implied. A particular ideology was intimately associated with this "methodological" plea for different subject matter. Historians had in effect sanctioned political and military conflict in human affairs, according to Eggleston, by spotlighting these conflicts. Scholars should instead help man realize that other aspects of life were both morally superior and more important.

> Politics is the superficial struggle of human ambitions crossed occasionally, but rarely, by a sincere desire to do good. . . . It often sails under false colors, and it will deceive the historian unless he is exceedingly vigilant. It likes to call itself patriotism. . . . But what is patriotism? It is a virtue of the half-developed. Higher than tribal instinct and lower than that great world benevolence that is to be the mark of coming ages.[116]

114 *Ibid.*, p. 47.   115 *Ibid.*, p. 38.
116 *Ibid.*, p. 40. Eggleston expressed his blend of dislike for scholarship in the service of patriotism, and of disinterest in politics in a letter to Herbert Baxter Adams, April 14, 1898: "I dont [*sic*] care for historical study for the sake of American citizenship. Living right at the door of Congress in this tire-

Mankind should be taught to progress beyond the igno-
bility of politics and to try especially to escape beyond
war, which was the extreme example of human disagreement and conflict. "We can not always cover our
pages with gore. It is the object of history to cultivate
this out of man; to teach him the wisdom of diplomacy,
the wisdom of avoidance—in short, the fine wisdom of
arbitration, that last fruit of human experience."[117] This
plea for minimizing the attention paid to war in written
histories was apparently part of a general desire to write
the history of the past in terms of what Eggleston
hoped would be the future—a future which would bring
greater rationality and increased resolution of conflict
by peaceful means to the human situation.

In 1900 Eggleston not only coined the phrase the
"New History" (under which the history of ideas would
first be publicized after the turn of the century), but
he also expressed many facets of the ideological position shared by these "New Historians." In his colonial
histories, Eggleston pioneered in the writing of the history of ideas and intellectual life in America. Just as
his views contrasted with those of Tyler concerning religion, war, science, human progress and Puritanism,
so did Eggleston's discussion of ideas differ in his histories of ideas from Tyler's. Whereas Tyler celebrated
the grandeur and decisiveness of thought in human affairs, Eggleston saw ideas mainly as an index of how
"progressive" and "modern" life was in the past. The

---

some time I don't seem to care much for American citizenship;
it is a brand that covers a discouraging lot of clap-trap. . . .
I am constitutionally not interested in politics living or dead."
For entire letter see W. Stull Holt, ed., *Historical Scholarship
in the United States, 1876-1901: As Revealed in the Corre-
spondence of Herbert B. Adams*, Baltimore, 1938, pp. 253-254.
   [117] *Ibid.*, p. 41.

study of the history of ideas in the United States in the twentieth century was to be undertaken first by the intellectual followers of Edward Eggleston (even though the followers never referred to their predecessor) rather than by the followers of Moses Coit Tyler.

JAMES HARVEY ROBINSON

PURITAN chroniclers and their eighteenth century successors represented with reasonable accuracy, as far as we know, the dominant attitudes and problems of their local communities. These writers, who were usually leading citizens, interpreted intelligently but in a common-sense way the apparent importance which ideas had in determining men's lives. It seemed obvious to the chroniclers that religious opinions had caused emigrations to the New World, and had influenced the character of society after settlement. Ideas were in this sense assumed to be important by early historians, but that assumption was not joined by analysis as to the precise nature of the role of ideas. And from Bradford through Bancroft, ideas were not focused upon for special treatment.

When American ideas were first featured in late nineteenth century histories by Moses Coit Tyler and Edward Eggleston, legacies from earlier American chroniclers remained. The colonial period, particularly in New England, was studied at length and religious beliefs were assumed to be causally powerful. In these pioneer American histories of ideas, as in earlier writings, common sense rather than intensive analysis, concern with the origin and development of the community or nation rather than detached theory, were characteristic.

In the most important American histories of ideas after 1900, theory and specialization of scholarship became increasingly evident, but even more obvious was the intimate relationship between the New Histories of ideas and the major currents of American social thought. The most influential American ideas concerning man and society, in the years between roughly the turn of the century and World War II, comprised a climate of opinion which can be called intellectually "progressive." Despite complexities, ambiguities, and outright disagreements in the intellectual climate of the period, it is possible to perceive a comparatively unified and coherent predisposition for progressive reform.

The philosophical fountain for this overflowing progressivism was William James' pragmatism and, perhaps even more, John Dewey's variant of pragmatism, instrumentalism. Dewey, whose mature intellectual years spanned the entire first half of this century, drew upon the method of modern science in an attempt to reform the quality of life. At the same time, archaic traditions were subjected by reformers to the stringent test of meeting present needs in areas such as education, law, social work, and government. To experiment freely with hypothetical solutions to current problems until solutions were found, was only to apply the scientific approach to everyday life, said Dewey. It has often been pointed out that ultimate goals were not emphasized by Dewey and other reformers as much as immediate techniques, probably because the ultimate goals were assumed to be agreed upon by the community. Pragmatism's, or instrumentalism's, accent upon "means," and its assumption that men would not disagree seriously as to "ends," marked progressive thought in almost all areas. In its analyses of the various "means" which individuals and societies use, pragmatic thought was empirically hardheaded; in its confident assumption of the ease by which agreements as to "ends" could be achieved, pragmatic thought was somewhat less hardheaded. A blend of slashing analysis and softer dream ran throughout pragmatism, pervaded progressivism generally, and permeated the heart of many of the most important histories of the period. It is easier today to see the leaps of faith of early intellectual progressivism than it is to recapture the excitement stemming from its early breadth of interest and its sense of the relevance of knowledge for everyday life. Out of intellectual progressivism's scholarly investigations and commitment to reform came most of the famous intellectual histories of the first half of the twentieth century.

A closer look at intellectual progressivism as the ideological source of many histories of ideas is possible through an examination of the writings of James Harvey Robinson (1863-1936). He was a historian of Europe rather than of the United States, he made his enormous reputation as a teacher and popularizer instead of as a researcher, but he became the best-known New Historian and publicist for the history of ideas in the United States. An examination of Robinson's writings, and a comparison with the earlier writings of Eggleston, also provokes the interesting question of why progressive histories of ideas were not written sooner.

Robinson was born a generation after the births in the 1830's of Tyler and Eggleston, and he received his first two degrees at Harvard. He followed the proper path for one of his period aspiring to be a professional political historian by going to Germany to complete his formal training. In 1890 he submitted to Hermann Eduard von Holst at Freiburg a revision of his earlier Harvard work entitled, "The Original and Derived Features of the Constitution of the United States."[1] Rob-

[1] For Robinson's biography, see Luther V. Hendricks, *James*

inson's first publications, while he was teaching during the 1890's at the University of Pennsylvania and later at Columbia, featured political-constitutional history and edited collections of documentary source materials —both characteristic of orthodox professional scholarship at the time. Robinson was preoccupied with medieval and early modern political history, and—for a few more years—he expressed little interest in expanding the scope of the subject matter of history, just as, in his academic work, he faced away from contemporary problems.

It might seem in one sense normal that Robinson should have devoted his scholarly energies along the same "fact-finding" and political lines which most professional historians were following at the time. He was a young man attempting to secure a place in his academic discipline. But, in another sense, Robinson's youthful orthodoxy which continued until his late thirties might be considered strange, for after 1900 he became increasingly reformist in his demands for a New History. Furthermore, there were several voices calling for a New History during the late 1800's which Robinson ignored, at least at the time.

Working in Robinson's own field of European history, Henry Thomas Buckle in his *Introduction to the History of Civilization in England* made a plea for present-minded histories which strikingly resembled Robinson's call for New Histories a half-century later. Hippolyte Taine, in his history of English literature, also anticipated a much later Robinsonian concern by

---

Harvey Robinson: Teacher of History, New York, 1946. For Robinson's ideas, see Harry Elmer Barnes, "James Harvey Robinson," *American Masters of Social Science*, Howard W. Odum, ed., New York, 1927, pp. 321-408; Morton White, *Social Thought in America: The Revolt Against Formalism*, New York, 1949, *passim*.

investigating the relationship between ideas and their environments. Among Robinson's own countrymen and fellow members of the American Historical Association, Henry Charles Lea, Andrew Dickson White, Moses Coit Tyler, and Edward Eggleston helped break down the narrow structure of political history which Robinson at the time supported. Tyler's wide sweep of source materials included all kinds of written records so that he announced his subject as the "intellectual history of a nation." Eggleston not only wrote a new kind of history, but entitled his presidential address to the guild "The New History."

Finally, there was an anticipation of Robinson's New History in certain social science scholarship of the late nineteenth century which attempted to contribute to the reform of society through an understanding of past and present historical processes. In the field of economics, for example, leaders in the formation of the American Economic Association in 1885, such as Richard Ely, argued that "this younger political economy no longer permits the science to be used as a tool in the hands of the greedy and avaricious for keeping down and oppressing the laboring classes."[2] The new economics, moreover, was historical in approach, for man's experience rather than classical theory was announced as the proper subject matter. It was indicative of the close relationship existent between historians and economists that the first meeting of the economists in 1885 was held jointly with the historians. Close too was the relationship between the sociologists and the economists during the late 1880's and 1890's. The leaders of the young discipline of sociology were members of the American Economic Association, and they expressed

[2] Richard Ely, "The Past and Present of Political Economy," *Johns Hopkins University Studies*, Second Series, III, March 1884, p. 64.

the same blend of enthusiasm for both science and reform. Sociology had to become empirically oriented and therefore aware of changing historical conditions, said Lester Frank Ward, the founder of American sociology, but at the same time the ultimate goal was to improve society.[3]

James Harvey Robinson was aware of the various late nineteenth century pleas for histories with broadened subject matter, and for scholarship geared to the improvement of contemporary society. But it was not until the turn of the century that he began to show a change of mind in this new direction. He then expressed increasing enthusiasm for a wider conception of the content of written history, for a new reliance on the emergent social sciences, and for histories relevant to the present. In his lectures at Columbia he created the first course in the United States entitled "intellectual history," and in *The New History* (1912), *The Mind in the Making* (1921), and *The Humanizing of Knowledge* (1924), Robinson repeated, systematized, and significantly extended Eggleston's plea for a New History.[4] Robinson protested against the "bias for political history" which resulted in "a great many trifling details of dynasties and military history which merely confound the reader and take up precious space." Vigorously Robinson publicized the need for a written history which would be of greater usefulness to the present day: "The present has hitherto been the willing victim of the past; the time has now come when it should turn on the past and exploit it in the interests of advance."

[3] For a convenient survey of the interrelationships of ideas and individuals in the emergent social sciences during the late nineteenth century, see Sidney Fine, *Laissez-Faire and the General Welfare State*, Ann Arbor, 1956, Chapters 7-8.

[4] *The New History*, New York, 1912; *The Mind in the Making*, New York, 1921; *The Humanizing of Knowledge*, New York, 1924, published for Workers Education Bureau of America.

Robinson's ideal histories were to be important to mankind, rather than being the scribblings of antiquarians.

When Robinson talked of his desired New History, he emphasized its usefulness to progressive social betterment.

> Society is to-day engaged in a tremendous and unprecedented effort to better itself in manifold ways. Never has our knowledge of the world and of man been so great as it now is; never before has there been so much general good will and so much intelligent social activity as now prevails. The part that each of us can play in forwarding some phase of this reform will depend upon our understanding of existing conditions and opinion, and these can only be explained, as has been shown, by following more or less carefully the processes that produced them.[5]

This exploitation of the past for the use of the present would come by virtue of the historian asking questions of contemporary significance, he said. The emphasis on explaining what will happen in the present and future through a study of the past implies laws or uniformities which have validity both in the past and in the future. Thus the social sciences were destined to contribute mightily to the New History. Robinson consciously apotheosized science's methods and achievements, and he hoped to make history more scientific:

> The historian is coming to see that his task is essentially different from that of the man of letters, and that his place is rather among the scientists. He is at liberty to use only his scientific imagination, which is quite different from a literary imagination. . . . He esteems the events he finds recorded, not for their dramatic interest, but for the light that they cast on the

[5] "The New History," *The New History*, pp. 8, 24, 23-24.

normal and generally prevalent conditions which gave rise to them. . . . In this respect history is only following the example set by the older natural sciences.[6]

In urging that history become more scientific, Robinson did not say that historical knowledge could ever become as precise or predictive as, say, knowledge of chemistry, but he pleaded for recognition of history's close relationship to all the sciences, and to the social sciences in particular. With characteristic open-mindedness, Robinson argued that

if history is to reach its highest development it must surrender all individualistic aspirations and recognize that it is but one of several ways of studying mankind. It must confess that, like geology, biology, and most other sciences, it is based on sister sciences, that it can only progress with them, must lean largely on them for support, and in return should repay its debt by the contribution which it makes to our general understanding of our species.[7]

A note of excitement ran throughout Robinson's frequent discussions of the social sciences, an excitement which stemmed from the conviction that the new knowledge derived from the social sciences had radically altered man's understanding of himself. Consequently, Robinson asserted that the New History "will avail itself of all those discoveries that are being made about mankind by anthropologists, economists, psychologists, and sociologists—discoveries which during the past fifty years have served to revolutionize our ideas of the origin, progress, and prospects of our race."[8]

Robinson's enthusiasm for the social sciences, his denigration of traditional history, his dream of model-

[6] "The History of History," *ibid.*, p. 52.
[7] "The New Allies of History," *ibid.*, p. 74.
[8] "The New History," *ibid.*, p. 24.

ing the study of history more closely upon the sciences, and his conception of the uses of the New History for reform were elaborations upon Eggleston and all harked back to Buckle. While there was no doubt diminished hope for scientific exactitude in Robinson's pleas for written histories, as compared with Buckle, there was increased hope for worldly reform. It is not far-fetched to observe that Robinson, by moving from traditional political history in the 1890's to his advocacy of the New History in the early 1900's, had paralleled in his intellectual life the move of many Americans in political allegiance from McKinley in 1896 to support of reform after 1900. Just as Robinson himself had changed his mind, so his interest in the history of thought became in part a study of how people changed their minds.

Robinson's specific interest in the history of ideas was related to his curiosity as to how humans "learned" and "re-learned," which, of course, includes changing their minds. Tyler gloried in the nobility of the early American ideas he described, and Eggleston excoriated the stupidity of the beliefs he depicted, but neither Tyler nor Eggleston pondered in print over theories of learning and intellectual change. Like Eggleston, Robinson looked to the present and to the future for an improvement over the past, but Robinson explained in considerable detail how the study of the history of ideas was going to contribute to man's improved state. Cultivation of the history of ideas was to show how certain ideas originated and developed historically in particular situations. By examining whether the present environment has changed, historians would then be able to show what function these and other ideas play in the present environment. For, asked Robinson,

> what more vital has the past to teach us than the manner in which our convictions on large questions

have arisen, developed and changed? We do not, assuredly, owe most of them to painful personal ex- cogitation, but inherit them, along with the institu- tions and social habits of the land in which we live. The content of a well-stocked mind is the product of tens of thousands of years of accumulation. Many widespread notions could by no possibility have orig- inated in modern times, but have arisen in condi- tions quite alien to those of the present. We have too often, in consequence, an outworn intellectual equipment for new and unheard-of tasks. Only a study of the vicissitudes of human opinion can make us fully aware of this and enable us to readjust our views so as to adapt them to our present environ- ment.[9]

The total historical environment responsible for ideas (and for nonintellectual aspects of man's past as well) was, to Robinson, comprised of psychological and intel- lectual components as well as material ones. This over- all environment demanded, in evolutionary fashion, cer- tain responses to it, but the historian should know not only the history of the responses—be they ideas or in- stitutions—but also the history of the causal conditions. Robinson explained, in 1912, that

contemporaneous religious, educational, and legal ideals are not the immediate product of existing cir- cumstances, but were developed in great part during periods when man knew far less than he now does. Curiously enough our habits of thought change much more slowly than our environment and are usually far in arrears.[10]

[9] *Ibid.*, pp. 102-103.
[10] *Ibid.*, p. 22. There is an Egglestonian tenor to Robinson's remark that these ideals grew up in the past "when man knew far less than he now does."

"Existing circumstances," including an understanding of the state of knowledge in the past, would thus be needed to understand the origin of religious, educational, and legal ideals. Robinson assumed that the existing historical environment prodded human thought to change, and he assumed that this was a good thing. He argued that a proper historical examination of the origin and development of ideas, in relation to their changing environments, would show whether or not present ideas were up-to-date and rightly adjusted to the contemporary environment. Robinson's discussion usually tended to emphasize the outmoded ideas which he hoped would be changed:

> Our respect for a given institution or social convention may be purely traditional and have little relation to its value, as judged by existing conditions. We are, therefore, in constant danger of viewing present problems with obsolete emotions and of attempting to settle them by obsolete reasoning. This is one of the chief reasons why we are never by any means perfectly adjusted to our environment.
>
> Our notions of a church and its proper function in society, of a capitalist, of a liberal education, of paying taxes, of Sunday observance, of poverty, of war, are determined only to a slight extent by what is happening today. The belief on which I was reared, that God ordained the observance of Sunday from the clouds of Sinai, is an anachronism which could not spontaneously have developed in the United States in the nineteenth century; nevertheless, it still continues to influence the conduct of many persons.[11]

Robinson's most emphatic utterances quoted here are to the effect that new, good ideas, which are well adjusted to present day conditions, need to be widely ac-

[11] *Ibid.*, pp. 22-23.

cepted for the cause of better, more efficient personal
and social action. But beneath this hope that new ideas
will be accepted that fit the environment, can be detected Robinson's belief that at some earlier time in
history it was the environment itself which called these
now out-dated ideas into being. In his pleas for changing
certain old ideas, it is quite true that he stressed the
current, temporary inapplicability of these ideas. But he
viewed their persistence not as testimony to their independent strength, but rather to the fact that temporarily
the new and different environmental conditions had not
as yet compelled these old ideas to be altered. Robinson thought that time would finally see the demise of
ideas hopelessly unrelated to their environment, and
that the environment would be ultimately responsible
for their demise as it was for their origin.[12] In this
strain of Robinson's thought, ideas were ultimately
creatures, rather than creators, of the environment.
Human thought was a tool which was fashioned by an
environmental crucible to help man adjust to his changing environment. Of all environmental components, and
Robinson emphasized that both psychology and the
state of knowledge were important components, he
thought the one most crucial was the economic factor.[13]

[12] The same phenomenon—the existence of ideas not in harmony with their environment—could obviously also have been
interpreted as evidence that ideas are strikingly independent of
environmental conditions.

[13] Robinson called the economic interpretation of history the
best "single explanation ever offered." See "The History of
History," *The New History*, pp. 50-51:

Few, if any, historians would agree that everything can be
explained economically, as many of the socialists and some
economists of good standing would have us believe. But in
the sobered and chastened form in which most economists
now accept the doctrine, it serves to explain far more of the
phenomena of the past than any other single explanation
ever offered. In any case, it is the economist who has opened
up the most fruitful new fields of research by emphasizing

It is striking that Robinson did not develop his assumption that historical environments significantly determine the character of human thought into a theory of the historical relativism of ideas. He did not because he, like Eggleston, was too much an evolutionist, too much a believer in the progressive improvement of human history. Robinson's conviction that society had evolved and was still evolving into a better society was the basic reason for the fact that he was an environmental interpreter but not a relativist. The same conviction was also related to the fact that Robinson did not emphasize an environmental interpretation as much when he referred to the origin and development of some ideas as when he discussed others.

The numerous quotations from Robinson already cited have revealed that when he emphasized the influence of some particular historic environment as an explanation for the origin and development of certain ideas, the ideas were most often those to which he was not sympathetic and whose replacement he was urging. "Outworn" ideas in the early 1900's concerning religion generally and Christianity specifically, ideas about education, capitalism, poverty, war, and the law were deprecated by Robinson as products of historic environments. In depicting various kinds of thinking, Robinson characterized, with obvious pejorative connotation, as "rationalizations" those ideas which people have unthinkingly absorbed from their environment:

> The "real" reasons for our beliefs are concealed from ourselves as well as from others. As we grow up we simply adopt the ideas presented to us in regard to such matters as religion, family relations, property,

---

the importance of those enduring but often inconspicuous factors which almost entirely escaped historians before the middle of the nineteenth century.

business, our country, and the state. We unconsciously absorb them from our environment.

Rationalizing ideas usually have their roots in self-interest: "*Rationalizing is the self-exculpation which occurs when we feel ourselves, or our group, accused of misapprehension or error.*" Or, again: "We are by nature stubbornly pledged to defend our own from attack, whether it be our person, our family, our property, or our opinion."[14] Throughout Robinson's comments emphasizing the decisive power of the environment in forming thought, a tenor of criticism of the resulting thought is evident.[15]

But Robinson did not always emphasize the power of the environment in originating and developing ideas. There was another strain in his remarks on the nature of ideas, a strain which stressed the creativity of ideas and their independence from any environmental influence. He expressed this view of human thought when referring to ideas he admired. Minimizing the influence of any environmental factors in influencing these ideas, Robinson labeled them "creative thought," in contrast to "rationalizations." Creative thought, he said,

> is not the defense of our own cherished beliefs and prejudices just because they are our own—mere plausible excuses for remaining of the same mind. On the contrary, it is that peculiar species of thought which leads us to *change* our mind.
>
> It is this kind of thought that has raised man from his pristine, subsavage ignorance and squalor to the

[14] *The Mind in the Making*, pp. 42-43, 44, 41.

[15] And, strangely enough, this critical tenor was present despite the fact that Robinson was virtually in the same breath urging that old ideas be brought into adjustment with new environments. The contradiction is explained only by the differing degrees of sympathy he felt for the ideas being discussed in each case.

degree of knowledge and comfort which he now possesses.

The most impressive examples of "creative intelligence" to Robinson were modern scientific ideas, "the most striking instances of the effects of scrupulous, objective thinking."[16] Whereas rationalizations were ideas as instruments in the sense that the environment molded them, creative ideas were instruments in a sense which defined their creative force as coming from thought itself. Creative thought was an instrument which could be used to change, to reform, the environment.

Robinson might be called an "environmental-relativist" when destructively criticizing ideas which he disliked, and a "progressive-absolutist" when praising ideas of which he approved. There were thus two sides to Robinson's conception of the influence of ideas in human affairs, but both sides were built on a common foundation: the faith or hope that man had improved and would continue to improve his situation significantly. Robinson's belief in progress was intertwined with his whole ideological position. He shared the progressivism of many later historians which was expressed by all of them in piecemeal fashion rather than in a philosophical system. Robinson viewed modern society in western Europe and in the United States as constituting the zenith in human achievement, and challengers of this alleged superiority—defenders of ancient Greece, for example—irritated Robinson considerably. He pointed out that "The Greeks had no telescopes, nor microscopes, nor thermometers, nor spectroscopes. Their knowledge was at best the result of what would seem to us crude and haphazard observation which tended to take the form of accepted authority." In addition to modern experimental science constituting evidence of

[16] *The Mind in the Making*, pp. 48-49, 55.

human progress, in Robinson's eyes, there was also strong evidence for progress in the fact that "the democratic spirit" continued to develop. Indeed, the newer social sciences were related to modern democratic thought, according to Robinson:

It is this appreciation of the common man which is reflected in our development of social sciences, undreamed of by the Greeks, and in the socializing of older subjects, such as psychology and ethics. Political economy was born in the eighteenth century; in the nineteenth anthropology developed on a large scale, together with the comparative study of religions, sociology, and social psychology.[17]

Robinson was equally optimistic about industrialism, urbanization, and increased communication. The industrial revolution provoked "unsuspected possibilities of social readjustment and the promotion of human happiness." He wrote:

Associated with these same economic changes is the development of world-commerce and of incredibly efficient means of communication, which have brought mankind together throughout the whole earth in a spirit of competition, emulation, and co-operation. It will not be many years before every one on the face of the globe can read and write and be in a position through our means of intercommunication to follow the course of events in every portion of the earth. This astonishing condition of affairs suggests boundless possibilities of human brotherhood.[18]

So deep was Robinson's optimistic belief in progress that he virtually equated "change" and "betterment." He stated that "history, *namely change*, has been mainly

[17] "Reflections on Intellectual History," *ibid.*, pp. 123-124.
[18] *Ibid.*, pp. 125, 126.

due to a small number of 'seers,'—really gropers and monkeyers—whose native curiosity outran that of their fellows and led them to escape here and there from the sanctified blindness of their time."[19]

Robinson thought that the progress achieved in the past had been largely unconscious, but it had become increasingly realized that man could consciously direct even more rapid progress: this realization was the birth of the idea of human progress.

> The nineteenth century proved conclusively that he [man] *had* been learning and *had* been bettering himself for hundreds of thousands of years. But all this earlier progress had been *unconscious*. For the first time, close upon our own day, progress became an ideal consciously proclaimed and sought. So, whatever the progress of man has been during the twelve hours which we assign to him since he became a man, it was only at about one minute to twelve *that he came to wish to progress, and still more recently that he came to see that he can voluntarily progress, and that he has progressed*. This appears to me to be the most impressive message that history has to give us, and the most vital in the light that it casts on the conduct of life.

The concept of progress thus seemed to Robinson "the greatest single idea in the whole history of mankind."[20] With the help of this idea, man could more efficiently bend history to his own ends. What these ends were, for Robinson, has perhaps already been suggested because Robinson's social thought permeated his historical writing.

Democratic social reform was of course important in

[19] *The Mind in the Making*, pp. 79-80.
[20] "The Spirit of Conservatism," *The New History*, pp. 251-252, 247.

Robinson's thought, and it was linked with pacifistic sentiment.[21] Robinson felt that "The abolition of poverty and disease and war, and the promotion of happy and rational lives" could be successful if people would simply look forward to the potential future rather than backward to what has always been. "The reformer who appeals to the future is a recent upstart," but "it is clear enough today that the conscious reformer who appeals to the future is the final product of a progressive order of things." Indeed, Robinson thought that "the long-disputed sin against the Holy Ghost has been found; it

[21] The precise extent of Robinson's pacifism is difficult to determine from his published writings. It is obvious that he thought World War I and American participation in it disappointingly irrational.

In *The Mind in the Making* (1921), while criticizing the great cost of the traditional, "muddling through" approach to social relations, Robinson brought up the First World War:

> An arresting example of what this muddling may mean we have seen during these recent years in the slaying or maiming of fifteen million of our young men, resulting in incalculable loss, continued disorder, and bewilderment. Yet men seem blindly driven to defend and perpetuate the conditions which produced the last disaster. (p. 13)

It seems also, but this is a matter of tone rather than explicit statement, that Robinson afterwards regarded American participation in World War I as a disastrous mistake. See his 1929 presidential address to the American Historical Association:

> Beginning with 1914 the old ways of historians were put to a fearful test. How did these old ways bear the test? Very badly, as I think we must all admit. Did such knowledge as historians have arduously accumulated of the past serve to make them wiser than their fellows? Hardly. In all countries they were unable to overcome their native susceptibility to the prejudices of their particular tribe. They applauded the old battle cries. They blew trumpets and grasped halberds. They gulped down propaganda which in a later mood they realized was nauseous. They were, in short, easily sold out, for their studies had not prepared them to assess the sudden emotional crisis much better than the man in the street. ("The Newer Ways of Historians," *American Historical Review*, xxxv [January 1930], 252.)

may be the refusal to cooperate with the vital principle of betterment. History would seem, in short, to condemn the principle of conservatism as a hopeless and wicked anachronism." Robinson argued that the "conservatives' " conception of a fixed human nature, and consequently the alleged impossibility of radical reform, was based upon faulty knowledge. He argued "that a great part of what has been mistaken for *nature* is really *nurture*." The anthropologist and psychologist had shown, according to Robinson, the importance of the physical and intellectual environment in forming human behavior. "Those things that the radical would alter and the conservative defend are therefore not traits of human nature but artificial achievements of human nurture."[22]

Thus Robinson's conception of knowledge derived from the social sciences was associated with his social views. Because "nurture" was so important, education was therefore a potent force in making society for good or ill, and Robinson was severely critical of the fact that

> we make no consistent effort to cultivate a progressive spirit in our boys and girls. . . . They are still so largely nurtured upon the abstract and the classical that we scarcely yet dare to bring education into relation with life. . . . They are reared with too much respect for the past, too little confidence for the future.[23]

From the social sciences, as well as from the natural sciences, Robinson drew support for his naturalistic or sociological view of religion. He wrote in the late 1920's that

[22] "The Spirit of Conservatism," *The New History*, pp. 263, 264, 265, 253, 254 (italics in original).

[23] *Ibid.*, p. 265. See also *The Mind in the Making*, pp. 18-23, for a criticism of traditional education and a plea for a more "progressive" education.

the intellectual climate in which religious beliefs and practices must hold their own underwent a sharp and surprising alteration in the early twentieth century. New, or previously over-looked, information about man, his origin and proclivities, his ancient ways and his observable habits in various stages of culture, promised to explain, or at least recast, the whole estimate of religious phenomena.[24]

Robinson asked whether it would "not be better in the interest of clarity to regard religion, not as a mystic and essential entity, but as a label which we attach to one division of our beliefs, emotions, and deeds?"[25]

Thus Robinson was critical of organized religion as being essentially superstitious, he was opposed to traditional education and in favor of "progressive" education, he attacked policies and practices which had led to American entry into World War One, and he was hostile to the economic status quo. These reformist ideas, which went to make up his ideological outlook, were joined by reformist pleas for the writing of history. In his "new history," Robinson gave an important place to the writing of the history of ideas. In the new histories of ideas for which Robinson pleaded, both the environmental analysis of outworn ideas and the celebration of creative thought received support from his belief in progress:

In the career of conscious social readjustment upon which mankind is now embarked, it would seem as

[24] From Robinson's essay, "Religion," in Charles Beard's symposium, *Whither Mankind*, New York, 1928, p. 264.

[25] *Ibid.*, p. 268. Also: "Paul says confidently that 'When I was a child, I spake as a child, I felt as a child, I thought as a child: now that I am become a man, I have put away childish things.' Alas, this does not take place with many of us. The majority of men and women do not revise many of their earlier impressions after thirteen or fourteen years of age. . . . This is rather especially true of religious beliefs." *Ibid.*, p. 278.

if the history of thought should play a very important part, for social changes must be accompanied by emotional readjustments and determined by intellectual guidance. The history of thought is one of the most potent means of dissolving the bonds of prejudice and the restraints of routine. It not only enables us to reach a clear perception of our duties and responsibilities by explaining the manner in which existing problems have arisen, but it promotes that intellectual liberty upon which progress fundamentally depends.[26]

Robinson's reformist ideas about society have been chosen from various areas because they were later to appear in several American histories of ideas—the same histories which were to express views similar to those of Robinson concerning the nature of ideas in history. In Robinson's writings, as in the writings of others, there was a welding together of social thought, conceptions of ideas in human affairs, and pleas for writing histories of ideas in a certain fashion. Robinson's importance to the development of the writing of American intellectual histories is that of a publicist who, in going beyond Eggleston by fervently arguing for the relevance of the study of historical ideas, issued precepts which were later carried into practice.[27]

[26] "Reflections on Intellectual History," *The New History*, pp. 130-131.

[27] James Harvey Robinson was the best-known publicist for the New History, and for the New Intellectual History. Equally active, if less famous, as a publicist for the New History generally, and for the history of ideas, was Harry Elmer Barnes. A student of Robinson between 1915 and 1920, Barnes went on to write more than Robinson in defense of the New History, but the defenses were roughly the same—except for Barnes' great sympathy for sociology. See Barnes, *The New History and the Social Studies*, New York, 1925; *History and the Social Intelligence*, New York, 1926.

CHARLES A. BEARD

All James Harvey Robinson's precepts for social reform, his two-sided view of the origin and development
of ideas in the past, and his plea for histories showing
how ideas grew found expression in the writings of his
younger friend and Columbia colleague, Charles Austin
Beard (1874-1948).[28]

Beard was the son of a "copper-riveted, rock-ribbed,
Mark Hanna, true-blue Republican"—so the historian
characterized his father—but after going to DePauw
College in Indiana and after seeing Chicago in the
1890's (with its shameful poverty and attempts to help
the unfortunate), the young Beard dedicated himself to
social reform.[29] As a graduate student in England in

[28] For Beard's life and work, see the following: *Charles A.
Beard: An Appraisal*, Howard Beale, ed., Louisville, 1954, col-
lection of essays by Eric Goldman, Harold Laski, Max Lerner,
Luther Gulick, George Soule, Richard Hofstadter, Walten Ham-
ilton, George Leighton, Merle Curti, Arthur Macmahon, George
Counts and Beale; Lee Benson, *Turner and Beard: American
Historical Writing Reconsidered*, Glencoe, Ill., 1960; Bernard
Borning, *The Political and Social Thought of Charles A. Beard*,
Seattle, 1962; Merle Curti, "A Great Teacher's Teacher,"
printed in Curti, *Probing Our Past*, New York, 1955, pp. 55-56;
Eric Goldman, "The Origins of Beard's Economic Interpreta-
tion of the Constitution," *Journal of the History of Ideas*, XIII
(April 1952), 234-249; Richard Hofstadter, "Beard and the
Constitution: The History of an Idea," *American Quarterly*, II
(Fall 1950), 195-213; Lloyd Sorenson, "Charles A. Beard and
German Historiographical Thought," *Mississippi Valley His-
torical Review*, XLII (September 1955), 274-287; Cushing
Strout, *The Pragmatic Revolt in American History: Carl Becker
and Charles Beard*, New Haven, 1958; B. T. Wilkins, "Frederick York Powell and Charles A. Beard: A Study in Anglo-
American Historiography and Social Thought," *American Quarterly*, XI (Spring 1959), 21-39; William Appleman Williams,
"A Note on Charles Austin Beard's Search for a General Theory
of Causation," *American Historical Review*, LXII (October
1956), 59-80.

[29] Quoted by Strout, from *Current Biography*, p. 88. For an
article on one of the DePauw teachers of Beard (and of his

1899, Beard helped found Ruskin Hall, Oxford's work-ingman's college, and he wrote and spoke in support of increased benefits for laborers.

> Let us hope [Beard wrote in 1900] that the new cen-tury will witness the triumph of the Co-operative ideal, and that humanity will have freed itself from the injustice, ignorance, and folly which to-day allow the few to live upon the toil of the many.[30]

"The central theme of history," said Beard in his first published volume which appeared in England in 1901, was mankind's triumph over "priestcraft, feudal ty-rants, and warring elements." Beard expressed the hope that, as the industrial revolution continued, "the people, instead of a few capitalists, will reap the benefits," and that modern technology would give "the material key to man's spiritual progress."[31]

After Beard returned to the United States at the turn of the century, his public service and reform ac-tivities continued. He was a leading member of the New York Bureau of Municipal Research and served as di-rector of its Training School for Public Service for sev-eral years; he resigned his academic position perma-nently at Columbia University during World War I in order to further the cause of academic freedom through dramatizing his protest of Columbia's dis-missal of faculty pacifists; he served actively on educa-

---

future wife, Mary Ritter), see Curti, "A Great Teacher's Teacher."

[30] Quoted by Strout, from Beard, "Co-operation and the New Century," *Young Oxford*, II (1900), 100. For Beard in Eng-land, see Burleigh Taylor Wilkins, "Charles A. Beard on the Founding of Ruskin Hall," *Indiana Magazine of History*, XII (September 1956), 77-84, and "Frederick York Powell and Charles A. Beard: A Study in Anglo-American Historiography and Social Thought."

[31] Quoted by Strout, pp. 89-90, from Beard, *The Industrial Revolution*, London, 1901, pp. 86, 53, 42.

tional commissions, such as the Commission on the Social Studies of the American Historical Association for which he wrote *A Charter for the Social Sciences in the Schools*, a plea for education to contribute to social reform.[32] After the First World War, Beard joined with Robinson, John Dewey, Herbert Croly, Alvin Johnson, and Thorstein Veblen to found, and teach in, the New School for Social Research. These activities of Beard the citizen revealed one aspect of the many-sided historian.

Beard began his dissertation, *The Office of Justice of the Peace in England and Its Origin and Development*, in England in 1898, and completed and published it in 1904.[33] The subject of the dissertation and its execution bore no similarity either to his own 1901 pamphlet, *The Industrial Revolution*, or to his later writings. *The Office of Justice of the Peace*, like James Harvey Robinson's pre-1900 scholarship, was orthodox political history. Not long after Beard joined the faculty at Columbia, he helped turn Robinson's *Introduction to the History of Western Europe* (1903) into the more radical and even more widely read *The Development of Modern Europe* (1907-1908). Beard and Robinson objected, in their Preface, to the irrelevance of traditional written history to contemporary needs and interests, and they objected also to the narrowness of traditional political-military history.

> In preparing the volume in hand [said Robinson and Beard] the writers have consistently subordinated the past to the present. It has been their ever-conscious aim to enable the reader to catch up with his own times; to read intelligently the foreign news in the morning paper . . . the writers have ventured to de-

[32] Volume 1 of sixteen volumes which comprised the Report of the Commission, New York, 1932.
[33] New York, 1904.

vote much less space to purely political and military events than has commonly been assigned to them in histories of the nineteenth century. On the other hand, the more fundamental economic matters have been generously treated,—the Industrial Revolution, commerce and the colonies, the internal reforms of the European states, even the general advance of science, have all, so far as possible, been given their just due.[34]

The Preface, with its attention to economics, showed the Beard influence, but it was characteristic of Robinson's New History that some emphasis was placed both on ideas (science and social reform being included) and also on the environment, the "reality" which was behind or underneath the ideas. The dominant focus, nevertheless, was on political history. The single chapter (of sixteen) in Volume 1 which was devoted to ideas, other than discussions of the church, concentrated on early modern scientific ideas and included a discussion of their implications for social reform. Entitled "The Spirit of Reform," the chapter described how modern scientific ideas liberated Europeans from "an unreasoning respect and veneration for the past," and helped them "to feel that the chief obstacles to progress were the outworn institutions, the ignorance and prejudices of their forefathers, and that if they could only be freed from this incubus, they would find it easy to create new and enlightened laws and institutions to suit their needs."[35] Similarly, in Volume 2 of Robinson's and Beard's *The Development of Modern Europe*, the only discussion of ideas (other than those associated directly with politics) concerned scientific thought and social reforms, for a total of roughly one chapter out of fifteen. Obviously the text was still largely

[34] *The Development of Modern Europe*, 2 vols., Boston, 1907-1908, Vol. 1, pp. iii, iv.
[35] *Ibid.*, 1, p. 157.

political history, varied slightly by intellectual and economic inquiries.

It was the economic inquiry, the economic aspect of the hard, basic "reality" which Beard pursued in much of his early American historical work. He investigated and emphasized one aspect—the economic—of the total historical environment (physical, intellectual, social, and economic) from which certain political ideas and institutions developed. There was a parallel between Robinson's interest in social science as a means of finding out how ideas are learned and transmitted, and Beard's interest in economics as the environmental origin of political thought. Both Robinson and Beard were here agreed that certain beliefs were best studied in relation to their environmental origins. The implications were considerable for studying the history of ideas, although Beard's scholarly work in the early 1900's did not consist of what is usually called intellectual history—so much of the scholarship concentrated on the economic and political background and the ideas discussed were wholly political.

Beard's most famous monograph, *An Economic Interpretation of the Constitution of the United States* (1913), was written as a corrective to traditional historical accounts which lacked "analysis of determining forces" in the environment which were responsible for the ideas which appeared in the Constitution:[36] "Nowhere in the commentaries [on the Constitution] is there any evidence of the fact that the rules of fundamental law are designed to protect any class in its rights, or secure the property of one group against the assaults of another." Beard argued that since "the primary object" of any government was "the making of the rules which determine the property relations of members of society,

[36] New York, 1913, 1935, p. 10. Quotations cited here refer to the 1935 edition.

the dominant classes whose rights are thus to be determined must perforce obtain from the government such rules as are consonant with the larger interests necessary to the continuance of their economic processes." Thus, wrote Beard at the outset of his examination of the economic factors behind the ideas which went into the American Constitution: "the social structure by which one type of legislation is secured and another prevented—that is, the constitution—is a secondary or derivative feature arising from the nature of the economic groups seeking positive action and negative restraint."[37]

Beard then attempted to show a correlation between property holding and political beliefs, or more precisely, certain types of property holding and certain kinds of political beliefs. As he concluded:

> the contest over the Constitution was not primarily a war over abstract political ideals, such as state's rights and centralization, but over concrete economic issues, and the political division which accompanied it was substantially along the lines the interests affected. . . . It may be truly said that the Constitution was a product of a struggle between capitalistic and agrarian interests.[38]

The heart of *An Economic Interpretation* was comprised of a collective biography of the members of the Constitutional convention, including mainly economic data, and there was little discussion of political opinions. However, one chapter out of eleven, roughly 6 per cent of the total pages, was devoted to "The Political Doctrines of the Members of the Convention," and here political views were briefly described. Perhaps Beard's

[37] *Ibid.*, pp. 11-12, 13.
[38] Beard, *Economic Origins of Jeffersonian Democracy*, New York, 1915, 1943, p. 3. Quotation cited here refers to 1943 edition.

method is best characterized, for present purposes, by noting that in a sense the purpose of the entire volume was to "explain" the brief chapter on "Political Doctrines." For Beard, the most illuminating way to explain these political ideas was through studying certain economic factors in the environment from which the political beliefs developed.

Beard's *Economic Origins of Jeffersonian Democracy* (1915) pushed the economic interpretation of the Constitution's formation into the period culminating in Jefferson's election in 1800. In this volume Beard devoted more attention to an analysis of the ideas of specific individuals, however, and there were separate chapters on the political ideas of John Taylor, Thomas Jefferson, and John Adams. In this respect, *Economic Origins* took at least a small step in the direction of *The Rise of American Civilization* (1927) in which Beard, in addition to applying an economic interpretation to the entire course of American history, for the first time widened the scope of his subject matter beyond politics to include social and intellectual life.[39] One-third of the pages of *The Rise of American Civilization* treated social and intellectual life, and the political history itself was related to social and economic phenomena.[40]

In part, Beard's discussion of thought in *The Rise* logically and consistently followed his economic approach in the *Constitution* and *Jeffersonian* volumes. Thus, Beard opened his characterization of colonial social and intellectual life:

> The prevailing class structure by which the provincial culture of America was so largely conditioned was derived in the main from the mother country.

[39] 2 vols., New York, 1927. Quotations cited here refer to 1930 one-volume edition.

[40] Chapters 4, 10, 16, of Volume 1; Chapters 25, 30 of Volume 2.

Although it is sometimes imagined, on the basis of schoolbook fictions, that the colonies were local democracies formed on the pure principles of a New World philosophy and founded on substantive economic equality, the facts of the case lend little color to that view.

Beard based much of his discussion of colonial intellectual life on the economic and social environment. Although ideas were not altogether ignored as causal agents historically, their influence was here minimized. New World religious doctrines contributed to a changing of the colonial family institution, for instance, but economic forces in the colonies were even more important.

Under the pressure of these forces and enlarged opportunities, bonds of kinship were snapped; branches of families and emancipated individuals scattered themselves among settlements all the way from New Hampshire to Georgia; and young men of ability made their way out of poverty with a speed that kept all society in ferment. By no social magic could any institution as secure as the English county family be maintained in America.[41]

Most of the thrust of the colonial section of *The Rise of American Civilization*, the motion which kept the story moving, came from economic factors, even in the brief descriptions of intellectual life. The same economic conditions which eroded colonial religious thought, were partially responsible for new eighteenth century beliefs.

The same fruitful economic development, that gave thousands of starving European peasants prosperity in America and poured treasures of specie and goods

[41] *Ibid.*, Vol. 1, pp. 125-126, 138.

into the markets of the world, opened up before the submerged masses of England and the Continent for the first time in their long history the possibility of attaining for themselves something beyond a bare pittance—some of the certainty, some of the pleasures and luxuries that had been enjoyed only by lords, merchants, and bishops. No philosophy of innate sin, of a baffled life, no promise of transports in heaven could stem the great desire of multitudes for the delights of this life enjoyed by their superiors—and all these strivings were secular in spirit and outcome.[42]

These beliefs in a different and better life were the new eighteenth century ideas in which Beard was most interested. And although Beard emphasized the economic roots and support of these new ideas which were to break down the old thought-world and build up the modern world of science and democratic reform, he, like Robinson, also attributed a special creativity, a nonenvironmental causal power, to these new ideas. Beard described as integral components of the modern spirit both social scientific thought and "the irresistible current" of scientific ideas generally.[43]

The only individual idea in *The Rise* to which Beard devoted extended treatment (more than seven pages) was the one which synthesized modern scientific thought and democratic reform ideas: the idea of progress. Beard did not deny that eighteenth century economic conditions contributed to the belief in progress, but he did emphasize the intrinsic causal force of the idea itself. He called the belief in progress "the most dynamic social theory ever shaped in the history of thought,"[44] and defined it as the belief in the "contin-

[42] *Ibid.*, p. 151.

[43] *Ibid.*, pp. 151-162. For quoted phrase, see p. 451.

[44] *Ibid.*, p. 443. For discussion of the idea of progress in Vol. 1, see pp. 443-447, 454-457.

ual improvement in the lot of mankind on this earth by
the attainment of knowledge and the subjugation of the
material world to the requirements of human welfare."
He discussed the close connection between democratic
reform and modern science which contributed to the
belief in progress:

> It is one of the significant phases of history that the
> development of political democracy during three rev-
> olutionary centuries was accompanied by the rise and
> growth of science and invention. . . . Yet the fact
> remains that political democracy and natural science
> rose and flourished together.

As Beard continued, he discussed the decisive influence of reform thought and of scientific ideas in trans-
forming the modern world:

> Democracy arrested the attention of idle curiosity and
> demanded that the man of microscope and test tube
> come into the street to invent, relieve, and serve.
> Science, on the other hand, helped to determine the
> course of democratic development. . . . Nothing was
> sacred to its relentless inquiry. Before it there was
> neither prerogative nor privilege.
>
> More than that, science pointed the way to pro-
> gressive democracy in its warfare against starvation,
> poverty, disease, and ignorance, indicating how
> classes and nations long engaged in strife among
> themselves might unite to wring from nature the
> secret of security and the good life. It was science,
> not paper declarations relating to the idea of prog-
> ress, that at last made patent the practical methods
> by which democracy could raise the standard of liv-
> ing for the great masses of the people. Finally sci-
> ence gave to man revolutionary concepts of the world
> and of his place in the great scheme of nature, feed-

ing the streams of thought which wore down ancient
institutions of church and state.[45]

Beard's tone—implicitly glorifying certain ideas—if
not his precise language, was here in marked contrast
to his earlier *Economic Interpretation* and *Economic
Origins*; it was also in contrast to other sections of *The
Rise of American Civilization*, which presented certain
ideas largely as expressions of economic environmental
factors. As he wrote in a discussion of the Glorious
Revolution of 1688, religious ideas were brought into
the seventeenth century argument as a "defense mech-
anism" by "men who were engaged in resisting taxes."
"All that was reasonable enough but the historian need
not tarry long with the logical devices of men in action."
Beard frequently reiterated his conviction that the
foundation of intellectual life was ultimately economic.

the worlds of fact and spirit evolve together; the
changing circumstances that mark the economic and
social development of nations into epochs also give
periods to the evolution of arts and letters. Divisions
are never sharp but they are undeniable. The America of cotton mills, blast furnaces, and a continental
empire was not the America of stage-coaches, hand-
looms, and seaboard villages.[46]

Specifically singling out one defense of the economic
status quo during the late nineteenth century, Beard interpreted the ideas contained in it, in Robinsonian
fashion, as little more than reflexes:

The capitalist system, in which the plutocracy flourished, like every other social organism, had to evolve
a scheme of defense and, as things turned out, the
task of justifying to man his own handiwork fell

[45] *Ibid.*, pp. 443-444, 737, 737-738.
[46] *Ibid.*, pp. 31, 762.

mainly to the economists in the universities that sprang up like mushrooms as the gilded age advanced. At Yale, William G. Sumner vindicated in lecture and treatise the economics of Manchester so acceptable to captains of industry eager to be left alone.[47]

When Beard applied his economic interpretation to beliefs, the result was an obvious minimization of the causal importance of ideas in human affairs. And despite his implied attribution of considerable creative causal force to certain scientific and democratic reform ideas, *The Rise of American Civilization* was in the main a study in economic interpretation. Thus Beard, at the same time that he contributed to the writing of the history of ideas by bringing American intellectual life into *The Rise*, simultaneously minimized the role of historical ideas by frequent application of his economic interpretation.

Beard's historical writings through the 1920's ordinarily emphasized the economic development of beliefs at the expense of their independent causal force—with the exception of some scientific and democratic reform ideas described in *The Rise*. By the early 1920's, however, if not before, certain new emphases appeared in Beard's work and remained in uneasy company with the older ones until the end of his life.

The most famous change in Beard's thought was his new espousal of the theoretical relativism of history.

[47] *Ibid.*, Vol. 2, p. 429. Symptomatic of Beard's wavering conception of the origin and development of ideas, reformist ideas which were critical of the same late nineteenth century status quo were not characterized by Beard as being simply reflexive. Rather, reformist ideas were signs that "social criticism had crept into scholarship. Indeed, university teachers were openly proclaiming that science had nothing to do with bolstering up or assailing any social order; its business, they said, was the search for truth—that corroding acid more disruptive to prevailing modes than any force except the discovery of new ways to easy profits." *Ibid.*, pp. 430-431.

Particularly in his presidential address to the American Historical Association, "Written History as an Act of Faith" (1934),[48] "That Noble Dream" (1935),[49] and *The Nature of the Social Sciences* (1934),[50] Beard criticized the nonrelativistic theory that written history could achieve objectivity in any scientific sense. Beard emphasized the subjective or relative factors involved in the historian's conception, selection, and interpretation of his materials when compared with the essential objectivity or detachment of the scientific method employed, for example, by the chemist. Thus, Beard's espousal of relativism was accompanied by a new emphasis on the difference between written history and the other social sciences on the one hand, and the "true" sciences on the other. When Beard discussed the uniqueness of history and the social sciences and stressed the relativism which these disciplines shared, he referred for support to contemporary European thinkers, including Croce, Mannheim, Riezler, Meinecke, and Heussi. Whether or not these Europeans actually stimulated Beard's relativism, their influence in any case was limited mainly to Beard's theoretical musings on history; his convictions on the validity of the economic interpretation of history did not vanish from his histories through adherence to a theoretical relativism.

Although Beard's new theories on historical relativism did not vitiate entirely his confidence in the economic interpretation of history, they were related to changes in Beard's writing after the 1930's. His historical relativism had emphasized the distinctions between historical and scientific scholarship. Beard argued that it was precisely the intellectual, by which

[48] *American Historical Review*, XXXIX (January 1934), 219-229.
[49] *American Historical Review*, XLI (October 1935), 74-87.
[50] Part VII of the Report of the Commission on the Social Studies of the American Historical Association.

he meant the mental or subjective, factor which made the study of history so different from the study of science. A new strain in Beard's writing appeared in the 1930's, a strain which emphasized that the gist of human history was not so much the environment, but the role of ideas in the environment. Beard wrote in the "History" chapter in *The Nature of the Social Sciences*:

> the central consideration of modern historiography becomes the relation between ideas and interests in history-as-actuality, the relation between individual and mass thought and action on the one side and total environment on the other. It is evident all about us and in the records of history that idea and interest, thought and deed, evolve together. . . . As Kurt Riezler says, there are no interests without ideas and no ideas without interests.

Beard in no sense renounced his view that the environment was important, but for the first time he dwelt upon the great significance of ideas as well.

> By casting off the determinism of empirical historiography, contemporary historiography makes room once more for the role of personality in history. If history is nothing except a "chain of causes" and individuals are merely atoms in the flow of things, then all of us, students and teachers alike, are mere puppets in a mechanical play. If, on the other hand, history-as-actuality is made in part at least by thought and purpose—by ideas—then there is room in the world for will, design, courage, and action, for the thinker who is also a doer. This does not mean that the individual is emancipated from all conditioning circumstances, that he can just make history out of his imagination; but it means that, by understanding the conditioning reality revealed by written history as

thought and description, by anticipating the spirit of the coming age, he may cut new paths through the present and co-operate with others in bringing achievements to pass. In other words, biography is restored to history by this emancipation of historical thought from complete bondage to "the chain-of-causation" idea.[51]

There had been anticipations, to be sure, of Beard's new interest in ideas. In the *Economic Origins of Jeffersonian Democracy* (1915) he treated the political ideas of a few individuals, and in *The Rise of American Civilization* he devoted considerable space to intellectual life, including relatively detailed descriptions of the ideas comprising the belief in progress. But Beard before the 1930's had made no statements suggesting the causal significance of ideas generally, and his economic interpretation of history pointed to their lack of importance. By the 1930's, in contrast, Beard paraphrased Kurt Riezler to the effect that "interests, both psychological and material, change under the impacts of ideas."[52] He continued, "To employ a figure, ideas march, divide, and come into conflict with themselves, with or without relation to the world of external events."[53]

Of whatever importance the theory of historical relativism was to Beard's increasing concern with the role of ideas after 1930, the rise of totalitarianism was apparently of equal or even greater significance. Beard first explicitly linked the threat of totalitarianism with the significance of human ideas in his Introduction to J. B. Bury's *The Idea of Progress* in 1932. In the spirit of his later statements celebrating the force of

[51] *The Nature of the Social Sciences*, pp. 60, 61.
[52] Beard and Vagts, "Currents of Thought in Historiography," *American Historical Review*, XLII (April 1937), 479.
[53] *Ibid.*, p. 461.

the intellect, Beard wrote that the "world is largely ruled by ideas, true and false." An "idea contains potential energy," he continued, for an idea "contains within itself a dynamic power to move individuals and nations, to drive them in the direction of effecting the ends and institutions implicit in it."

Ideas had to be accorded importance, said Beard, because constitutional government depends on it.

> Constitutional and democratic government is impossible unless the significance of ideas is recognized. It is founded on the assumption that all social conflicts will be fought out within the framework set by the fundamental law through the exchange of ideas. To government by opinion there is no other alternative except government by violence.[54]

Beard was here pointing up the importance of "ideas" in two respects. First, and explicitly, he was saying that ideas are the means by which differences are resolved in constitutional governments, and therefore the ideas themselves are of some importance. But second, and implicitly, Beard was committing himself to an idea or value—constitutional and democratic government—and his general statements on the transcendent power of ideas suggested that he thought that such ideas as constitutionalism were of tremendous inherent importance. This emphasis in 1932 was in fundamental contrast with Beard's statement in 1913 that "the rules of fundamental law" embodied in the United States Constitution were designed simply "to secure the property of one group against the assaults of another." This contrast in emphasis may not amount to an explicit contradiction, but it is nonetheless dramatic and significant.

The rise of totalitarianism was apparently what

[54] "Introduction" to J. B. Bury, *The Idea of Progress*, New York, 1932, pp. ix-x.

shocked Beard into a new emphasis upon the importance of devotion to "abstract" ideas or values, a devotion which made the ideas or values assume a new significance. Thus, Beard's increasing respect for the Constitution during the era of totalitarianism—a respect expressed in 1943 in *The Republic* in which he suggested that the "greatest triumph" of the writers of the Constitution was their achievement of constitutional government and avoidance of military despotism—represented an increased respect for ideas without regard to their possible origin.[55]

During these years after 1930, when he was concerned about totalitarianism and its threat to the United States, Beard published two histories of ideas, and an examination of them will reveal to what extent his changed views about the significance of ideas were expressed in his writing. His first book, *The Idea of National Interest* (1934), treated a narrower range of thought than his second book and concentrated on one major concept in American foreign relations. Despite the spotlight on an idea, that of "national interest," Beard did not in this volume show any reduced confidence in his former view that thought was best understood in relation to the environment from which it came. Beard's avowed attempt was to investigate American ideas on the "national interest" through actual behavior rather than through words.

Instead of presenting a detailed analysis of a few thinkers on the idea of national interest, Beard focused on the practical conduct of foreign affairs and on comments about trade and foreign policy by politicians, publicists, and businessmen. Beard opened *The Idea of National Interest* by quoting Charles Evans Hughes, who declared that "foreign policies are not built upon

[55] Beard, *The Republic: Conversations on Fundamentals*, New York, 1943, p. 21.

abstractions. They are the result of practical conceptions of national interest arising from some immediate exigency or standing out vividly in historical perspective."[56] Beard brought out the exigencies of American experience which provoked the practical conceptions resulting in United States foreign policy. The story was told as a historic battle between an agrarian, Jeffersonian conception of national interest and a commercial, Hamiltonian view. Two interests conflicted, as well as two practical conceptions of "national interest," and it was clear that Beard thought the conflict of interest (mainly economic) caused the conflict in ideas: "Public policies, as Secretary Hughes pointedly remarked, are not abstractions. They are not manufactured in the Department of State by phantoms. They are the products of concrete experiences with concrete economic phenomena."[57] In 1934, ideas in the area of foreign relations at least were described by Beard as being rooted largely in economic conditions.[58]

[56] Beard, *The Idea of National Interest*, New York, p. 1.

[57] *Ibid.*, p. 112. The most detailed examination of ideas was a chapter, "Moral Obligation in National Interest," in which Beard analyzed the intellectual composition of altruism or morality in American foreign policy. He apologized for devoting a chapter to exposition of ideas, apart from the behavior or background associated with the ideas: "To take the words and ideas associated with moral obligation out of the context of which they are a part, or away from the events and conditions which they describe, is ordinarily an exercise of dubious validity. And if the purpose in doing so were to subject them to a critical analysis and appraisal, the undertaking would be specious indeed." *Ibid.*, p. 401.

[58] Friedrich Meinecke's *Die Idee der Staatsräson,* 1924, translated into English as *Machiavellism: The Doctrine of Raison d'état and Its Place in Modern History*, London, 1947, Douglas Scott, tr., furnishes opportunity for comparison with Beard's study of the ideas of national interest, and reveals what a different written history emerged from Meinecke's contrasting conviction as to the intrinsic interest and importance of ideas, independent of the environment. Beard was aware of his disagreement with Meinecke in this respect; for he criticized

Beard's second contribution to the history of ideas after 1930 was the only volume in which he tried to locate the central streams of American thought. Published in 1942 as the concluding fourth part of "The Rise of American Civilization" series, *The American Spirit: A Study of the Idea of Civilization in the United States* was Beard's version of a usable American past in a time of totalitarianism. Beard's admiring return to the American past as the era of totalitarianism advanced into the late 1930's has not been the object of intellectual fascination as has been his advocacy of conti-

---

Meinecke for being too abstract, for failing to see that the most important pressures on governments in their foreign relations are not abstractions, but "imperial and trade rivalries, foreign investments, inter-governmental debts, defaulted bonds, or disorders in backward countries." (*The Idea of National Interest*, p. 15.) Meinecke wrote his history of the idea of statism from a detailed examination of the thought of seventeen European thinkers, with only slight attention paid to their economic environments. Meinecke's detailed analysis of ideas was rooted in a conviction that ideas possessed great interest and significance. The study of the history of ideas, said Meinecke,

> marshalls together and presents what the thinking man has made of what happened to him historically, how he has mastered it intellectually, what sort of intellectual consequences he has drawn from it.
>
> By converting experiences into ideas, Man frees himself from the pressure of experience, and creates the fresh powers which fashion life. Ideas are the highest points, to which Man can attain, in which his observing mind and his creative strength unite together and achieve a collective performance. For their own sake (as well as for the sake of their efforts) they are worthy of being looked at from the point of view of universal history. A history of opinions (Herder already remarked) "would really be the key to the history of deeds." The ideas which guide historical life, do certainly not indeed spring solely from the intellectual workshop of the great thinkers; on the contrary, they have a much broader and deeper origin. But it is in this workshop that they are condensed and solidified; it is there, in many cases, that they first assume the form which will have an effect on the progress of events and actions of men. (*Machiavellism*, pp. 20-21.)

nental isolation in foreign policy. Beard's isolationist foreign policy, however, was only his special solution to problems posed by threats to America's existence—an America which, Beard increasingly felt, stood for certain humane ideas or values as much or more than it stood for an amoral battle of economic forces. Beard's search in *The American Spirit* for beliefs which made American society so different from the society of totalitarian countries was quite in contrast with his search in the early 1900's for the economic explanations of the writing of the Constitution.

Beard announced in the Preface to *The American Spirit* that, having dealt previously with "the outward aspects of civilization in the United States," this book would focus on "the interior aspects." "This volume represents," he wrote, "an effort to grasp, through an examination of the written and spoken word, the intellectual and moral qualities that Americans have deemed necessary to civilization in the United States." The Preface explained that the central intellectual synthesis which Beard had found at the heart of American history was "the idea of civilization": Beard thought that "no idea, such as democracy, liberty, or the American way of life, expresses the American spirit so coherently, comprehensively, and systematically as does the idea of civilization."[59]

Both the method and the viewpoint of *The American Spirit* were imbedded in the idea which Beard chose as his focus: "the idea of civilization." It was an idea, or complex of ideas, about man and society in the past, present, and future. By way of definition, Beard wrote:

> This idea of civilization, in a composite formulation, embraces a conception of history as a struggle of human beings in the world for individual and social

[59] *The American Spirit*, New York, 1942, p. v.

perfection—for the good, the true, the beautiful—
against ignorance, disease, the harshness of physical
nature, the forces of barbarism in individuals and in
society. It assigns to history in the United States, so
conceived, unique features in origins, substance, and
development.[60]

In other words, Beard's inclusive idea of civilization
was made up of all the democratic reform thought and
all the scientific knowledge which provided the intellectual foundation for the idea of progress—as Beard
had outlined it earlier in *The Rise*. He portrayed the
American idea of civilization as one of the world-views
characterized by the "optimism, life-affirmation, and
activism that proclaim the ethical will to overcome suf-
fering and other evils and make the good or better prevail in individual behavior and in social arrangements."[61]
Under the threat of totalitarianism, Beard clearly implied the great worth of American social values as inherently humane beliefs of virtually timeless worth.

Beard presented the idea of civilization, describing
its birth in England, France, and the United States in
the eighteenth century, and its unique later development in America. Almost 600 of the book's nearly 700
pages were devoted to tracing the idea's development
in the United States, from Thomas Jefferson to John
Dewey. Beard discussed, for more than two or three
pages each, the ideas of civilization expressed by approximately fifty thinkers. The book's index listed 200
other individuals whose ideas were more briefly discussed. Obviously Beard's method was to sketch briefly
the ideas held by many individuals, and most of the
people he chose to discuss were contributors to reformist thought which was basic to his idea of civilization.

Beard was more concerned with celebrating humane

[60] *Ibid.*, p. 672. [61] *Ibid.*, p. 3.

ideas in this volume than with "explaining" the environmental roots of inhumane ideas. He did not, however, altogether ignore the relation between certain beliefs, to which he was unsympathetic and with which he contrasted the idea of civilization, and certain economic environmental factors of self-interest. Thus, the post-Civil War idea of "individualism" was a belief which was used "especially in relation to economic activities and vested rights."[62] Again, "terrific momentum was given to the idea of individualism," Beard wrote, "by its utility to the most powerful private interests in the country." He continued: "Capitalists eager to rush forward in the business of making money and owners of property content with their possessions, or desirous of more, snapped up the doctrine as a 'scientific' justification for their activities and accumulations." By contrast, when Beard discussed a belief which was part of the sympathetically viewed idea of civilization, namely, the doctrine of individual freedom, no environmental self-interest factors were mentioned. Beard then simply emphasized that "the idea of individual freedom had been one of the major forces in American civilization as fact," and that it "was a creed of seasoned strength."[63]

The American Spirit surveyed the course of American history as a movement toward a secular, democratic, collectivist, isolationist future: the conflict portrayed was that between the representatives of light, whose ideas helped propel Americans forward, and the representatives of darkness, whose thoughts attempted to preserve the social, economic, political, and intellectual status quo. Beard's answer to the totalitarian challenge was for Americans to commit themselves yet more fully to domestic democratic social progress.

In this book, despite his celebration of democratic reform thought without special emphasis upon environ-

[62] *Ibid.*, p. 333.　　　　[63] *Ibid.*, pp. 334, 333.

mental origins, Beard did not customarily analyze ideas in detail. His characteristic technique, even in dealing with ideas to which he attributed considerable causal influence and for which he had sympathy, was to sketch ideas on the run, so to speak, rather than to settle down with them in detailed analysis. Beard's brief descriptions of ideas, together with the fact that his histories dealt largely with "explaining" ideas in terms of the economic environment, in a sense made his total contribution to the writing of intellectual history negative. To put it another way, Beard's overall approach actually minimized the role of ideas.

But to say that Beard minimized the role of ideas in history, and to add that he was inconsistent even in that, does not diminish his importance in the development of the writing of American histories of ideas. He was the Buckle of American historical writing, the first to suggest the possibility of making systematic studies of the relationship between ideas and their material environment. Eggleston and Robinson had written about the desirability of establishing such a relationship, but Beard was the first actually to attempt the task. One's own judgment on the profundity of environmental interpretations of thought will obviously influence his evaluation of Beard's worth as a historian of ideas.[64] Environmental interpreters of history have rightly regarded Beard as an outstanding pioneer and will continue to do so.

CARL BECKER

Carl Becker (1873-1945) revealed in his historical

---

[64] It is no coincidence that the two most approving estimates of Beard as a historian of ideas have been made by historians who subscribe to the essential validity of Beard's economic interpretation of history. See the essays cited above by Howard Beale and William Appleman Williams.

writings that it was possible to share with Robinson and Beard many ideas about society, to adhere to much of their theoretical conception of the origin and development of ideas, and yet to focus on ideas in detail and at length.

Becker, like Robinson and Beard, was born and raised in the Midwest—in and near Waterloo, Iowa. After a year at Cornell College in Iowa, he attended the University of Wisconsin and graduated in 1896. After early graduate work there with Turner, Haskins, and Ely, Becker spent the academic year of 1898-1899 at Columbia doing work with James Harvey Robinson and Herbert Levi Osgood. From this time on—Becker did not receive his Ph.D. from Wisconsin until 1907— he taught, briefly at Pennsylvania State and Dartmouth, for a longer time at Kansas, then at Minnesota, and finally at Cornell.[65]

Becker seems to have been in fundamental agreement with most aspects of Robinson's and Beard's ideological positions, although he lacked their enthusiasm. Before World War One, according to his most recent biographer, Becker shared the "Progressive Faith."[66] He was, in addition, critical of American expansion overseas after the War of 1898, and he suggested that the Philippine occupation occurred "in order to" pour profits into certain big corporations.[67] Although Becker

[65] No American historian has attracted such sensitive commentators as Becker: George Sabine, Preface to Becker's *Freedom and Responsibility in the American Way of Life*, New York, 1945; Charlotte Watkins Smith, *Carl Becker: On History and the Climate of Opinion*, Ithaca, 1956; Cushing Strout, *The Pragmatic Revolt in American History: Carl Becker and Charles Beard*, New Haven, 1958; Burleigh Taylor Wilkins, *Carl Becker*, Cambridge, 1961.

[66] Wilkins, *Carl Becker*, p. 92.

[67] *Ibid.* Becker's biographer has concluded that he "must have voted for Wilson at least once, and for Franklin Roosevelt possibly in 1936, probably in 1940 and 1944. But, as his 'pro-

saw more problems than did Robinson in defining the
reformist "progress" which *The New History* publicized,
yet Becker adhered to the essential Robinsonian hope for
a better world. Disturbed by the difficulty of formulating an objective "definition of progress," Becker's comments in reviewing *The New History* suggested his
basic agreement with Robinson:

> If conscious efforts toward social regeneration are to
> issue in anything more than temporary expedients,
> the distinction between what is natural and perma-
> nent in human society and what is artificial and tem-
> porary must be drawn again in some manner or
> other. But to be in any way effective the distinction
> must be based upon genuine scientific knowledge as
> well as upon emotional faith.

Looking to the emergent social sciences, as did Robinson and Beard, Becker expressed the hope in 1912 that
the "newer sciences of mankind" would contribute to
the problem of defining "progress."[68]

Becker, in addition to sharing a good part of Beard's
and Robinson's reformist hope, expressed sympathy for
an economic interpretation of history,[69] and supported
"revisionist" interpretations of World War One during
the 1920's and early 1930's.[70]

Becker resembled Robinson and Beard in other aspects of his thought as well. Skeptical concerning or-

---

test' votes for Debs [1920] and Thomas [1932] suggest, he
was not a party man." See *ibid.*, p. 12.

[68] Review of Robinson's *The New History*, *The Dial*, LIII
(July 1, 1912), 21.

[69] See, for example, "The Marxian Philosophy of History,"
in *Everyman His Own Historian*, p. 114; "Lord Bryce on Modern Democracies," in *ibid.*, p. 44.

[70] Burleigh Taylor Wilkins marshalls evidence to show Becker's fundamental agreement with the "revisionists," Sidney Fay
and Harry Elmer Barnes. See *Carl Becker*, pp. 125-140.

ganized religion, Becker left the Methodist church while an undergraduate. An admirer of the Enlightenment *philosophes*, Becker sympathized with their contribution to "the rise of history and science," which, as he wrote in *The Heavenly City*, "were but two results of a single impulse, two aspects of the trend of modern thought away from an overdone rationalization of the facts to a more careful and disinterested examination of the facts themselves."[71]

Above all, Becker contributed to the cluster of ideas which comprised Beard's and Robinson's ideological position by his attacks on the claims of the traditional "objective," "scientific," political history which the New History was designed to replace. Becker did not, like Eggleston, Robinson, and Beard, criticize traditional histories for their uselessness and narrowness of scope; rather, Becker argued the functional or instrumental nature of all historical studies. He wrote in 1913 that

> the historians of any age are likely to find those aspects of the past interesting or important which are in some way connected with the intellectual or social conditions of the age in which they live; so that the historical work that is most characteristic of any time may be regarded as embodying an interpretation of the past in terms of present social interests.
>
> Historical thinking is . . . a social instrument, helpful in getting the world's work more effectively done.

Late nineteenth century scholarship, according to Becker, was produced by an environment which was conducive to "objective," "scientific," political histories.

> This attitude of objectivity—the thoroughgoing renunciation of the present, the disposition to reconstruct the past as a whole, to know it for itself alone,

[71] *The Heavenly City of the Eighteenth-Century Philosophers*, New Haven, 1932, p. 20.

to "justify that which is just by the judgment of experience"—undoubtedly this attitude was well suited
to the spirit of the two decades after 1870. The re-
splendent vision of Perfectibility, vouchsafed to the
generous minds of the eighteenth century, was much
dimmed after 1815, and again after 1848. . . . When
all the old foundations were crumbling, historians
held firmly to the belief that facts at least could not
be denied; and in these days of acrid controversy, the
past, studied for itself, as a record of facts which undoubtedly happened, was a kind of neutral ground,
and excellent refuge for those who wished to sit tight
and let the event decide.

Since written histories have usually been functionally
or pragmatically related to the circumstances of origin,
according to Becker, so new contemporary circumstances called for new interpretations and methods in
historical scholarship.

During the last two decades there has been a revival
of faith in the possibility of social regeneration, a
revival, one might almost say, of the optimistic spirit
of the eighteenth century. Out of the wreck of old
creeds, there is arising a new faith, born of science
and democracy, almost the only vital conviction left
to us—the profound belief, namely, in progress; the
belief that society can, by taking thought, modify the
conditions of life, and thereby indefinitely improve
the happiness and welfare of all men.

Becker's relativistic view of the writing of history supported Eggleston, Robinson, and Beard not only in undercutting the old histories, but also in showing the contemporary relevance of the New Histories as well.
Becker concluded his discussion of the new reform
spirit:

As this faith strengthens, it finds expression in the imperative command that knowledge shall serve purpose, and learning be applied to the solution of the "problem of human life." And so there comes, ever more insistently, this question: What light does the past throw on the present and the future?[72]

Becker's conception of written history as a product of its environment included, of course, a relativistic view of the "truthfulness" of historical accounts. His theory of the relativism of written histories, not only traditional ones but New Histories as well, was original for an American historian. It went much further than Robinson ever did, and Beard did not express his adherence to historical relativism until the 1930's.[73] Becker's assertion that historians' "truths" were relative to their environmental origins, was part of a larger assertion of relativism that "truth" and "falsity" could not be attributed to ideas or beliefs in the past except with reference to the practical uses to which the ideas were put. As Becker wrote in 1913:

The latest fashion among psychologists and philosophers seems to be to regard the individual intelligence, not as an instrument suited to furnish an absolute test of objective truth, but rather as a tool

[72] "Some Aspects of the Influence of Social Problems upon the Study and Writing of History," *American Journal of Sociology*, xviii (March 1913), 641, 642, 663-664.

[73] For Becker's statements as to the necessary relativism of written histories see: "Detachment and the Writing of History," originally published in *Atlantic Monthly*, cvi (October 1910), 524-536, reprinted in Phil Snyder, ed., *Detachment and the Writing of History: Essays and Letters of Carl L. Becker*, Ithaca, 1958, pp. 3-28; "What Are Historical Facts?" originally read as a paper in 1926, printed in *Detachment and the Writing of History*, pp. 41-64; "Everyman His Own Historian," originally his presidential address to the American Historical Association, 1931, reprinted in Becker's *Everyman His Own Historian*, New York, 1935, pp. 233-255.

pragmatically useful in enabling the individual to find his way about in a disordered objective world. In like manner, one may conveniently regard the general intellectual activity of any period—the common ideas and beliefs, the prepossessions and points of view—as having had its origin in practical interests, and as deriving its validity from the service it renders in solving the problems that grow out of community life.[74]

Becker openly voiced this theoretical relativism in his historical scholarship, as well as in his speculative essays. Concluding his single history of ideas in America, *The Declaration of Independence: A Study in the History of Political Ideas* (1922), Becker gave classic expression to the view that ideas are conceived pragmatically, as human instruments in man's struggle to survive and prevail:

> To ask whether the natural rights philosophy of the Declaration of Independence is true or false is essentially a meaningless question. When honest men are impelled to withdraw their allegiance to the established law or custom of the community, still more when they are persuaded that such law or custom is too iniquitous to be longer tolerated, they seek for

[74] "Some Aspects of the Influence of Social Problems," pp. 641-642. For another example, from one of Becker's written histories, see his *Beginnings of the American People*, Boston, 1915, reprinted by Cornell University Press, 1960, pp. 83-84. In a discussion of Protestant ideas, Becker wrote:

Ideal constructions are doubtless the psychic precipitates of social experience, and the Protestant theory was but the reasoned expression of the middle-class state of mind. Thwarted by the existing world of fact, the leaders employed their practical and dexterous intelligence to create a new world of semblance, a world of the spirit, in which the way was illumined by the light of reason, and the individual rather than the social conscience gave the sense of right direction.

some principle more generally valid, some "law" of higher authority, than the established law or custom of the community. To this higher law or more generally valid principle they then appeal in justification of actions which the community condemns as immoral or criminal. They formulate the law or principle in such a way that it is, or seems to them to be, rationally defensible. To them it is "true" because it brings their actions into harmony with a rightly ordered universe, and enables them to think of themselves as having chosen the nobler part, as having withdrawn from a corrupt world in order to serve God or Humanity or a force that makes for the highest good.[75]

His relativistic statement went as far toward making ideas mere rationalizations as any of Beard's portrayals of ideas in, for example, *The Idea of National Interest*. Becker did not specifically emphasize the economic interests behind ideas, nor did he emphasize ideas as part of any other nonintellectual environment; in both respects he differed from Beard. Nevertheless, Becker expressed a concept of ideas in *The Declaration of Independence* in 1922 which denied attribution of "truth" or "falsity" to the ideas except in functional terms. Becker asked, as Beard had asked in his studies of the economic origins of American beliefs: how effective were the ideas as instruments?

Becker's method of describing historical ideas was in sharp contrast to Beard's, however, despite their similar conceptions of the origin and development of thought. Notwithstanding Becker's view that ideas expressed in the Declaration of Independence were largely rationalizations, he gave them lengthy and detailed analysis.

[75] *The Declaration of Independence: A Study in the History of Political Ideas*, New York, 1922, 1958, pp. 277-278.

Had Becker proclaimed their eternal validity and universal relevance to mankind, he could not have shown more concern for describing the ideas in depth.

The Declaration of Independence: A Study in the History of Political Ideas described the ideas on which the Revolutionary manifesto was based, traced how the ideas got into the document, showed how they appeared in final form, and traced their reception later. Becker devoted little space to possible nonintellectual determinants, such as economic interests which might have been correlated with the ideas.

The ideas which Becker found to be elemental were, most basically, the natural rights philosophy inherited from Locke, and, next in importance, the newly enunciated view that the colonies were voluntary members of a federation of independent states. It was Becker's contention that neither of these fundamental assumptions was expressed explicitly in the Declaration, but that everything expressed depended on them. Long separate chapters were devoted to detailed analyses of each of the two fundamental assumptions. The idea of natural rights according to Locke was described, as was the gradual appearance in the decade before the American Revolution of the idea that membership in the Empire was voluntary and that the colonies could withdraw voluntarily.[76] The chapter which most closely related ideas to the environment was that on the colonial theory of the Empire. The environment consisted of political events, as the Revolution approached, which affected the conceptions of the Empire. Becker continued to dwell upon the changing imperial theories in detail, while noting that events moved the colonists into an increasingly radical position in relation to England.[77]

[76] For discussion of the natural rights philosophy, see Chapter 2, pp. 24-79; the theory of the Empire, Chapter 3, pp. 80-134. Both chapters together equal almost half of the book.

[77] See Chapter 3, pp. 80-134.

Two long chapters described the process of composition of the Declaration, how it evolved from draft to draft, and its literary qualities. Through a close textual analysis, Becker argued that the appeal was to the head rather than to the heart, that Jefferson's prose was cold and detached rather than warm and immediate as was, for instance, Lincoln's. Becker's examination of the prose style with which ideas were expressed epitomized the difference between Becker's method of treating ideas and Beard's technique—despite their common adherence to a pragmatic conception of ideas as instruments. In Beard's enthusiasm for relating the environmental "interest" behind each idea, there was no time for so peripheral a matter as the style in which ideas were expressed.

Detailed analysis was a characteristic Becker technique when he was writing about ideas, and he focused this technique on underlying assumptions rather than solely on explicit meanings. In *The Heavenly City of the Eighteenth-Century Philosophers* (1932), Becker's contribution to the study of European thought, he made fashionable the term "climates of opinion," by which he meant "those instinctively held preconceptions in the broad sense."[78] Becker had been examining these "instinctively held preconceptions" in the *Declaration of Independence* a decade before when he described the natural rights philosophy and the conception of Empire which lay behind the Declaration.[79]

[78] *The Heavenly City*, p. 5.
[79] The text has occasionally suggested similarities between the European scientific historians Buckle and Taine and Americans who sought to investigate the relationship between ideas and their environments in order to determine the role of ideas in history, e.g., Draper, Eggleston, Robinson, and Beard. Although Becker held enough characteristics in common with the progressive New Historians to consider him one of their number, the European historian he most resembled was Leslie Stephen. It was Stephen who conceived of his *History of English Thought*

Becker's interest in the unsaid premises of human thinking was perhaps related to his theory of relativistic knowledge and relativistic value. In a sense, the development of the "climate of opinion" notion was the methodological parallel to Becker's theoretical relativism. For the idea of changing climates of opinion showed one fundamental way in which relativistic "truths" succeeded one another. Or, to put it another way, "climates of opinion" revealed what exactly it was that was relativistic—it was this changing "climate." To examine these intellectual preconceptions was therefore to examine deeply, far beneath the more superficial level of explicit talk or behavior. Separable from relativism, which was one of Becker's legacies, was his legacy of a technique of writing the history of ideas by searching for prevailing "climates of opinion."

Becker's interest in shifting climates of opinion and in implicit assumptions contributed to his formulation of the subject of historiography—the history of history —as a part of the history of ideas generally. Becker had, of course, early manifested an interest in how history was written, and he concluded from his knowledge of the process that claims for the "objectivity" of historical scholarship were invalid. Allowing for individual differences within a given time and place, Becker concluded that the relativism of historical knowledge stemmed from the varying climates of opinion in which

---

in the Eighteenth Century as being an investigation of "the spirit of an age," a synonym for the climate of opinion. And it was Stephen who analyzed ideas in detail without reference to environmental relationships. Further, Stephen anticipated Becker's central theme, in *The Heavenly City*, of the underlying continuity between an older body of thought on one hand, and, on the other, newer ideas which avowedly attack it in devastating fashion but which actually assume and perpetuate much of the older way of looking at the world. But it was Becker and not Stephen who presented this approach persuasively to American historians.

histories were written. Becker's 1913 article, "Some Aspects of the Influence of Social Problems and Ideas upon the Studying and Writing of History," was a pioneering attempt to relate the writing of history to more general currents of ideas. After a quarter-century of writing book reviews which frequently made the same attempt,[80] Becker explicitly urged in his 1938 essay, "What Is Historiography?" that historiography should be conceived "as a phase of intellectual history," forgetting "entirely about the contributions of historians to present knowledge and to concentrate wholly upon their role in the cultural pattern of their own time."[81] Becker objected to the fact that historiography—studies of historical writing—had been concerned mainly with providing "a neat balance sheet of the contributions which each historian has made to the sum total of verified historical knowledge now on hand." This approach, mourned Becker as historian of ideas, resulted in little more than studies of "the gradual emergence of historical truth objectively considered."[82] Becker's conception of historiography as a part of the history of ideas was intimately related to his historical relativism. Historiography according to Becker's precepts became as relative as his view of intellectual history or general history.

In the case of Becker's historiography, as in the case of Becker's role as a historian of ideas generally, his sig-

[80] See, for example, Becker's review of Robinson's *The New History, The Dial,* LIII (July 1, 1912), 19-21; H. G. Wells' *Outline of History, American Historical Review,* XXXII (January 1927), 350-351. The essay, "What Is Historiography?" was a long review of Harry Elmer Barnes' *History of Historical Writing.*

[81] "What Is Historiography?" *American Historical Review,* LXIV (October 1938), 20-28; reprinted in Snyder, ed., *Detachment and the Writing of History,* pp. 65-78. Quote appears in Snyder, p. 73.

[82] *Ibid.,* pp. 66, 75.

nificant place in this study rests upon rather slight scholarly production, and a large part of that production consisted of precepts. Except for reviews and for "The New History" chapter of *The Heavenly City*, Becker never actually wrote any historiography—either American or European. Similarly, his writing on the history of ideas in America was restricted virtually to *The Declaration of Independence*. Nevertheless his method, which he elaborated and made more explicit in *The Heavenly City*, was a significant contribution.

Carl Becker contributed to the rise of the New History, which included the New Intellectual History, through his criticisms of the old "scientific" history. Working from a general ideological position similar to Robinson's and Beard's, Becker expressed a conception of ideas as instruments with functional origins and uses. But Becker's method of actually writing about ideas was a deviation from New History practices, as expressed by Robinson or Beard. Becker's technique of discussing ideas was to provide detailed "internal" analysis of the ideas themselves, quite irrespective of social and economic environmental factors. Beard, by contrast, emphasized the "external" relation of ideas to the "interests" served by the ideas. The theoretical relativism Becker expressed concerning the nature and role of ideas did not lead him to Beard's technique of describing human thought. Becker's relativism, implicit in his interest in changing "climates of opinion," did, however, contribute to his formulation of the subject of historiography—the study of historical writing—as part of the general subject of intellectual history.

Becker's ideological position changed in several significant respects during the years immediately preceding, and during, the Second World War. In the face of totalitarianism, Becker modified his emphasis upon a theoretical relativism in favor of an emphasis upon virtually "absolute," "universal" ideas or values in man's history. There were, he decided, after all, "some generalities that still glittered," and in *New Liberties for Old* he wrote of the eternal worth of a core of humane values which, though including the values of democracy,

> are older and more universal than democracy and do not depend upon it. They have a life of their own apart from any particular social system or type of civilization. They are the values which, since the time of Buddha and Confucius, Solomon and Zoroaster, Plato and Aristotle, Socrates and Jesus, men have commonly employed to measure the advance or the decline of civilization, the values they have celebrated in the saints and sages whom they have agreed to canonize.[83]

At the same time that Becker was modifying his relativism in the late 1930's, he was also revising his sympathy for pacifism. When he decided to assert the virtually "absolute" worth of certain humane beliefs, he also decided that the United States had to intervene on the side of England and France in World War Two. Totalitarianism compelled Becker, as it also forced Beard, to modify the theory of relativism. It was perhaps ironic that environmental factors—the presence of totalitarianism in Becker's and Beard's environment—impelled a modification of their emphasis upon environmental interpretation. The two historians came to minimize their former environmental relativism and to emphasize instead the virtually "universal" validity of certain values or ideas.

The half-century journey of Robinson, Beard, and Becker from the old history to the New, from politics to ideas, and from reformist confidence in the future to apprehensive grasping at native American traditions,

[83] New Haven, 1941, pp. 149-150.

mapped the land in which the most famous of the progressive histories of ideas would be written. Robinson had popularized a rationale for writing histories of opinion; Beard had published histories in which ideas were characteristically related to economic environments; Becker analyzed ideas more intensively, but made only a brief study of American thought. It was left to Vernon Louis Parrington and Merle Curti to write broadscale histories of American thought from a progressive point of view and based on the concept of ideas as instruments.

VERNON LOUIS PARRINGTON

VERNON LOUIS PARRINGTON'S *Main Currents in American Thought* (1927-1930) was the first history of ideas in America written from a viewpoint generally similar to Robinson's, Beard's, and Becker's, including their ideological views and their conception of ideas as instruments. Indeed, Parrington's two volumes, plus his incomplete and posthumously published third volume, made the first attempt to survey the entire course of American thought from any perspective.

Parrington (1871-1929), like Eggleston, Robinson, Beard, and Becker, was born, raised, and partially schooled in the Midwest. Parrington was born in Illinois and raised in Kansas where he attended the College of Emporia prior to transferring to Harvard as a junior in the class of 1893. He returned to Emporia where he taught and received his M.A. He then taught at the University of Oklahoma from 1898 to 1908; for the remaining two decades until his death, Parrington was professor of English at the University of Washington in Seattle.[1]

[1] For Parrington's life, see the following writings by students and colleagues: Russell Blankenship, "Vernon Louis Parrington," *Nation*, CXXIX (August 7, 1929), 141-142; James L. Colwell, "The Populist Image of Vernon Louis Parrington," *Mississippi Valley Historical Review*, XLIX (June 1962), 52-66; E. H. Eby, "Vernon Louis Parrington," *Main Currents of American Thought*, Vol. 3, pp. v-xxi; Joseph B. Harrison, "Ver-

He was raised in a Republican family, but esthetic rather than political concerns preoccupied Parrington during his youth. Although he expressed publicly no interest in politics through the election of 1896, he later pointed to that particular election as the event which first focused his attention upon politics. By early 1897, Parrington drew on the writings of William Morris and John Ruskin, no longer for esthetic guidance alone but for political thought. "The old Greeks were right, I think, in applying the name 'idiot,' even had they used it in its modern sense, to the educated man who took no interest in affairs of state," Parrington wrote in 1897. He then went on to criticize the business leadership of society on the grounds that businessmen were selfishly materialistic.[2] As the century neared its end, Parrington's new-found political interest was reformist and increasingly permeated with an economic interpretation of history. During the twentieth century he became specifically Beardian in his view of American development and of the history of ideas in the United States. Yet Parrington, in contrast to Beard, was fearful of big government as well as of big business and emerged more a Jeffersonian than a technocratic admirer of the modern machine age.

Parrington's interpretation of American history from the seventeenth century to the Civil War was generally Beardian. This point of view, which would later find expression in Parrington's histories, was already suggested in a letter he wrote to his former Harvard classmates a decade before the volumes were published: "The past five years [since c. 1913] I have spent in study and writing, up to my ears in the economic in-

non Louis Parrington: American Scholar," *Washington Alumnus*, XL (Winter 1950), 10-11.

[2] Quoted by Colwell, "Vernon Louis Parrington," p. 64.

terpretation of American history and literature, getting the last lingering Harvard prejudices out of my system." As Parrington continued, he made it clear that his economic interpretation was closely related to strong sentiments favoring democratic reform.

> I become more radical with each year, and more impatient with the smug Tory culture which we were fed on as undergraduates. I haven't been in Cambridge since July, 1893. Harvard is only a dim memory to me. Very likely I am wrong in my judgment, yet from what little information comes through to me I have set the school down as a liability rather than an asset to the cause of democracy. It seems to me the apologist and advocate of capitalistic exploitation—as witness the sweet-smelling list of nominees sent out yearly for the Board of Overseers.[3]

These reformist ideas found clear expression in *Main Currents in American Thought*. Parrington's theme was the conflict between progress and reaction, in which reason, optimism, democracy, and intellectual freedom were joined in combat with irrationality, pessimism, aristocracy, and religious dogmatism. In Volume One, Parrington characterized Puritan religious ideas as inert and useless mountains of rock serving mainly as a bastion to wall New England in and close from its sight the expanded horizons of a changing post-Renaissance world. "Unfortunately," Puritan ideas comprised,

> an absolute theology that conceived of human nature as inherently evil, that postulated a divine sovereignty absolute and arbitrary, and projected caste divisions

[3] Quoted by Thomas J. Pressly, "Vernon L. Parrington and the Writing of American Literary History," MS, Widener Library, Harvard University, 1946, p. 1, from *Secretary's Sixth Report Harvard College Class of 1893*, Cambridge, 1918, pp. 220-221.

into eternity—a body of dogmas that it needed two hundred years' experience in America to disintegrate.[4]

The eighteenth century happily developed an ampler body of thought, with a more generous view of man's ability to shape his institutions anew in order to promote justice and liberalize his society.

> It asserted that the present evils of society are the consequence of vicious institutions rather than of depraved human nature; and that as free men and equals it is the right and duty of citizens to re-create social and political institutions to the end that they shall further social justice, encouraging the good in men rather than perverting them to evil.[5]

By the time of the Revolution, "the liberal impulses in the background of the American mind assumed a militant form and purpose."[6]

After arriving at a Jeffersonian and Jacksonian zenith, American democracy, according to Parrington in Volume Two, was confronted by a new acquisitive spirit in the nineteenth century. Private self-interest and consolidation smothered the liberating impulses set loose by Revolutionary thought. Despite the ideas and the work of humanitarians like Channing and Parker, a licentious acquisitive spirit had triumphed, and this spirit characterized the Civil War era. The Northern "imperialistic" industrial capitalism vanquished the Southern "imperialistic" agrarian slavocracy. Hope for Jeffersonian democracy originally had rested with the yeomen-farmers of the new West. But unfortunately, the Western agrarian freeholder was also subjugated to the new spirit in America. Though he had "an econom-

---

[4] *Main Currents of American Thought*, 3 vols., New York, 1930, Introduction, Vol. 1, p. iv.
[5] *Ibid.*, p. v. [6] *Ibid.*, p. 180.

ics equalitarian in temper, decentralizing in impulse,"
and although he was "nourished on the idealism of the
Declaration of Independence," nevertheless the settler
in the West had interpreted this idealism "to mean the
natural right of every free citizen to satisfy his acquisitive instinct by exploiting the natural resources in the
measure of his shrewdness."[7]

In his final, uncompleted third volume, Parrington
clearly dissociated himself from the spirit of post-Civil
War America, feeling that liberal democracy, except in
the abortive third-party movements, had reached a
nadir. In contrast to Beard's and Robinson's more optimistic embracement of technology as a liberating force
in modern American experience, Parrington manifested
distinct feelings of alienation from the business-oriented,
middle-class-dominated character of modern American
life. Democratic idealism had slowly decayed, and Parrington traced the cause of the decay to three sources:
economic consolidation, scientific determinism, and an
enervating pessimism—all the result of a drying up of
imaginative liberal thought through "the custodianship
of America by the middle class." And in a significant
return of his old rancor, Parrington took a parting shot
at New England by paralleling the modern wasteland
of intellectual stagnation to the narrow-minded world
of earlier Puritanism:

> Thus after three hundred years' experience we have
> returned, intellectually, to the point from which we
> set out, and the old philosophy brought to the new

[7] *Ibid.*, Introduction, Vol. 2, pp. v-vi. Parrington's interpretation of the Civil War was "the same as Beard's in all essentials," as Thomas J. Pressly concluded in *Americans Interpret
Their Civil War*, Princeton, 1954, p. 212. Beard's classic interpretation was published the same year (1927) in *The Rise of
American Civilization*, but of course Beard's earlier studies in
economic interpretation were published while Parrington was
working on *Main Currents*.

world from the compact societies of Europe, with its doctrine of determinism and its mood of pessimism, has come back in changed form to color the thinking of our generation.[8]

Parrington, though himself critical of the specific character of modern American life, had not only refused to give up on democracy, but he censured those, such as Mencken, who had abandoned Jeffersonian and Jacksonian dreams. Despite the fact that Parrington traced some of the loss of faith in democracy to intellectuals, he nevertheless (perhaps as an alienated intellectual himself) viewed with optimism the rebellion of intellectuals from dominant middle-class life during the 1920's. He found "hope" in the fact that "intelligent America is in revolt. The artist is in revolt, the intellectual is in revolt, the conscience of America is in revolt." Parrington fervently prayed that they would be able "to unhorse the machine that now rides men and to leaven the sodden mass that is industrial America."[9]

While he was writing Volume Three in the 1920's, Parrington obviously felt himself more alienated than ever from middle-class America, but yet hopeful that the intellectual elite could lead Americans in reform. He expressed, in addition to reform hopes, disillusionment with Americans generally for their stupidity. In a 1923 letter to his Harvard classmates, Parrington wrote:

Thank God, at any rate, we teachers are not as the Philistines, who believe whatever the newspaper would have them believe. . . . I often wonder what becomes of the fine young men and women who annually make their cheerful plunge into the outside scramble. Some of them turn out Babbitts, I sup-

[8] *Main Currents*, Foreword, Vol. 3, p. xix.
[9] *Ibid.*, p. xx.

pose, in spite of our warnings; but not all I am sure. There is far more intellectual ferment among the better undergraduates today than there was in our provincial time, [when the Class of 1893 was in college] and a goodly number of keen, well-trained minds now go out to help leaven the American lump.[10]

Yet he suggested, on the positive side, in his projected Introduction to Volume Three, that

not too hastily should we abandon our earlier faith: the eighteenth-century conception of environment as a creative influence in determining character is a vital idea not yet adequately explored. Even morons may be traced back to adenoids or diets of salt pork and whisky or to later machine labor, and aristocracies are still seen to be economic. And aristocratic albinos may well breed mobs and morons. Jefferson was not as foolish as many of his disciples have been, and Jeffersonian democracy still offers hope. Education begins to fail—except education to individualize and to summon forth the potential intelligence of the younger generation.[11]

These views of Parrington about past and contemporary American society went to make up his ideological position, one which was similar in many respects to those of Robinson, Beard, and Becker.[12]

Parrington's conception of the origin and development of ideas in history was also similar to the conceptions held by Robinson, Beard, and Becker. Parrington expressed most fully his theory of the "origin and sig-

[10] Quoted by Pressly in Widener Library MS, p. 19, from *Secretary's Seventh Report Harvard College Class of 1893*, Cambridge, 1923, p. 219.

[11] *Main Currents*, Introduction, Vol. 3, pp. xxviii-xxix.

[12] For Parrington's attitude toward war, see two comments suggesting that he thought that no war was ever worth the cost: Vol. 1, p. 178; Vol. 3, p. 43.

nificance" of ideas in an essay written in 1917; this essay was published in 1953 by his son.[13] "Ideas are not godlings that spring perfect-winged from the head of Jove," Parrington protested. Instead, "they are weapons hammered out on the anvil of human needs." He adhered, in other words, to a concept of ideas as instruments in man's struggle to prevail. Parrington emphasized in particular the influence of the environment in forming thought. "To love ideas is excellent," he said, "but to understand how ideas are conditioned by social forces, is better still." Men "fashion themselves ideas for swords to fight with. To consider the sword apart from the struggle is to turn dilettante and a frequenter of museums." The most important aspect of what "we call vaguely social forces" was, according to Parrington, the economic: "To understand those forces is the economist's first business; for such knowledge, he is confident, will explain many things which have gone too long unchallenged."[14]

Parrington repeated briefly his view of the nature of ideas in the Introduction to Volume One. The "political, economic, and social development of the country" comprised the determining environment from which ideas are created and developed historically.[15] He thus echoed Robinson and Beard in offering an environmental theory of the origin of thought. He echoed them in practice as well as in theory, for he also emphasized the influence of the nonintellectual environment most when he discussed ideas toward which he was unsympathetic.

Parrington clearly revealed this emphasis on the influence of the environment in his first volume, "The

[13] "Vernon Parrington's View: Economics and Criticism," Vernon Parrington, Jr., ed., *Pacific Northwest Quarterly* (July 1953), 97-105.

[14] *Ibid.*, p. 99.

[15] *Main Currents*, Vol. 1, p. iii.

Colonial Mind, 1620-1800." John Cotton, "the most authoritative representative in New England of the ideal of priestly stewardship" was treated by Parrington with more sympathy than most leaders of the Puritan oligarchy. Parrington was drawn by the fact that "Cotton seems to have been something of a Puritan intellectual, with an open-minded curiosity that made him receptive to new ideas and tempted him to play with doctrines that were intolerable to his bigoted associates." But the "open-minded" Cotton was eventually intimidated by a stingy environment. "Unfortunately, his daily contact with narrow-minded and intolerant men gave an unhappy bias to his later career." The roots for the "unhappy bias" were to be found not in Cotton's simply having made up his mind one way or the other, but rather in his environmental background: "his theocratic dreams were conditioned by the facts that he was both a Calvinist and a Carolinian gentleman. The fusion of these two influences resulted in the unique political theory of an ethical aristocracy, consecrated to moral stewardship in the state."

This background, both intellectual and social, led Cotton to ally himself with the status quo when Anne Hutchinson and Roger Williams proposed change in the New England intellectual and social order. Despite Parrington's considerable sympathy for Cotton, the Puritan was portrayed finally as "not a catholic thinker" but rather a captive of the unprogressive old ways. He was explained to a large extent by his environment: "It was no fault of John Cotton's that he was the child of a generation reared under the shadow of absolutism, fearful of underling aggression, unable to comprehend the excellence inhering in the democratic faith."[16]

Samuel Sewall was treated in the same manner by Parrington. He offered an environmental "explanation"

[16] *Ibid.*, pp. 27, 29, 30, 37.

of Sewall's ideas as being a series of habitual responses to his environment. Presenting Sewall primarily as a man of affairs rather than of great intellect, Parrington sketched an economic environment provoking mental reflexes: "To say that Sewall possessed either an economic or political philosophy would be too generous an interpretation of his opinions. The views which he upheld vigorously were little more than prejudices." Sewall, according to Parrington, always defended his own economic and political interests, partly because self-interest demanded it and in part because he by nature opposed all changes.

> A man so cautious by nature, and with so large a stake in the existing order, could not fail to be a conservative, content with a world that justified itself by the prosperity which it brought him, and which it would bring to others, he doubted not, if they governed their conduct with equal prudence. He desired no innovations in church or state; established forms answered his needs and filled the measure of his ideal. The existing system was approved by all the respectable people of the community; there was everything to gain in upholding it, and likelihood of loss in suffering power to pass into the hands of a royal governor or of the ignorant poor. And so, determined by complex motives, by habit, by class ties, by economic interest, and by honest liking, Samuel Sewall went with the stream of conventional orthodoxy, strong for the old theocratic principles, seeing no need for readjustments to meet changing conditions.[17]

Parrington's description of Sewall's thought sounded much like James Harvey Robinson's definition of "rationalization." Equally similar was Parrington's char-

[17] *Ibid.*, pp. 92, 94-95.

acterization of Increase Mather, who was dealt with less charitably than Sewall.

Mather's thought, as described by Parrington, was little more than the conditioned reflex of an unresilient mind to a stagnant environment. Parrington berated Mather for the timidity and self-interest which kept him from questioning "the sufficiency of the established system."

> All his life he was inhibited from bold speculation by his personal loyalties and interests. As a beneficiary of things as they were, certain to lose in prestige and power with any relaxing of the theocracy, it would be asking too much of human nature to expect him to question the sufficiency of the established system of which he was the most distinguished representative. Not to have approved it would have been to repudiate his habitual way of thinking, his deepest prejudices, his strongest convictions. He had been molded and shaped by the theocracy; it was the very marrow of his bones; as well demand that pig iron turn molten again after it comes from the matrix. The ore of which he was fashioned was excellent, but once molded it was rigid; there would be no return to fluidity. And so determined by every impact of environment, by every appeal of loyalty, and by a very natural ambition, Increase Mather became a stout upholder of the traditional order, a staunch old Puritan Tory of the theocratic line.[18]

Ideas which held little personal appeal for Parrington were likely to be described as related to the environment, usually socioeconomic in nature, which influenced their development.

But Parrington was not consistent in the way he described the origin of ideas. On occasion, he character-

[18] *Ibid.*, pp. 99-100.

ized ideas as originating and developing independently
of any social and economic environment. The relationship between Parrington's ideological position and his
inconsistent treatment of the origin and development of
historical ideas and thinkers is this: ideas for which he
had sympathy were more likely to be depicted with
little or no reference to the environment, whereas ideas
he disliked were more likely to be related to and "explained" by the environment from which they came.
Ideas Parrington considered democratic, secularizing,
and contributing to religious freedom, for example,
were usually described as originating independently of
their environment. Aristocratic social, political, and economic ideas, on the other hand, were more often discussed in relation to the pressures of the environment
which supposedly produced them. Despite an avowedly
environmental approach to ideas, then, Parrington was
likely to regard ideas to which he was sympathetic as
constituting "thinking" independent of the social and
economic environment.

Roger Williams' ideas, for example, were described
and praised without any reference to environmental
origins. Williams "lived in the realm of ideas, of inquiry and discussion; and his actions were creatively
determined by principles the bases of which he examined with critical insight." Williams' ideas were thus
conceived without reference to emotional self-interest
or environmental pressures, and their end-results were
actions "creatively determined by principles." Also admirable was the fact that Williams' ideas were concerned with political and economic, rather than theological, issues:

> Much of his life was devoted to the problem of dis-
> covering a new basis for social reorganization, and
> his intellectual progress was marked by an abundant

wreckage of obsolete theory and hoary fiction that strewed his path. He was a social innovator on principle, and he left no system unchallenged; each must justify itself in reason and expediency or be put aside.[19]

Ideas were instruments here, but only in the sense that they were used to create a better social situation for man. Ideas were instruments, in the treatment of Cotton, Sewall, and Mather, in the sense that the immediate environment fashioned them originally and also in the sense that the ideas were then used to perpetuate the existent social situation.

Parrington's interpretation of Franklin was close to that of Williams, although he did comment that, while Franklin's thought reflected an admirable "new social ideal," his life signified the influence of "a rising class." But Parrington emphasized the "new social ideal," almost never referring to social determinants in Franklin's world. Indeed, Franklin seems to have transcended his environment to become a free and "unbiased" man of ideas.

Although Franklin's origins, whether Boston or Philadelphia, were narrowly provincial, his mind from early youth to extreme old age was curiously open and free, and to such a mind the intellectual wealth of the world lies open and free. From that wealth he helped himself generously, to such good effect that he early became an intellectual cosmopolitan, at ease with the best intellects and at home among the diverse speculative interests of the eighteenth century: the sane and witty embodiment of its rationalism, its emancipation from authority, its growing concern for social justice, its hopeful pursuit of new political and economic philosophies, its tem-

[19] *Ibid.*, pp. 64, 66-67.

pered optimism that trusted intelligence to set the world right. No other man in America and few in Europe had so completely freed themselves from the prejudice of custom. The Calvinism in which he was bred left not the slightest trace upon him; and the middle-class world from which he emerged did not narrow his mind to its petty horizons. He was a free man who went his own way with imperturbable good will and unbiased intelligence.

Later in the same volume Parrington wrote:

He was concerned not with property or class interests, but with the common welfare; and in his quick sympathy for all sorts and conditions of men, in his conviction that he must use his talents to make this world better and not exploit it, he reveals the breadth and generosity of his nature.[20]

Thus Parrington did not express a consistent concept of the nature and role of ideas in history. Despite his frequent statements in support of an environmental interpretation of human thought, he sometimes expressed a concept in which ideas developed independently of any environmental influence, thus exercising a creative causal force in human affairs. When championing ideas, he abandoned an environmental view and characterized these ideas as largely independent in origin and creative in causal importance.

Parrington continued in Volume Two to "explain" those ideas which he disliked by discussing them in terms of the influence of environment (or frequently to dismiss them as "prejudices"). And again, when he was more sympathetic to the ideas he described, Parrington did not attribute them to environmental formation but emphasized instead their "creativity" and "orig-

20 *Ibid.*, pp. 165, 178.

inality." John P. Kennedy, Alexander Stephens, Webster, Clay, and Fisher Ames were prejudiced men influenced by, as well as serving, narrow interests. But Bryant's was "a self-pollenizing nature" despite his early "environment of intolerant Federalism and an equally intolerant Calvinism." Furthermore, his ideas were "creative, and determined all his thinking."[21]

In Volume Two discussion of the West as an influence on American ideas provides further illumination of Parrington's conception of thought. The presence of a free Western environment helped, rather than hindered, the growth of "good" ideas. But this environment was largely negative. In other words, that which was conducive to the growth of "good" ideas was precisely the absence of traditional environmental social and economic forces. And as soon as the Western void was filled by considerable numbers of people, this Western environment too became inimical to the growth of ideas to which Parrington was sympathetic. So Jeffersonian agrarian ideas were at first "springing up naturally" on the Ohio frontier. But the Hamilton-Clay industrial psychology soon became prevalent in the West and changed humane "opportunity" to narrow "opportunism." "From the determining factors . . . of abundant wild lands, rapid increase in population, and an elastic credit, operating on a vast scale, came the optimistic, speculative psychology of the new West."[22] Parrington explained that Lincoln, like Jackson, developed his "instinctive democracy" from "the equalitarian West"; but Whiggery had made fatal inroads in the West by Lincoln's time, so that he was also "shaped by an environment in which the new philosophy of progress had displaced the older agrarianism."[23]

This dual attitude toward the development of ideas

[21] *Ibid.*, Vol. 2, pp. 239, 240, 241.
[22] *Ibid.*, pp. 137, 140.   [23] *Ibid.*, p. 152.

appeared again in Parrington's third volume. Even though their Brahmin environment was similar, Wendell Phillips did not absorb the "Back Bay prejudices" of Thomas Bailey Aldrich because "something deep within him, a loyalty to other and higher ideals, held him back. . . . An instinctive love of justice held him back." Henry George was a physiocratic liberal thinker "created by the impact of frontier economics upon a mind singularly sensitive to the appeal of social justice." But his Western contemporary, Mark Twain, "never was at home in the world of catholic thought, but all his life he suffered from the petty inhibitions of his origins. He could not throw off the frontier."[24]

Parrington's ambivalent attitude toward the nature of ideas was not unique among American historians sharing his social views, as the prior discussions of Robinson, Beard, and Becker have shown. But Parrington was unusual in the art, the literary mastery, with which he implemented his conception of historical ideas. Parrington was a more imaginative writer than any other historian discussed in this study, and his literary craft both illuminates, and is illuminated by, an understanding of his conception of ideas as well as of his ideological position. Kermit Vanderbilt's sensitive examination of Parrington's literary art has made clear how gifted a "historian-as-writer" Parrington was, and, at the same time, how intimately associated Parrington's art and mind were—effectively using his literary imagination as a weapon in fighting for his portrayal of ideas and also, of course, for his social views.[25]

[24] *Ibid.*, Vol. 3, pp. 58, 141, 125, 88.

[25] For Vanderbilt's analysis of Parrington's literary imagination, see R. A. Skotheim and Kermit Vanderbilt, "Vernon Louis Parrington: The Mind and Art of a Historian of Ideas," *Pacific Northwest Quarterly*, LIII (July 1962), 100-113. The discussion of Parrington's literary style, which follows, is taken from Vanderbilt.

The literary structure of *Main Currents* was shaped as a dramatic series of dialogues between men of conflicting ideas. The dominant personalities who figured as opponents in Parrington's pages were John Cotton and Roger Williams, Adam Smith and Quesnay, Hamilton and Jefferson, Jackson and Clay, Emerson and Webster, Spencer and Haeckel; or, phrased as group conflicts, the aristocrat and the republican, privileged minority and democratic majority, frontier democracy and Wall Street Whiggery, the middle class and the proletarian masses, producer and middleman, versatile frontiersman and specialized factory-hand. Again, phrased as abstractions, the warfare of ideas was waged between regimentation and freedom, centralization and decentralization, capitalism and agrarianism, economic realism (English), and egalitarian idealism (French), cash psychology and commodity value, profit and consumption, rights of property and rights of man, exploitation and social justice. Parrington's two-sided conception of the historic role of ideas found expression in the dramatic literary structure of his histories.

Within the dramatic structure erected by Parrington, the literary imagery acted out the ideas according to the way he conceived them. This metaphor of a voyage through the "main currents of American thought," was used throughout to insure a dynamic sense of unity to all three volumes. Parrington used it variously and often and always with a sense of its fitness in his epic story of the role of ideas in American history. What is most striking in his "currents" imagery is the way in which "liberal" ideas were *the currents*, while ideas to which Parrington was unfriendly were described as "reefs," "barriers," "foundering bark," "barnacled craft," "dragging anchor," or as "moral squalls" or "chill winds." Emerson was described as "a child of the romantic revolution" who "understood quite clearly how the waves of humanitarian aspiration broke on the reefs of property rights." Again, "fortunately the old Puritan anchors were already dragging, and Emerson was pretty well adrift when the romantic surge caught him and sent him far along new courses." The currents of European idealism swept into Emerson's New England environment because

at last the old barriers gave way, and into this narrow illiberal world, that had long fed on the crusts of English rationalism and Edwardean dogmatism—dry as remainder biscuit after voyage—broke the floods that had been gathering in Europe for years, the waters of all the streams of revolution that were running there bank-full.[26]

Daniel Webster and his Constitutionalism had the misfortune to be "launched between tides on a stormy sea and his stately bark foundered in the squall of Abolitionism." The old Tie-Wigs of the early nineteenth century were "blind sailors navigating the Dead Sea of Federalist pessimism."[27] Better seamanship could be expected later in the century from ex-riverboat pilot Mark Twain, "trimming his sails to the chill winds blowing from the outer spaces of a mechanistic cosmos." For a courageous spirit like Whitman's, nothing would serve but complete immersion in the congenial and life-giving currents of common-man democracy: "He sank into experience joyously like a strong swimmer idling in the salt waves."[28] John Marshall ("last of the Virginia Federalists"), however, preferred the secure comfort of his office on dry land: "The turbid waters of frontier leveling and states-rights democracy washed fiercely about him, but he went on quietly with his self-appointed work." Oliver Wendell Holmes, also a land-

[26] *Main Currents*, Vol. 2, pp. 395, 389, 317.
[27] *Ibid.*, pp. 316, 278.   [28] *Ibid.*, Vol. 3, pp. 98, 70.

lubber, was (as a rationalist) at least willing to open his windows and look out to sea: "He kept the windows of his mind open to the winds of scientific inquiry that were blowing briskly to the concern of orthodox souls. Many a barnacled craft was foundering in those gales, and Holmes watched their going-down with visible satisfaction."[29]

Holmes, the freethinker with the windows of his mind open to the winds of doctrine and even at times a respectable "puller down of worm-eaten structures," suggests another persistent and fruitful image of Parrington's. His lack of sympathy for a life devoted to gestures of consolidation rather than to progressive social action, led him naturally to the image of conservative ideas constituting a "theocratic temple," an "impregnable citadel," or a "jerry-built house." Again, conservative thought was a house of intellect close-shuttered and surrounded by high walls to keep out all liberalizing gusts of fresh air (but meanwhile collecting cobwebs in the rafters and rotting away at the timbers). And the occupants, in their turn, were self-satisfied bookworms eschewing a life of arduous activity in the open air in favor of a cloistered existence among their musty libraries, stale cupboards, privileged teacups, and bad-smelling professors' pipes.

Parrington's rhetoric, when describing the environments which produced thoughts and thinkers for which he had little sympathy, forcefully and imaginatively implemented his conception of environmental determinism. Jonathan Edwards "like Cotton Mather before him . . . was the unconscious victim of a decadent ideal and a petty environment";[30] Henry Clay was "the unconscious tool of powerful economic interests," and was, like Calhoun and Webster, "a victim of changing

[29] *Ibid.*, Vol. 2, pp. 20, 454.
[30] *Ibid.*, Vol. 1, p. 162.

times."[31] When Parrington warmed to his assignment, the environment and the victim merged in the image. Increase Mather "closed the windows of his mind against the winds of new doctrine"; Timothy Dwight's mind "was closed as tight as his study windows in January";[32] James Russell Lowell's mind withered in "the stagnant atmosphere of his Elmwood study," while the doors at nearby Craigie House were "shut securely against all intrusion. The winds of doctrine and policy might rage through the land, but they did not rattle the windows of [Longfellow's] study." The nineteenth century neo-Calvinists spent their days in "spinning cobweb systems between the worm-eaten rafters, quite oblivious to the common-sense world" outside their walls, and their illustrious pupil Hawthorne likewise wasted his talents in "spinning cobwebs about the old Puritan rafters."[33] Parrington was kinder to Melville, however, who, though imbued with no passion for social reform, still implied in his novels a strong indictment of acquisitive middle-class ideals. Nor had President Woolsey of Yale in the Gilded Age given up the "stale Connecticut Calvinism, molding in the corner of the cupboard."[34]

This animus toward the polite academic world which safely divorced itself from progressive thought ("Provocative social thinking and the American university seem never to have got on well together")[35] appeared again when Parrington characterized Francis Lieber's Federalist political opinions as being "as studiously conventional as a professor's gown." Hugh Legaré discovered "no other than a juridical romanticism . . . in the bottom of his scholar's cup." Lowell's mind was "as cluttered as a garret" and whatever political principles

[31] *Ibid.*, Vol. 2, pp. 143, 144.
[32] *Ibid.*, Vol. 1, pp. 99, 361.
[33] *Ibid.*, Vol. 2, pp. 468, 440, 323, 444.
[34] *Ibid.*, Vol. 3, p. 124.   [35] *Ibid.*

he had "he discovered in the smoke of his professor's pipe."[36] A similar image appeared in the sketch of the well-educated Southerner, William Gilmore Simms: "He never realized what a clutter of useless luggage he carried into his study. It is a pity that he constricted himself to the shell of an outworn order." And the great casuist, Henry James, remained "shut up within his own skull-pan": "Like modern scholarship he came to deal more and more with less and less."[37]

By contrast, the men whom Parrington admired were "thinkers" and he characterized them as open-air pioneers or fearless navigators on adventurous, uncharted currents of thought, unhampered by constricting and formative pressures of environment. John Cotton, despite his penchant for "cloistered scholarship," gave signs of breaking out of the Puritan mold. As a man who could occasionally flirt with liberalizing ideas, he became a vigorous seaman "tacking in the face of adverse winds." Roger Williams was an "unshackled thinker" and "an adventurous pioneer, surveying the new fields of thought laid open by the Reformation."[38] Sam Adams, though well-read, was not a "bookman" like the Mathers, and his extensive reading in political theory was spread largely through his pages. Despite his debt to an endless number of sources, his was a creative intellect, and "the elusive 'meanders and windings' of his thought, veering and tacking as the winds blew" were the movements of a free, creative, and well-ventilated mind.[39] Similar praise of other heroes—Jackson ("never a bookish man") and preeminently Jefferson ("the man of affairs kept a watchful eye on the philosopher in his study")—echoed Parrington's ad-

[36] *Ibid.*, Vol. 2, pp. 95, 120, 460, 467.
[37] *Ibid.*, p. 126; Vol. 3, p. 241.
[38] *Ibid.*, Vol. 1, pp. 30, 64-65.
[39] *Ibid.*, pp. 236-237.

miration for the man of action, the man in the open air.[40]

The imaginative use of language was an integral part of Parrington's unforgettable sketches of historic figures and their ideas. Parrington's zestful interest in the people he discussed was clearly shown in the generous amount of space he allotted to them; in Volume One, for instance, the twenty-seven individuals given separate sketches received an average of more than ten pages each. This somewhat detailed consideration of thinkers and thoughts was in contrast to Beard's method, despite their common emphasis on the importance of the social and economic environment in forming ideas. To Beard, a belief in the decisiveness of the environment in developing ideas meant that ideas themselves deserved little analysis. To Parrington, however much he agreed theoretically with Beard, the ideas of his leading characters were simply too fascinating, the drama they enacted too exciting, to let go without fairly detailed treatment.

If Parrington's belief in the importance of the environment might have led him to devote less space to ideas, so his interest in imaginative literature might have led him to write pure literary history. Parrington was an esthete before he became a political reformer, and his esthetic inclinations did not vanish in later years as he became interested in political and economic reform. Parrington continued to write poetry until his death and of course to teach—not history, but rhetoric and literature. *Main Currents of American Thought* was subtitled *An Interpretation of American Literature* and the subject matter was more often literary than, for example, scientific, legal, or educational. From the standpoint of the study of the history of ideas, it is worth stressing that Parrington described mainly writers (omitting altogether no significant literary figure),

[40] *Ibid.*, Vol. 2, p. 147; Vol. 1, p. 343.

national political figures, and outstanding social thinkers. To a historian of ideas, this may not appear to
cover enough fields to deserve the title, *Main Currents
of American Thought*. To literary historians and readers focusing on the subtitle, *An Interpretation of American Literature*, however, Parrington's broad conception
of "literature" and his discussion of writers in terms of
their political and social thought were the more striking features.[41]

Of the four hundred pages comprising Volume One,
less than sixty pages were concerned in any way with
describing imaginative literature, such as a discussion
of the Hartford Wits or Philip Freneau, and even these
pages were pervaded with an attempt to locate the social thought of each author. Volume Two included discussions of John P. Kennedy, William Alexander Caruthers, Poe, William Crafts, William Gilmore Simms,
Charles Brockden Brown, Robert Montgomery Bird,
Washington Irving, James Kirke Paulding, Cooper,
Melville, Robert Treat Paine, Whittier, Emerson, Tho-
reau, Hawthorne, Longfellow, Holmes, and James Russell Lowell. These discussions, however, were focused
largely on the social thought of each writer, rather than
on his literary qualities. These sketches totaled approximately one hundred and thirty pages in a volume almost
five hundred pages long. There were, to be sure, a few

[41] John Higham concluded that Parrington "remained a captive of his own academic discipline," and that his "emphasis
still lay on imaginative letters." Higham, "The Rise of American
Intellectual History," *American Historical Review*, LVI (April
1951), 461. Morris Cohen, on the other hand, complained in
a contemporary review (1931) that Parrington's approach gave
esthetically superior literature no more attention than inferior
works. *New Republic*, LXV (January 28, 1931), 303. Stanley
Williams made the same point in *New England Quarterly*, IV,
(April 1931), 352-354. These three commentators all shared
high opinions of Parrington's volumes: they are cited only to
show their contrasting expectation and evaluation of his treatment of imaginative letters.

pages of literary evaluation and characterization of literary technique, but Parrington's treatment of writers generally focused on their social thought, and their social thought was, as he announced, grounded in social, economic, and political history.

Because Parrington's approach was to relate literature to the history of ideas, and because he emphasized the social and economic determinants influencing the history of ideas, it is justifiable to compare him with Hippolyte Taine. Indeed, Parrington's student and editor, Harold Eby, has indicated his teacher's reliance upon Taine.[42] Of course, Parrington's work was ambitious, wide-ranging, and coherent, without being, as was Taine's, grandiose and doctrinaire. Yet Parrington was the American Taine, just as Beard was America's Buckle. The differences which divide the two Americans from the Europeans do not vitiate the comparisons so much as simply suggest the less systematic, less philosophical character of American historical writings.

Despite the fact that some historians claimed that Parrington leaned too much on imaginative literature and too little on other areas of intellectual activity, and some literary historians asserted that he ignored esthetic criteria in discussing writers, his *Main Currents* was no doubt the most famous American history of ideas ever published. His synthesizing vision of the long sweep of the American past, the urgency and relevance of the ideas which his lively prose communicated— these characteristics were enthusiastically noted by reviewers.[43] A "great book," wrote Stanley Williams after

[42] *Main Currents*, Vol. 3, p. vii. From Georges Brandes' *Main Currents in Nineteenth Century Literature*, 1872-1890 (in Danish), 1901-1905 (in English), it is not apparent that Parrington took anything but the title.

[43] See, for examples of contemporary reviews, Percy Boynton, *New Republic*, LI (July 6, 1927), 181-182; Leon Whipple, *Survey*, LV (January 1, 1931), 396; Joseph K. Hart, *Survey*,

the posthumously published third volume was out.[44]
To Charles Beard, Parrington's first two volumes constituted important evidence that America was "coming-
of-age."[45] The first two volumes were awarded the Pulitzer Prize for history in 1928. When a sample of
over one hundred American historians were asked in
1952 to name their "most preferred" American histories published between 1920 and 1935, Parrington's
Main Currents received more votes than any other.[46]
Whether because Parrington's social thought was attractive, or because he viewed and described ideas in
such a way as to illuminate the role of thought in American experience (or probably because of a combination
of the two), *Main Currents* was adjudged a masterpiece.[47]

LVIII (August 1, 1927), 474-475; Kenneth Murdock, *Yale Review*, XVII (January 1928), 382-384.

[44] In a review in *New England Quarterly*, IV (April 1931),
352-354.

[45] In a review in *Nation*, CXXIV (May 18, 1927), 560-562.

[46] John W. Caughey, "Historians' Choice: Results of a Poll
on Recently Published American History and Biography," *Mississippi Valley Historical Review*, XXXIX (September 1952),
289-302. Caughey reported that Turner's 1920 *The Frontier
in American History* received 83 votes, to 84 for *Main Currents*.
Beard's *The Rise of American Civilization* was fourth, behind
Walter Webb's *The Great Plains*. Caughey's letter to the historians suggested that the "preferred" books be "best for reference or for reading or for both purposes," and that they be
judged by "accuracy of findings, contribution to knowledge,"
etc. (Caughey, p. 291.)

In the late 1930's, Parrington's *Main Currents* was one of
the works selected by a group of politically left-wing intel-
lectuals who selected a dozen books to appear in *Books That
Changed Our Minds*, Malcolm Cowley and Bernard Smith, eds.,
New York, 1939. The other writers included were: Spengler,
Lenin, Beard, Franz Boas, Dewey, Veblen, Sumner, Turner,
Henry Adams, I. A. Richards, and Freud.

[47] There were indications that a younger generation of American historians was less enthusiastic about Parrington's *Main
Currents* in the years after World War Two. John Higham

The Progressive Tradition, II

MERLE CURTI

In the same poll of historians which picked Parrington's *Main Currents* as the "most preferred" written history published between 1920 and 1935, Merle Curti's (1897—) *The Growth of American Thought* was selected as the "most preferred" work appearing between 1936 and 1950.[48] It is fitting that a survey singling out Parrington should at the same time honor Curti, for both expressed a progressive outlook and shared a similar view of ideas as instruments in history. Curti may in fact be viewed, at the risk of losing sight of his individuality to be sure, as a composite of Eggleston, Robinson, Beard, Becker, and Parrington—a composite in which the common features of all are retained and

---

(born 1920), for example, wrote in 1951:

> today the book appears as a noble ruin on the landscape of our scholarship . . . much of it has become obsolete. . . . Parrington at times miscast his heroes and made villains of men who deserved fairer understanding. The splendor of his rhetoric often concealed a looseness of meaning, and a few of his boldest generalizations have proved the most mistaken. . . . Parrington's themes and materials did not fulfill his intention of surveying the main currents in American thought. He showed slight interest or competence in metaphysics and theology; he scarcely touched scientific thought and development, or the rise of the social sciences; he ignored legal thought, intellectual institutions, and the nonliterary arts. (Higham, "The Rise of American Intellectual History," pp. 460-461.)

Richard Hofstadter (born 1916) wrote in 1960 that although "I suspect that to some degree Parrington influenced me, I don't think much of him now. . . . In digging into his work on the one particular that interested me—the Physiocrats' influence on Jeffersonians—I found him totally wrong. That helped me get Parrington out of my system." (From "Interview: Richard Hofstadter," *History: 3*, New York [September 1960], 140-141.)

[48] *The Growth of American Thought*, New York, 1943; 2nd edn., 1951; 3rd edn., 1964. Curti was also awarded the Pulitzer Prize in history for his book.

the unique characteristics of each are missing. Their shared confidence in humanity's future through the application of modern intelligence to social problems was also Curti's confident hope. Their conception that ideas are best approached by viewing the environments in which they developed was also Curti's. He too, however, sometimes wavered, as they did, in his application of environmental interpretations and often treated "enlightened" ideas without reference to nonintellectual environmental factors. As might be expected of a composite or representative figure, Curti was more systematic and less erratic than his predecessors. He broadened the scope of the subject matter in his histories to include material previously left out, and he more consistently related beliefs to their social contexts. Although Curti's successors might criticize his histories for being encyclopedic, and might claim that his relation of belief to context was merely mechanical, his position during the 1940's as the foremost historian of American opinion was secure. His high reputation stemmed both from his own achievement and from the prestige of the progressive tradition in the writing of history.

However, depicting Curti as nothing more than a composite figure made up of the characteristics common to progressive historians would be to miss his special blend of these characteristics. He had Robinson's energy and willingness to teach, combined with Beard's to write. Lacking Parrington's intense despair of the 1920's, and without Becker's wry detachment, Curti was an activist. Further, his activism flowed along institutional lines to a remarkable degree, and in a sense his many-sided leadership in the historical profession around 1950 marked the culminating institutionalization of progressive scholarship.

Curti was born and raised in Nebraska, and received all his academic degrees from Harvard. After teaching at Smith and Columbia Teachers College, he was appointed professor of history at the University of Wisconsin in 1942, where he has remained. In a long writing and teaching career which began in the 1920's, Curti has become the elder mentor of American intellectual history in the United States. He has also become the elder statesman, and, on occasion, the embattled defender, of the general ideological position enunciated by Robinson, Beard, Becker, and Parrington. To list Curti's publications is to indicate the nature of his social views.

Curti's earliest work in the 1920's and 1930's was concerned almost entirely with pacifist ideas and peace movements. His doctoral dissertation became, in 1929, *The American Peace Crusade, 1815-1860*; in 1931 *Bryan and World Peace* was published; and *Peace or War: The American Struggle, 1636-1936*, came out in 1936.[49] These books of Curti's were sympathetic to the pacifist ideas they described and it was obvious that he chose to portray the fate of pacifism in the past at least partly in order to increase the understanding and possible success of peace movements of the future. Pacifist ideas were presented as beliefs which could operate as creative instruments to change the world:

> Men weary of struggle and of war dream of peace. Even in ancient times these dreams of peace were written down. The vision of the time when swords shall be beaten into ploughshares and spears into pruning hooks has remained since Biblical times vividly in the minds of lovers of humanity.

As Curti wrote, his sympathy was manifest. As he continued, it became clear that he hoped pacifist dreams

[49] Durham, 1929; *Smith College Studies in History*, Vol. xvi, 1931; New York, 1936.

would receive widespread support and "determine" future behavior.

> Dreams alone, however, will not permanently satisfy a continuing need. A characteristic of waking dreams which continue to possess the imaginations of men is that they are likely to stimulate the dreamers to action. Men do not rest content with the world as it is. Constantly they seek to change it. Slowly it changes. These changes often represent plans, dreams if you will, which after centuries become realities.[50]

Curti sympathetically described, after a search of personal manuscripts, newspapers, periodicals, and broadsides, the body of pacifist thought which emerged in the United States:

> Perhaps the most striking contribution of early organized pacifism was the development of a body of brilliant arguments against war. . . . While the arguments against war in the earlier years were chiefly religious, moral, and philanthropic, they tended to become less and less an expression of the general spirit of liberalism and romanticism. They tended to become increasingly realistic and to make greater use of economic and political considerations. . . . Increasing attention was given, for example, to the wastefulness of war and to the burdens it inflicted on the working classes.[51]

This "body of brilliant arguments against war" was clearly, to Curti, an example of independent, "rational," and critical thinking.

The failure of these pacifist ideas to prevail historically was attributed by Curti not to defeat by other inde-

[50] *The American Peace Crusade*, p. 3. Curti here mentions "need" but it is the "need" of peace rather than of conflict and war; it is a hope or a belief, not an environmental "need."
[51] *Ibid.*, p. 225.

pendent, "rational" ideas, but instead to unfavorable environmental conditions which supported "irrational," "rationalizing" pro-war opinions. Among the various psychological and intellectual factors in the environment, by 1936 Curti came to stress the economic factor in particular:

> peacemakers have not adequately fought the economic forces that make for war. . . . Some aspects of the capitalistic order have undoubtedly promoted peace. But by its very structure this system, based on a profit-making economy, has also favored the forces of war. The desire for profits has played an important part in the willingness to float war loans. . . . In short, while individual capitalists have sincerely desired peace, war has been functional to the capitalistic system itself.[52]

Referring specifically to World War One, Curti concluded that "by and large friends of peace failed to appreciate the importance of economic interests in committing nations to war."[53]

The "irrationality" of war, "in the face even of the most logical arguments," was a recurring theme in the writings of Curti.[54] Speaking in 1936 of the Civil War, Curti referred to the "hysteria" and "all the rationalizations which led to a whole-hearted acceptance of the war."[55] Commenting in 1936 on American entry into the First World War, Curti praised LaFollette's attack on the Wilson administration during arguments over intervention—"one of the greatest speeches ever heard in a crisis at Washington"—in which LaFollette

[52] *Peace or War: The American Struggle*, pp. 307, 308.
[53] *Ibid.*, p. 231.
[54] *The American Peace Crusade*, p. 227.
[55] *Peace or War: The American Struggle*, p. 51. The specific rationalization to which Curti referred was the idea that for Northerners "Compromise with slavery, in short, seemed worse than war."

punctured the broad, idealistic assumptions that Wilson had made in declaring that this was a war for democracy, a conflict which we could no longer avoid. He showed that not Germany alone, but all the belligerents were at fault, not only in causing the war but in bringing about the situation which had so gravely injured our interests and our pride. Had we remained truly neutral, had we cut off our commerce from all belligerents, or had we enforced our commercial rights equally against all antagonists, we would not now stand on the brink of war.[56]

Thus Curti revealed, in his early histories, not only a sympathy for pacifism and for the economic interpretation of war, but he also expressed an ambivalent attitude toward the role of ideas in history. On occasion, when referring to pacifist thought, he suggested the possible power of ideas. Yet at other times, when accounting for the lack of popularity for pacifist sentiments, he stressed the power of the environment to mold thought.

Curti's sympathy for pacifist ideas was but part of an overall reform outlook, and from the middle thirties on, Curti's publications broadened in scope. *The Social Ideas of American Educators* (1935) stressed the relation between the ideas of educators and the American social and economic system. Individuals whose ideas contributed to secularization and democratization were treated more sympathetically than were individuals who retarded these reforms. Both the reformers and their opponents were criticized explicitly by Curti insofar as they failed to realize the limiting defects of the American social and economic structure, for "education cannot rise above the existent social system and the virtues sponsored by that system."[57] Emphasizing the impor-

[56] *Ibid.*, pp. 253-254.
[57] *The Social Ideas of American Educators*, Report of the American Historical Association Commission on the Social Stud-

tance of economic conditions, Curti commented, in the course of a sympathetic review of Becker's ideas in 1935, that

> while the economists were taking historians to task for their indifference toward economic influences, Mr. Becker was pointing out that most of our political troubles, domestic and international, were due to the fact that the political structure of the modern world was out of harmony with its economic organization.[58]

Curti espoused Becker's theoretical relativism, but not to the detriment of "absolute" beliefs in social reforms. Curti was in fundamental agreement with Becker that "the writing of history is functional to the needs of the day as those needs are seen by Mr. Everyman," but Curti emphasized that the historian "should think of success not merely in terms of conformity to the temper of Mr. Everyman; he must under certain circumstances be a guide as well as a fellow traveler." Curti thought "Becker would probably admit all this," but he nonetheless stressed James Harvey Robinson's (and Beard's, he might have added) precept "that the historian should select and emphasize those memories of the past that will impel men consciously to seek and build a more desirable future."[59]

Curti's synthesis, *The Growth of American Thought*

---

ies, Vol. 10, New York, 1935, p. 424. Pageant Books published a 1959 edition which includes a chapter on ideas since 1935.

[58] Curti's review of Becker's *Everyman His Own Historian: Essays on History and Politics, American Historical Review*, XLI (October 1935), 117.

[59] *Ibid.*, p. 118. For another example from the mid-1930's of Curti urging a historian, with whom he was in fundamental agreement, to be more explicit and positive in dedication to histories pointing the way clearly to social reform, see Curti's review of Henry Steele Commager's *Theodore Parker*, in *New England Quarterly*, IX (September 1936), 540-542.

(1943), carried the social views of the earlier volumes into all areas of American intellectual life. Curti's *magnum opus*, like Beard's *The American Spirit* and Parrington's *Main Currents*, was organized in terms of the conflict between reform ideas which looked forward in history and antireform ideas which looked backward. Curti's *The Growth of American Thought*, like Beard's *The American Spirit*, was not only a historical Bible for reformers, it was also a book for free men in an era of totalitarianism. It was a statement of what Americans had achieved, and it seemed to Curti—as it had come to seem also to Beard and Becker when totalitarianism threatened the United States—that America had developed ideas and institutions which were particularly good and even of virtually "absolute" value.

> As war crept closer [Curti concluded in ending his 1943 volume], always against the wish of the great majority of the American people, as step by step aid was given to the democracies resisting the totalitarian onslaught, a larger number of men and women, both among the intellectual leadership and the rank and file, realized that fascism menaced much that Americans had long held precious. The traditional American love of individual freedom, opposition to regimentation, devotion to fair play and the doctrine of live and let live, and above all, loyalty to the ideal of a moral law—these values seemed clearly jeopardized. As intellectuals wondered whether democracy and the life of the mind could survive the totalitarian menace abroad and the ominous fascist-like patterns of thought at home, and as more and more plain folk sensed that what was at stake was their way of life, the Japanese struck at Pearl Harbor.[60]

These ideals, so cherished in a time of crisis, were con-

[60] *The Growth of American Thought*, p. 751.

tributed in large part by American social reformers of the past, and they continued to be cherished after World War Two, a time when Curti feared that Americans were losing sympathy with the historic dreams of their social reformers. Curti criticized the postwar tendency of Americans to be content with too little.

> We can of course say that the ideals so generously and eloquently expressed in the American experience assumed too much and must be pared down. But let us not pare down too much! For if we do, we confess our bankruptcy. We also confess that we do not choose to take our stand with those great and bold spirits, known and unknown, recorded and unrecorded, who have helped develop the higher values of civilization and who have struggled for their realization. The American phase of that struggle has been especially full of promise, not only for Americans, but for millions of men and women the world over.[61]

In addition to defending the old social ideals in an era of cautious cold war which threatened to make them appear dispensable luxuries, Curti also answered increasing attacks on historical relativism and histories which emphasized democratic themes.[62]

Even this brief indication of Curti's social thought shows his adherence to the overall ideological position developed by Robinson, Beard, Becker, and Parrington; it also suggests—without demonstrating at length—his adherence to their interpretation of ideas. Curti empha-

[61] "Human Nature in American Thought: The Retreat from Reason in the Age of Science," printed in *Probing Our Past*, New York, 1955, p. 170.

[62] See, for example, Curti's presidential address to the Mississippi Valley Historical Association in 1952, "The Democratic Theme in American Historical Literature," reprinted in Curti, *ibid.*, pp. 3-31; Curti, *et al.*, reply to C. Destler's article in *American Historical Review*, LVI (January 1951), 450-452.

sized the crucial importance of the environment in forming human attitudes, such as sentiments favoring war,
but he also stressed the significance of the intellect in
directing man's actions and controlling his environment.
In other words, he placed an exceedingly great emphasis
on the power of the environment in shaping ideas, and
at the same time emphatically expressed the hope that
ideas could significantly transform the world.

Curti's greatest emphasis, however, was on the influence of the environment on ideas and he explicitly declared this to be the basis of his method of discussing
ideas. He developed, more than any other historian, an
explicitly environmental view of ideas, in which ideas
are seen formed as instruments through man's relation
to his environment. The ideas are what they are because
of the thinker's environmental situation: the "situation"
includes, of course, what it is that the thinker needs or
wants, but these needs or wants also tend to be explained in part environmentally. Thus this particular
view is, in important respects, an environmental one in
which ideas as instruments are formed by specific conditions. As Curti summarized his interpretation of ideas
in 1937:

> The doctrine that men seek ideas to justify their ac-
> tivities and to promote their interests, that they think
> as they live, is hardly startling. If this is true, it
> should follow that the vitality of ideas depends at
> least in part upon the effectiveness with which they
> function, on their usefulness to the interests which
> they serve. Ideas might be expected, then, to flourish
> when they answer a need and to wane when that
> need is no longer urgent. Although it is now almost
> thirty years since John Dewey asserted that thinking
> can best be explained in terms of functional relation-
> ships to human problems and needs, students of in-

tellectual history have for the most part been little influenced by this concept. Nor have they been much affected by the still older but related contention that ideas are always associated with particular interests, and that the latter, broadly defined, have a way, in the never ending conflict with antagonistic interests, of adopting, modifying, and even inventing ideas serviceable to themselves.[63]

This functional or environmental view of ideas in history seemed the common sense of the matter to Carl Becker a quarter of a century earlier when he wrote "Some Aspects of the Influence of Social Problems on the Writing of History." All it meant to Becker was that the "truth" or "falsity" of ideas was relative to the situation: when Becker wrote of ideas in history, he devoted no more space to the environment from which ideas developed than he would have if the environment had been largely irrelevant. Curti, by contrast, drew a different inference from the theoretical functionalism which both he and Becker espoused. When Curti wrote of ideas he devoted considerable space to the environmental conditions with which the ideas were associated. This method was in contrast to a detailed analysis of the ideas themselves. As Curti said of *The Growth of American Thought*, "it is thus not a history of American thought but a social history of American thought, and to some extent a socio-economic history of American thought."[64] This method and approach tended to emphasize the adaptability of ideas to the environment rather than the independent creativity of the ideas, and this was exactly the way Curti had interpreted Dewey's instrumentalism in the article quoted above. Curti executed his

[63] "The Great Mr. Locke, America's Philosopher, 1783-1861," *Huntington Library Quarterly* (1937), reprinted in Curti, *Probing Our Past*, p. 72.
[64] *The Growth of American Thought*, p. vi.

avowed method with remarkable consistency. In *The Growth of American Thought*, he did not ordinarily probe into the "interiors" of ideas, but instead focused on "the functional or instrumental nature of intellectual activities within changing social climates and shifting situations."[65] Ideas—whether formal philosophical ones or pervasive, popular thought on diverse topics from science to sports—were briefly indicated against the social and economic background.

Whether or not a historian may be said to analyze the "interiors" of ideas is, of course, only a matter of degree, and, merely because Curti was particularly interested in the relation of thought to its social and economic context, does not mean that he had no interest in the components of an idea. What Curti's technique did preclude, however, was lengthy, detailed analysis of ideas. Brief, succinct descriptions were instead characteristic.[66] And because Curti attempted to touch upon a

[65] From Curti's Preface to the 1951 edition of *The Growth of American Thought*, p. xviii.

[66] The one Curti intellectual history in which he narrowed his focus to a few thinkers and described their ideas individually in separate chapters—which allowed for more detailed study of each figure—was *The Social Ideas of American Educators*. This method was an unusual one for Curti. But even in *The Social Ideas of American Educators*, the social and economic environment figured most crucially as an explanation of why ideas developed, succeeded, or failed.

In the original Introduction to *The Growth of American Thought* (1943), Curti stated that analysis of the composition of ideas would be "valuable," although he indicated that he had not made that kind of analysis. In the Preface to the second edition (1951), Curti said that such "internal" analysis as others had carried out had revealed "unsuspected depth and richness in American thinking," and he suggested that a combination of the "internal" and environmental approaches held "great promise." In the Preface to the third edition (1964), he repeated the statement that "a combination of these two main approaches is highly desirable." He also added in the third edition, however, that since 1950 "the main emphasis in scholarship has been on the systematic inner analysis of ideas," which

vast number of areas of intellectual activity, as well as because he tried to relate them to socioeconomic circumstances, brief descriptions of ideas were mandatory.

The treatment of the colonists' idea of the Indian or of white supremacy, exemplified Curti's technique: after the idea was succinctly etched, it was "explained" or related to the environmental factors which had virtually created it.

The fact that the Atlantic seaboard settlers pushed westward in search of farms jeopardized the Indians' hunting grounds and made conflict inevitable.

When the conflict became particularly bloody, when the white men, hysterically fearful for their lives and for those of their women and children, indulged in brutal recriminations and even in massacres, they found it necessary to justify their actions on moral and rational grounds. In their efforts to enslave the Indians the whites had already elaborated a rationale of white superiority. This rationale was now extended: the Indian was condemned as a savage incapable of becoming civilized and Christianized. He was, in the words of Cotton Mather, a rabid animal, perfidious, bloody, cruel, a veritable devil in the flesh, an agent employed by Satan himself to overcome God's chosen people. If such vituperations were less necessary in periods of equilibrium, it was still easy to regard the Indian as an inferior species to be forced onto a reservation or pushed farther into the wilderness when the land hunger of the whites pressed too heavily on his preserves.[67]

Curti's method of describing colonial ideas of the

"reflects dissatisfaction with [Curti's own] assumption that the instrumentality of ideas is a valid and useful key to understanding them."

[67] *The Growth of American Thought*, p. 20.

proper family relationship followed the same environmental or functional technique:

> The general Biblical prescription for family relationships continued to be taken more or less seriously in most quarters. Scripture taught that the primary social unit was the patriarchal family. Children were enjoined to give absolute obedience as well as their labor to their parents; woman, in accordance with St. Paul's teaching, was in her original nature weaker than man and therefore subordinate to him in all things. Such a pattern of thought, which was generally accepted in Christian circles save among Quakers and related sects, provided little experience within the family in democratic living. Yet this general conception of family relations served human needs fairly well in a new society. The Biblical command to multiply and replenish the earth and the stipulation that a youth's labor belonged to his father were congenial precepts in view of the economic value of children in a new land where labor was scarce.[68]

Similarly, when he described the Puritan view of children—which characterized child nature, like all human nature, as "depraved, unregenerate, and corrupt"— Curti noted that the Puritan view "imbued the child with all the qualities of mature adults." He went on to point out how functional such an idea of children was to the New England environment.

> Such a conception of child nature favored appeals to emulation in the training of youth. In a society that was marked by a hard struggle for existence if not by an increasing competitiveness, emulation in character training was useful in promoting a successful adjustment to social environment.[69]

[68] *Ibid.*, p. 68. [69] *Ibid.*, pp. 61-62.

These examples taken from Curti's presentation of colonial thought do not in themselves suggest an approach remarkably different from Beard or Parrington, since the specific ideas mentioned were not ones for which Curti had much sympathy. But Curti did not treat environmentally only those ideas for which he had no special liking. His "environmental" or "functional" method was practiced more consistently than is the case with any other American historian of ideas. Curti's portrayal, for example, of "the Rise of the Enlightenment" —he was sympathetic to the Enlightenment mentality— revealed his characteristic method. Following a description of what Curti held to be the fundamental components of Enlightenment thought, he continued:

> The ideas of the Enlightenment answered new needs resulting from new ways of life. The rising middle classes needed ideas quite different from those that had served the priestly and feudal classes. Natural science was a more useful instrument in guiding them in their mercantile enterprise than the revealed word. The pursuit of commerce called for religious toleration, the civil liberties, respect for property, and security of property from arbitrary taxation. The middle classes no less wanted individual freedom for enterprise. As Harold Laski has insisted, they needed to be released from the hampering economic doctrines that a religious and feudal society had imposed against taking interest and "undue" profits. They required not an organic, regulatory state, but one invested with mere police powers. An environment allowing for personal freedom, so necessary to commerce and trade, came to be regarded as the natural environment, the one in accord with the great harmonious mathematical laws of the universe itself. A philosophy of free will rather than of predestination, one

which assumed that reason and natural law enabled man to control his environment and mold his destiny, seemed reasonable to men with such ideas. Optimism and faith in progress stood high in the scale of values of the middle classes. Thus the doctrines of the Enlightenment provided these classes, especially the trading folk, with ideas congenial to their interests.[70]

Curti also tried to locate the environmental origins of humanitarian thought during the Enlightenment:

In Europe humanitarianism was largely, but by no means exclusively, a middle-class phenomenon; and this was inevitably true in America, where the middle classes dominated. The social sympathies of the middle classes with those less fortunate than themselves may have resulted in part from the fact that these social groups were dynamic, recruited from beneath and on the make, and thus somewhat better able to think in terms of social improvement than the traditionally static classes of long-established privilege.[71]

Yet another example of Curti emphasizing the social and economic roots of intellectual activity of which he approved, was his discussion of the late nineteenth and early twentieth century rise of modern learning. Even acknowledging all the "intellectual" reasons for the increased specialization and professionalization of learning, Curti observed,

scholars would not have organized and zealously attended their annual meetings of their learned societies or published their technical monographs had not the new urban and industrial civilization made all this specialization and professionalization possible. Money would not have poured into institutions for

[70] *Ibid.*, p. 105.   [71] *Ibid.*, p. 120.

the advancement of knowledge had not the economy
of the nation developed to the point which permitted
it and made it seem necessary and good.[72]

It was symptomatic of Curti's emphasis upon the power
of the environment to form ideas that the "advancement of knowledge" was seen by the community to be
not merely "necessary" but also "good."

The consistency of Curti's environmental treatment
of ideas in *The Growth of American Thought* was remarkable. It is not surprising, however, to find that his
consistency was not complete—Curti had in his earlier
writings emphasized the independent origin and causal
power of certain ideas. It was a feature of his ideology
as well as of his method that he sometimes maximized
the decisive influence of thought that he particularly
admired and minimized its dependence on any environmental factors.

When Curti described the growth of scientific ideas
during the mid-nineteenth century, for instance, he emphasized the importance of environmental conditions
which compelled the positive development of science.
But he also placed stress on pure intellect itself. "In
this period, as in other times," he wrote, "sheer curiosity and disinterested love of truth for the sake of truth
exerted a powerful sway over scientific investigators."[73]
Scientific thought was here understood as the product
not of any social and economic forces but simply of independent minds searching for truth. Similarly, there
was noticeably greater attribution of intellectual independence in chapters discussing Enlightenment thought
than in sections describing "the conservative reaction"
to Enlightenment ideas, although Curti never omitted
environmental factors altogether.[74] Discussion of ration-

[72] *Ibid.*, p. 581.   [73] *Ibid.*, p. 322.
[74] Chapters 5, "The Rise of the Enlightenment," and 7, "The

alism and deism in religious thought, of the philosophy of natural rights, and of humanitarian reform values emphasized the extent to which intellectual and moral considerations determined the development of the various ideas. Curti mentioned, for instance, that humanitarian beliefs against slavery in the late 1700's were aided by the economic "fact that slavery no longer appeared to be profitable." But he went on to place stress upon a purely intellectual and moral consideration: "there was also a widespread conviction that slavery was uncongenial if not contradictory to republican principles, that it stood in the way of realizing the rights of man."[75]

Curti's treatment of "the conservative reaction" to Enlightenment thought emphasized "that it was the substantial merchants and planters and the professional men most closely associated with them who were the chief critics of the Enlightenment."[76] When Curti described the "conservative" late eighteenth and early nineteenth century doctrines of the inequality of man and of respect for established institutions, he usually correlated the doctrines with the privileged members of the status-bound society who expressed them:

> John Adams shared with many others of similar temperament and class affiliations or sympathies the veneration bestowed on institutionalism and legalism by Burke in his *Reflections on the French Revolution.* This respect for established institutions, for the authority of the past, for law, found its most important expression, perhaps, in the judicial thought of John Marshall. As chief justice of the Supreme Court . . . Marshall lent powerful support to the defense of property interests.

Expanding Enlightenment," in contrast to Chapters 8, "The Conservative Reaction," and 9, "Patrician Direction of Thought."
 [75] *Ibid.*, p. 170.   [76] *Ibid.*, p. 186.

Curti singled out the Yazoo Fraud case, in which Marshall

> ruled that even though a legislature steeped in corruption had bestowed public lands on private investors, such a bestowal was a sacred contract. Thus judicial authority upheld the irrevocable nature of contract in spite of fraud against the public interest. The sanctity of the contract as a defense of property rights against the public interest long remained as a testimony of the victory of private over public interest.[77]

Since Curti was critical of these ideas he related them somewhat more closely to social and economic conditions: it seemed that Curti was always looking for the environmental roots of thought, but found them more often when examining "conservative" thought. Curti pointed out, for example, that "social and political conservatives" in general contributed to the belittlement of the "claims of natural science." "This was especially true," he wrote, "when these claims appeared to challenge orthodox religion or the established social order."[78] In the same vein, Curti noted that some "conservatives" were "favorable toward science" when its application would advance their interests, but that they showed less "zeal for applying science to inventions for the increased well-being of man" generally.[79]

Similarly, when Curti described early nineteenth century legal thought, including arguments over perpetuating the common law, he told how "social and political liberals objected to the common law." The beliefs of these critics were attributed by Curti to intellectual and moral principles, without regard to social and economic considerations: "These radicals, influenced by the eight-

[77] *Ibid.*, pp. 191-192.   [78] *Ibid.*, p. 204.
[79] *Ibid.*, p. 208.

eenth-century concept of rationally made legal codes corresponding to natural rights, favored the rejection of common law and the establishment of an American law based on natural rights." But, continued Curti, "virtually all conservatives" supported the common law, and he singled out as an explanation their economic position. "What made this law especially congenial to conservatives was that it met so well the needs of the directors of an expanding commercial and industrial society."[80]

In discussing reform agitation at the end of the nineteenth century and the beginning of the twentieth, Curti commented that the "growing interest of men and women in social amelioration reflected changing social and economic conditions."[81] Conditions were bad, and much thinking was directed to their improvement. There was a relationship between the environment and the thought which emerged from it, in other words, but not in the sense that the environment controlled the thought—indeed, it was just the reverse, for the environment was so bad that ideas tried to change it. Curti was here picturing ideas as instruments, not in the sense of an instrument being formed by the environment, but in the sense of the instrument reforming the environment. Thought was thus celebrated in Curti's chapter on "Formulas of Protest and Reform." But in the chapter following, "The Conservative Defense," somewhat more emphasis was placed on the formation of specific beliefs by the social and economic environment, which implicitly minimized the creative power of ideas. Curti remarked that reform sentiments did not prevail during the late 1800's against the "conscious and articulated defense of the existing order by conservatives." This defense was supported by some because, as Curti approvingly quoted E. A. Ross, "Those who have the sunny rooms in the social edifice have . . . a powerful ally in the suggestion of Things-

---

[80] *Ibid.*, p. 237.   [81] *Ibid.*, p. 606.

as-they-are."[82] The ideas which comprised the "conservative defense" were thus in part responses of privileged position. As reform attacks were made, "industrial leaders and their defenders began to elaborate theoretical defenses." Curti here stressed ideas as instruments in the sense of being formed by functional demands. "Gradually," he wrote of the spokesmen for the status quo, "they came to use the slogans, symbols, and ideas in the general cultural heritage which promised to be most suitable to their needs."[83]

It can be said, therefore, that *The Growth of American Thought* revealed a slight discrepancy in its method of describing ideas. Like Robinson, Beard, Becker, and Parrington, Curti was more apt to emphasize the environmental origins and functional development of thought for which he had little sympathy, and he was more likely to minimize any environmental interpretation when discussing ideas he particularly admired. Important as this discrepancy was in Curti's writings, the extent to which he was successful in relating ideas to their environments was nevertheless crucial. To the extent that he consistently portrayed thought functionally, and he did so more consistently than any other American historian of ideas, he implemented what he understood to be Dewey's instrumentalism.

Curti became perhaps the best known representative of the socioeconomic approach to ideas, in part because he provided considerable data concerning the social and economic context in which thought functioned. But Curti's distinction was derived too from his great breadth of scope which included diverse areas of intellectual life not previously incorporated into large-scale histories of ideas. "Most striking," wrote Richard Shryock in reviewing *The Growth of American Thought*, "is the catholicity of interests, the broad conception of what

[82] *Ibid.*, p. 633.   [83] *Ibid.*, p. 634.

constitutes the cultural life of a people."[84] Curti expanded Eggleston's and Beard's comments on science and education, Curti summarized activities in the arts and architecture, and, above all, he focused on nonelite thought, or popular and minority group attitudes generally, on diverse topics. So wide was Curti's sweep in *The Growth* that the volume was almost an encyclopedia of American beliefs. This quality of inclusiveness, with popular culture prominently included, made *The Growth of American Thought* different from Parrington's *Main Currents of American Thought* and gave historians some reason to think the study of American ideas was developing significantly.[85]

Popular culture was precisely the focus of Curti's major scholarly publication after World War Two, *The Making of an American Community: A Case Study in a Frontier County.*[86] This Trempealeau County study was not a history of ideas, but, rather, an investigation of the extent of "democracy" in one Wisconsin county between 1840 and 1880. Yet the inquiry, including in particular the chapters on "The Social Creed" and "Educational and Cultural Opportunities," involved some analysis of beliefs. To this extent, the study was an offshoot of the desire to explore ideas in their social and economic context. The investigation of popular opinion, inferred partly through behavior and pursued with the aid of techniques and insights from the social sciences, made the Trempealeau County volume in part a lega-

[84] *American Historical Review*, xxxix (July 1944), 732-735.

[85] Reviews of Curti's *The Growth* talked as if the book's inclusiveness was a significant step forward for scholarship, not because the specific information was new, but because Curti related it to American intellectual life generally. See, for example, in addition to Shryock's review, Harold Whitman Bradley's in *Mississippi Valley Historical Review*, xxxi (June 1944), 113-114.

[86] Palo Alto, 1959.

tee of the New History precepts issued a half-century earlier.

Curti's scholarship as a whole has been a fulfillment of Robinson's plea for a New Intellectual History. Curti perpetuated Robinson's enthusiasm for ideas as creative forces and as historical syntheses on the one hand, and on the other, his enthusiasm for the social and economic environment as the critical force in forming human thought. The social and economic environment was the behind-the-scenes determinant in *The Growth of American Thought. The Making of an American Community* simply featured on stage the socioeconomic conditions which Robinson, Beard, Becker, Parrington, and Curti had always thought were so important. The Trempealeau County study (with its long chapters on "Making a Living on the Farm," "Making a Living in Town," and "Social and Economic Structure"), like Beard's work in economic interpretation, was thus a consistent part of the shared conception of the nature of history and the role of historical ideas.

Curti's attempt to apply social science techniques to historical research on a wider scale than he or his predecessors had done previously was the outstanding feature of the Trempealeau book. Absent from the heart of the volume was the explicit concern for reform so characteristic of the bulk of Curti's scholarship. But the attempt to make written history more scientific, in the sense of ascertaining the relationship between environmental conditions and the beliefs which emerged from them, had always been present in progressive histories of thought. Assuming science as well as the flow of history to be on their side, the reformers usually saw no contradiction between the use of more scientific methods and better written history. In Buckle's and Taine's pioneering pleas for scientific histories which featured the role of ideas, the central place went to the relation of thought to its environmental origin. Robinson perpetuated the emphasis even as he coupled it with American progressivism. Beard's use of collective biography, as well as his general attempt to tie ideas to interests, marked his histories almost as much as his reformist sympathies. Similarly, Parrington's progressive masterpiece, which he originally titled "An Economic Interpretation of American Literature," harked back to Taine's *History of English Literature* in its attempt to indicate the environmental origins of thought. Curti was thus underlining a persistent concern of his own and his predecessors' earlier works when he called upon the methods of the social sciences to study the extent of democratic beliefs and practices in their social and economic contexts in Trempealeau County. The legacy of the New Intellectual History was environmental analysis (sometimes phrased in scientific terms) as well as reform sympathy.

SAMUEL ELIOT MORISON

WHILE Edward Eggleston, James Harvey Robinson, Charles Beard, Carl Becker, Vernon Louis Parrington, and Merle Curti were expressing in their writings a distinctive ideological position and a distinctive conception of ideas, which became the dominant tradition of American histories of ideas during the first half of the twentieth century, some challenges to these progressive views were also voiced. Quietly, without any initial manifesto, several historians during and after the 1920's made individual contributions to the study of American ideas and intellectual life which expressed (implicitly or explicitly) views of society and theories of ideas different from those held by the progressive scholars. Three such dissenting historians—whose only predecessor was the late nineteenth century pioneer, Moses Coit Tyler—were Samuel Eliot Morison, Perry Miller, and Ralph Gabriel. From the 1920's to World War Two these dissenting historians gradually built up a body of writings which stood in contrast to those of the dominant group; during the 1940's and 1950's, as the era of totalitarianism seemed to many to lend support to the views of the dissenters, Morison, Miller, and Gabriel expressed their views most explicitly.

Samuel Eliot Morison (1887—), not exclusively or even most significantly a historian of ideas, nevertheless contributed during the late 1920's and 1930's to the development of a description and assessment of the American intellectual experience different from that of Eggleston, Robinson, Beard, Becker, Parrington, and Curti. Morison's studies of America's intellectual past were focused solely upon New England Puritanism, and they all revealed a strong sympathy and respect for Puritanism. By contrast, the ideas of the Puritans had been generally ignored by Beard and Curti, and had been explicitly disparaged by Eggleston and Parrington.

Morison was descended from an old New England family, he was Boston bred and Harvard schooled, and he taught history at Harvard throughout his career. His studies of Puritan life and thought, *Builders of the Bay Colony* (1930), *The Founding of Harvard College* (1935), *Harvard College in the Seventeenth Century* (1936), and *The Puritan Pronaos* (1936),[1] were among the early attempts to put Puritanism back into the structure of American histories as a crucial and esteemed intellectual foundation. "My attitude toward seventeenth-century puritanism," wrote Morison in 1930, "has passed through scorn and boredom to a warm interest and respect. The ways of the puritans are not my way, and their faith is not my faith," he continued, "nevertheless they appear to me a courageous, humane, brave, and significant people."[2] Working at Harvard

[1] Boston, 1930; Cambridge, 1935; 2 vols., Cambridge, 1936; New York, 1936 (republished with slight revisions as *The Intellectual Life of Colonial New England*, 1956, Cornell University Press reprint, 1960).

[2] Boston, p. vi. There is some evidence to suggest that, on occasion at least during the 1920's, the younger Morison was more critical of Puritanism, and more sympathetic to economic interpretation, than he was later. See his review of T. J. Wertenbaker's *The First Americans, 1607-1690*, in *New England Quarterly*, I (July 1928), 412, in which Morison wrote that after reading Wertenbaker's "chapter on the paucity of formal religious life in Virginia, and reflecting on the great men produced at the lowest religious ebb, one wonders whether the Puritan Church was not a blight to New England. Certainly the

with Kenneth Murdock—whose very sympathetic biography of Increase Mather in the 1920's had provoked Parrington to say that the book must have been "conceived in the dark of the moon, a season congenial to strange quirks of fancy"[3]—Morison, according to his own later statement, consciously attempted to revise what he saw as the prevailing unsympathetic estimation of Puritan intellectual life. Morison wrote in the 1950's that he felt impelled during the late 1920's and 1930's "to counteract the disparaging and, for the most part, inaccurate accounts of New England colonial culture that had been published during the previous forty years."[4] The 1920's, of course, witnessed Menckenian attacks on Puritanism as the source of all that rebellious intellectuals did not like about American life, and the same postwar decade saw the publication of James Truslow Adams' popular histories of New England which argued that economics, rather than ideals, comprised the driving force of Puritanism.[5]

Morison's sympathetic view of the Puritans rested in part on his conviction that they took the life of the mind seriously and lived it successfully:

What is not sufficiently known or appreciated is this: puritanism not only did not prevent, but stimulated an interest in the classics, belles-lettres, poetry, and

---

burden of proof is now cast upon protagonists of the New England Way." See also Morison's favorable review of *The Rise of American Civilization*, *New England Quarterly*, I (January 1928), 94-98.

[3] Parrington, Vol. 1, p. 98.

[4] *The Intellectual Life of Colonial New England*, Preface to second edition, p. v.

[5] Morison constantly expressed disagreement with Adams in his writings. For the most famous conflict, see the Appendix to Morison's *Builders of the Bay Colony*, in which he presented his case that religious ideas, not economic considerations, determined Puritan colonization in the New World.

scientific research. Neither pioneer hardships nor other restrictions were ever so great as to prevent the burgeoning of genuine intellectual life in that series of little beachheads on the edge of the wilderness, which was seventeenth-century New England.[6]

This conclusion as to the quality of Puritan intellectual life was accompanied by a conviction that Puritan ideas were the most important factors in early New England history. He wrote that "the dynamic force in settling New England was English puritanism desiring to realize itself."[7] The specific religious doctrine of Puritanism was not in itself particularly appealing to Morison, but he was attracted by the fact that religion and ideas were taken seriously by the Puritans. "After three hundred years," Morison said, "it no longer seems so important what sort of religious faith the puritans had, as that they had faith."[8] This Puritan faith, together with the will to prevail, had carried the early New Englanders to success despite an unfriendly physical environment. "Nature seemed to doom Massachusetts to insignificance," he commented. "With a tithe of the bounty that Nature grants more favored lands, the Puritan settlers made their land the most fruitful not only in things of the Spirit, but in material wealth."[9]

Part of Morison's belief that ideas were significant causal factors in history rested upon his view that nonintellectual environmental forces were not sufficient to "explain" ideas which developed. He devoted one of his earliest essays, "Squire Ames and Doctor Ames," to a study of two brothers with similar social and economic backgrounds who came to express opposing ideas. Morison later wrote of this article:

[6] *The Intellectual Life of Colonial New England*, p. 4.
[7] *Ibid.*, p. 6.
[8] *Builders of the Bay Colony*, p. 129.
[9] *The Maritime History of Massachusetts, 1783-1860*, Boston, 1921, p. 7.

Deterministic historians are fond of explaining persons and ideas by material things such as background, education, and class interests. I wrote this essay, in part, to poke fun at them. For here were two brothers living cheek-by-jowl in the village where they were born, both Harvard graduates, one a lawyer and the other a physician, but at opposite poles in politics.[10]

Thus Morison's sympathy for Puritan New Englanders was accompanied by his conception of ideas as important historical determinants. Morison's writings were obviously similar to Moses Coit Tyler's, rather than to those of his contemporaries, the progressive historians. Further, an examination of several aspects of Morison's social thought which combined to comprise his overall ideological outlook reveals distinct conflict with the ideological positions expressed by Eggleston, Robinson, Beard, Becker, Parrington, and Curti.

One area of conflict, for example, was that of attitudes toward the history and future role of formal education in the United States, and in this area Morison explicitly criticized the writings of Beard and Curti. Morison published during the 1930's several volumes on the history of Harvard, in which he sympathetically evaluated early New England education in much the same spirit as he interpreted the Puritan experience generally. He concluded that no contribution of Puritanism to New England and to the United States was more important than the gift of "a learned clergy and a lettered people."[11] This devotion to learning, which gen-

[10] The essay was originally printed in *New England Quarterly*, I (January 1928), 5-31. It was reprinted, with introductory comments in *By Land and By Sea*, New York, 1953, Chapter 8.

[11] *The Founding of Harvard College*, Cambridge, 1935, p. 45.

erated the founding of Harvard College, was rooted in the Puritans'

> brave religious faith, serenely overriding all prudent objections and practical difficulties, [and it was this faith] that carried the puritan fathers, through poverty and struggle, into so ambitious and so excellent an enterprise. "To advance *Learning* and perpetuate it to Posterity," was their high purpose; posterity dared not fail to achieve the design so confidently pricked out on their white shield of expectation.[12]

This praise for Puritan educational thought included a sympathy for the classical education which, according to Morison, was transmitted by the New England schools from the seventeenth century to the twentieth, until, as he said in 1936, it was "mangled and thrown aside by the professional educators and progressive pedagogues of our own day and generation."[13] The twentieth century, wrote Morison even more graphically in 1961, had "hatched the ugly duckling of John Deweyism, which continues to befoul American education to this day."[14] Morison criticized the interpretation by Beard and Curti that Puritan education was basically religious indoctrination or propaganda for the governing class.[15] Morison's views on education were part of his tendency to look favorably upon established traditions, rather than to look with optimistic favor upon change, and both his views on education and his sympathy for established traditions differed from the attitudes manifested in the writings of Beard and Curti. A crucial responsi-

[12] *Ibid.*, p. 350.
[13] *The Puritan Pronaos*, p. 16. The second edition, *The Intellectual Life of Colonial New England*, contains a nearly identical phrase on p. 17.
[14] Morison, *The Scholar in America: Past, Present, and Future*, New York, 1961, p. 15.
[15] *The Puritan Pronaos*, pp. 64-65; p. 67 in the second edition.

bility of American public education, wrote Morison in 1961, is to instruct students "in the tradition of western civilization," rather than, "as Progressive Education has done in its misdirected zeal for immediate effects and 'togetherness,' to make young people acquainted only with the world around them." "This," he concluded, "is a major cause of the emotional malaise of our times. As Paul Tillich has pointed out, the young person of today, 'living in a world hardly touched by the traditions . . . inescapably becomes skeptical, both from a religious and from a cultural point of view.' "[16]

Views toward war formed an even more important part of the complex of ideas on which Morison differed from the progressive historians. Morison, unlike Beard, Becker, Parrington, and Curti, did not express during the 1920's and 1930's any sympathy for an economic interpretation of past wars nor any sympathy for pacifism. Later, in the 1940's, Morison participated in the Second World War, became the official historian of the United States Navy for that war, and published criticisms of historians—particularly Beard—who since the First World War had "ignored wars, belittled wars, taught that no war was necessary and no war did any good," and whose "zeal against war did nothing to preserve peace."[17]

In 1950, in his presidential address to the American Historical Association, Morison made his most explicit statement of his ideological position. He urged that American historians and thinkers appreciate the importance of established traditions and beliefs:

A historian owes respect to tradition and to folk-memory; for "History is corrected and purified tra-

[16] Morison, *The Scholar in America*, p. 25.

[17] "Faith of an Historian," *American Historical Review*, LVI (January 1951), 266, 267. The address appears in almost the same form in *By Land and By Sea*, pp. 346-359. Quotations appear there on p. 351.

dition, enlarged and analyzed memory." . . . in many works written in the 1920's and 1930's, there are no great men or leading characters, only automata whose speeches, ideas, or aspirations are mentioned merely to give the historian an opportunity to sneer or smear.[18]

Morison asserted that these histories contributed to a weakening of American traditions and values by undercutting the respect which was given them; historic ideals and great men of the past were in effect "debunked" in these works by an environmental approach emphasizing material factors. The rise of totalitarianism made it imperative that Americans know what ideals they were willing to defend, but instead there was "American spiritual unpreparedness for World War II," according to Morison. "Pacifism, disillusion, and a disregard for settled values were rampant in literature, on murals and the screen, and over the air."[19] Modern history had thus justified to Morison his position, and he could record with relief, in 1950, that "the age of 'debunking' has passed . . . a new generation both here and in Europe is sounding and elucidating national and sectional traditions."[20] Morison, like Tyler, looked to community traditions established by the past for inspiration and guidance in the present and future. Morison's source of authority in the past, as well as the specific precepts elicited from the past, contrasted markedly with the viewpoint of his progressive contemporaries.

The intellectual studies in which Morison expressed his social thought, and his view of Puritan ideas as important historical determinants, were not studies of the

[18] "Faith of an Historian," p. 270; p. 354 in *By Land and By Sea.*

[19] "Faith of an Historian," p. 267; pp. 351-352 in *By Land and By Sea.*

[20] "Faith of an Historian," pp. 270-271; p. 355 in *By Land and By Sea.*

internal content and structure of ideas. But neither were they studies of the socioeconomic background from which ideas took shape. Rather, Morison's studies were largely of the biographical and educational aspects of Puritan intellectual life. *Builders of the Bay Colony* (1930) was comprised of biographical sketches of the founding generation of Massachusetts Bay Puritans, with an emphasis placed upon their ideas. Morison's depiction of the Puritan outlook was in essential agreement with that given by the original Puritan chroniclers themselves. For example, he took issue with any materialist interpretation of the Puritan migration from England. "My own opinion, one arrived at by considerable reading of what the puritans wrote, is that religion, not economics nor politics, was the center and focus of the puritan dissatisfaction with England, and the puritan migration to New England."[21]

The similarity between Morison's views, and those of the original Puritan chroniclers—which were those of the ruling Puritan oligarchy—was suggested also in his description of the problem of intellectual dissent in the early Bay Colony. Morison argued that religious unity and communal security, not freedom of thought, comprised the issue when Puritans were faced with dissidents. "The colony had not been founded with a view to establishing religious liberty. . . . Toleration had never been offered or promised to the immigrants."[22] Therefore, according to Morison, historians need not become excited about Puritan uniformity of thought. Dissenters were free to leave New England if they wished. But more than this, declared Morison in speaking of Anne Hutchison's banishment, "the historian may be permitted to doubt the value of doubt in all times and places. It is at least arguable that the suppression

[21] *Builders of the Bay Colony*, p. 346.
[22] *Ibid.*, p. 116.

of the gifted lady was necessary to preserve all that the puritans had to give, or bequeath."[23] In singling out the problem posed by dissident thinkers in an insecure society, and by sympathizing with the censors rather than the censored, Morison explicitly differed both in description and evaluation with the treatment given to the same subject by Beard, Parrington, and Curti.[24]

The Puritan Pronaos: Studies in the Intellectual Life of New England in the Seventeenth Century (1936) surveyed the nature of Puritan intellectual life as it was expressed in the school system, higher and lower, the

[23] *Ibid.*, p. 125. Morison commented elsewhere to the same effect that Puritan uniformity of thought produced good results: "Rhode Island, the colony of religious liberty, democracy, and intense individualism, had no school system or compulsory education laws throughout the colonial period." (*The Puritan Pronaos*, p. 67.)

Again: "A mere reference to the France of Louis XIV or the England of Elizabeth is sufficient to prove that intolerance does not necessarily crush literary expression; and, conversely, the two English colonies that adopted a tolerant polity in the seventeenth century, Rhode Island and Maryland, were conspicuously barren in letters." (*The Intellectual Life of Colonial New England*, p. 154.)

For other examples of Morison's irritation at sympathy extended to dissidents against Puritan orthodoxy see: Morison's review of three books dealing with Anne Hutchinson ("a woman whom he [the reviewer] finds more tedious the more often her story is told"), *New England Quarterly*, III (April 1930), 358; *The Founding of Harvard College*, pp. 175-180; Morison's review of L. H. Gipson's *The British Empire Before the American Revolution*, Vol. 6, *New England Quarterly*, xx (March 1947), 117-121.

[24] See Beard's *The Rise of American Civilization*, Vol. 1, pp. 56-57; Parrington's *Main Currents*, Vol. 1, pp. 24, 29, 49-50; Curti's *The Growth of American Thought*, p. 56. Morison's view of the claim for free speech in mid-twentieth century America was that it should be allowed to all who did not advocate force and violence. Similarly, he thought that the academic freedom to teach extended to all those who would allow others freedom. He intimated that he favored allowing Communists to speak in public, but not to teach in colleges. See Morison, *Freedom in Contemporary Society*, Boston, 1956, pp. 45, 136.

printing and distribution of books, and the state of libraries. Chapters were devoted also to "Theology and the Sermon," "Historical and Political Literature," "Verse," and "Scientific Strivings," but the focus in these chapters, as in the others, was not solely on ideas but on the overall state of activity in these various intellectual areas.

"Theology and the Sermon" indicated the nature of the federal or Covenant system which was preached, and the Half-Way Covenant which replaced it, but Morison also discussed at equal length the literary style of the sermon as well as the technique of delivery. "Historical and Political Literature" assessed the writing of "histories, biographies, chronicles, and original narratives of secular experience." The assessment was concerned not with the ideas expressed by these historical writings—other than to note that they all tried to show God's special interest in New England—but in describing the literary form of the writings. In treating "Verse," as in discussing theology and history, Morison's focus was on the development of the particular discipline, rather than on the development of particular ideas. He consistently concentrated on intellectual activity itself, not the social and economic background to it, but he did not concentrate on the content of ideas so much as on the development of institutions (schools) and genres (verse, historical writings) of intellectual activity.

Morison's survey of intellectual life in colonial New England, like that of Moses Coit Tyler—in sharp contrast with Edward Eggleston's—was a study in impressive achievement. The Puritan intellectual contribution lay above all in "providing a framework and setting up values that later generations could use and respect." Rather than dwelling upon Puritan superstition and ignorance of modern science, as did Eggleston, Morison argued that the "puritan creed, an intellectualized form of Christianity, stimulated mental activity on the part of those who professed it," and that the ministry "maintained an open mind and a receptive attitude toward the scientific discoveries" of the seventeenth century.[25] "Religion proved a stimulus rather than a restraint" to the growth of scientific knowledge, according to Morison, "because the clerical leaders of the community were well-educated men, curious about what was going on, eager to keep in touch with the movements of their day, receptive to new scientific theories."[26] To take a specific case, Morison cited the "new astronomy, which had to fight the church and the clergy in almost every other country," and yet these new scientific views were "accepted by and even propagated by the clergy in New England."[27] In the same vein, Morison explained that certain Puritan limitations, such as the witchcraft episodes, were the common results of seventeenth century conditions and were not caused by Puritanism in particular.

Morison made his major contribution in studies of Puritan education. In *The Founding of Harvard College* (1935), Morison traced the importation of European theories and practices to the new college at Cambridge. By studying the European origins of Harvard education at length, Morison made his history of a colonial college a chapter in early modern European intellectual history. He described how "the traditional Arts and Philosophies and learned Tongues were taught," and how "the standards, forms, and amenities of English universities were reproduced, so far as the slender means and austere principles of New England would permit." There were hard times, "when the colonies were ravaged by Indian wars, and encroaching

[25] *The Intellectual Life of Colonial New England*, p. 273.
[26] *Ibid.*, p. 241.   [27] *Ibid.*, p. 247.

materialism all but squelched learning," but, noted Morison with satisfaction, "the torch never went out."[28] He emphasized the determination of the early Puritans to successfully perpetuate their educational institution despite difficult environmental conditions:

Harvard College was established at a place which had been a wilderness eight years before, in a colony whose history was less than ten years old, and by a community of less than ten thousand people. The impulse and support came from no church, government, or individual in the Old World, but from an isolated people hemmed in between the forest and the ocean, who had barely secured the necessities of existence. No similar achievement can be found in the history of modern colonization; and in the eight centuries that have elapsed since Abelard lectured by the Seine, there have been few nobler examples of courage in maintaining intellectual standards amid adverse circumstances than the founding and early history of the puritans' college by the Charles.[29]

Morison described in great detail the indecision about various sites for the new college, the possible means of financial support, and the selection of its first teacher and president. People rather than ideas received the most intensive examination as they did in all Morison's studies of intellectual life. He continued his description of curricular ideas, college organization, and student life through the 1600's in the two volumes of *Harvard College in the Seventeenth Century* (1936).

The story of early Harvard was an inspiring one to Morison, as was the story of early New England generally. He described the achievement of an intellectual life at Massachusetts Bay, an achievement gained de-

28 *The Founding of Harvard College*, p. 4.
29 *Ibid.*, p. 148.

spite the inhospitable environmental factors of intellectual isolation, economic poverty, and a small population. Thus Morison studied ideas and intellectual institutions in relation to their nonintellectual environment, but what he emphasized was the decisive effect of thought upon the environment. He denied the allegation of progressive historians that the decisive influence moved in the other direction. The only sense in which Morison viewed ideas pragmatically was in interpreting ideas partly in terms of their impact on environments.

Morison's admiration for early New Englanders (part of a Tyler-like traditionalism on social issues generally) and his celebration of the power of thought were the basis of his challenge to the progressive historians of ideas. The challenge was above all an affirmation of Morison's view of the world, and a dissent from the ideological position of the progressive scholars. Morison offered little challenge to the way progressives actually wrote histories of thought except for his allegations concerning the independence of ideas from social and economic determinants. That is, Morison devoted no more space to the "internal composition" of ideas in his histories than did Eggleston, Beard, or Curti. Moreover, Morrison was less concerned than Parrington or Becker with the content of ideas. In other words, Morison's denigration of nonintellectual environmental influences was not accompanied by analyses of ideas in depth in his histories.

PERRY MILLER

Morison's challenge to progressive historians was more ideological than methodological, but Perry Miller (1905-1963), a younger colleague, issued a bold challenge primarily through his study of the content and structure of Puritan ideas. Miller, born and educated in

Chicago, taught English at Harvard from 1931 to his death, and he expressed a conception of the nature and role of ideas similar to Morison's. Miller also showed great respect for Puritan ideas, although he, being an atheist, emphasized even more than did Morison that "respect for them is not the same thing as believing in them." Miller wrote that he never intended to be a Puritan apologist, that he merely started at the beginning of the American experience, and that the beginning happened to be theological and intellectual. "This was not a fact of my choosing," he said, "had the origin been purely economic or imperial, I should have been no less committed to reporting."[30]

Miller found ideas at the "beginning" (and in every other phase of American history which he studied), and he expressed his admiration for "the majesty and coherence of Puritan thinking."[31] More than this, Miller implied that the Puritan view of life was in some sense true. "Puritanism failed to hold later generations," he wrote, "largely because the children were unable to face reality as unflinchingly as their forefathers."[32] Further, he emphasized that ideas were crucial in all periods of human history. Part of Miller's respect for the Puri-

[30] Miller, *Errand Into the Wilderness*, Cambridge, 1956, p. ix. Miller was here being less than completely frank, as Donald Fleming has pointed out. Virginia, not Massachusetts, was the "beginning" chronologically, but "a preponderantly economic situation did not meet his specifications for a theme." See Fleming, "Perry Miller and Esoteric History," *The Harvard Review*, II (Winter-Spring 1964), 26. Miller would probably have agreed with Fleming's point, although Miller did once argue that not even Virginia's settlement could be understood "unless the cosmological and religious premises of the epoch are taken into account." See Miller, Preface to "Religion and Society in the Early Literature of Virginia," in *Errand Into the Wilderness*, p. 100.

[31] From 1959 Preface to Beacon paperback edition of *Orthodoxy in Massachusetts, 1630-1650*, originally published by Harvard University Press, 1933, p. xx.

[32] *The New England Mind: The Seventeenth Century*, Cambridge, 1939, 1954, p. 37.

tans stemmed from the fact that these New England colonists took their theological concepts and intellectual life seriously. He was critical of scholars who did not treat ideas seriously as did the New Englanders:

> historians are apt to slide over these [theological] concepts in a shockingly superficial manner simply because they have so little respect for the intellect in general. I have difficulty imagining that anyone can be a historian without realizing that history itself is part of the life of the mind; hence I have been compelled to insist that the mind of man is the basic factor in human history.[33]

Miller's conviction that "the mind of man is the basic factor in human history," and his admiration for Puritan intellectual achievement, paralleled Morison's views, albeit with less sentiment. Miller did not express himself in print on the full range of social issues which have been cited in the cases of the other historians discussed, but his views—when expressed—were in opposition to many of those of the progressive historians. Miller was critical, for example, of the relativistic implications of the "progressive education" concept of "the school as a service to society." Dewey had influenced "schools to make a kind of citizen who, because of his training, without any supernatural assistance, will behave in ways useful to society,"[34] Miller wrote, and he suggested that such a conception allowed society to control and curtail the schools in potentially harmful ways. After 1945, according to Miller, this potential threat, which was not sufficiently appreciated by those who developed the concept of "education to serve society," became an actual danger because of society's

[33] *Errand Into the Wilderness*, p. ix.
[34] Perry Miller, "Education Under Cross-Fire," in John W. Chase, ed., *Years of the Modern: An American Appraisal*, New York, 1949, p. 182.

changing temper. Miller did not share the implicitly hopeful reformism of progressive education.

The same opportunities for change which excited the progressives, whether in education or in the interpretation of history, made Miller grow cautious. He suggested that the "presentistic"

> "new history," written in terms of economic factors, or of class warfare, or of sectionalism and the frontier, has a way of becoming as quickly dated as has [Jonathan] Edwards' history in terms of the Old Testament.[35]

Nor did Miller share, at least in his early writings, the enthusiasm for the social sciences which was felt by the progressive historians. In 1933, introducing the first portion of his study of the New England mind, Miller wrote, with tongue in cheek:

> I lay myself open to the charge of being so very naive as to believe that the way men think has some influence upon their actions, of not remembering that these ways of thinking have been officially decided by modern psychologists to be generally just so many rationalizations constructed by the subconscious to disguise the pursuit of more tangible ends.

Miller's conviction that ideas significantly influence behavior, and that the way to understand ideas is to study the ideas themselves, led him to declare in the same introductory statement that he had "attempted to tell of a great folk movement with an utter disregard of the economic and social factors."[36] Several years later, in the same vein, Miller criticized historians who "have tended to minimize the importance of abstract theology

[35] *Jonathan Edwards*, New York, 1949, Meridian Books paperback reprint, 1959, pp. 310-311.

[36] *Orthodoxy in Massachusetts, 1630-1650*, Cambridge, 1959, p. xi.

and of the pulpit," historians who thought "that whatever the theology, Puritan conduct can be explained without it." While admitting that a neglect of theological ideas "has the advantages of appealing to an age that has no relish for theology, and of making the task of writing about New England appreciably simpler," he added:

It would perhaps be unkind to suggest that historians, particularly those known as "social and economic," are not prone to be themselves conspicuous examples of the Augustinian piety, and are therefore the more inclined to discount spiritual motives.[37]

Finally, it seemed to Miller, Puritan thought was important enough to deserve careful analysis irrespective of nonintellectual environmental relationships. "I assume," he wrote, "that Puritanism was one of the major expressions of the Western intellect, that it achieved an organized synthesis of concepts which are fundamental to our culture, and that therefore it calls for the most serious examination." Consequently, he said, he had "deliberately avoided giving more than passing notice to the social or economic influences."[38]

Miller did not in his later scholarship actually ignore all environmental interpretations of ideas—as an examination of his written histories will show—but his characteristic emphasis was on the power and importance of ideas, rather than on the environment from which they came. In addition to a conviction that ideas were significant historically (in the sense of causing things to happen), Miller also revealed an interest in ideas for what they *were*, regardless of what they *did*—if the ideas possessed "quality": "there is, I am convinced, a perspective in which the speculations of a serious and

[37] *The New England Mind: The Seventeenth Century*, p. 47.
[38] *Ibid.*, p. viii.

competent (all the more if he be a great) thinker have an intrinsic worth that has nothing to do with their direct impact upon politics or programs.[39] To this extent, Miller interpreted ideas less pragmatically than any other American historian of ideas. For not only did he frequently disregard the pragmatic social and economic origins of ideas, but he also (sometimes) expressed disinterest in the pragmatic worldly consequences of ideas. The progressive historians of ideas were ordinarily pragmatic both in their interpretations of the origins of ideas, and also in their view that the meaning of an idea was to be found largely in its worldly consequences. Even Samuel Eliot Morison, who denied the decisive influence of social and economic environmental factors in the formation of ideas, nonetheless described the effect of ideas in terms of impact upon the social and economic environment.

Miller's interest in thought for its own sake, his belief nonetheless that thought is of decisive historical importance, and his admiration for Puritan ideas in particular were expressed in five volumes devoted to the colonial New England mind: *Orthodoxy in Massachusetts, 1630-1650* (1933); *The New England Mind: The Seventeenth Century* (1939); *The New England Mind: From Colony to Province* (1953).[40] Individual biographies were devoted to *Jonathan Edwards* (1949) and *Roger Williams* (1953). Miller's detailed analysis of Puritan ideas was unprecedented; no one had allotted

[39] Miller, ed., *American Thought: Civil War to World War I*, New York, 1954, p. vii.

[40] Cambridge, reprinted in 1954. The chronological order of publication is not the proper chronological order of the story as Miller relates it. *The New England Mind: The Seventeenth Century* is really an analytical overview, or summary of the "mind" without regard for its changes. These changes are dealt with in *Orthodoxy in Massachusetts*, followed chronologically by the subject matter of *The New England Mind: From Colony to Province*.

so much time and space to studying the structure of Puritan thought. Indeed, the depth of Miller's analysis of ideas was unprecedented in any period of American thought.

Miller's portrait of the Puritan mind differed in crucial respects from that drawn by Parrington, and from those portraits briefly drawn by Beard and Curti. Miller did not depict the Puritan mentality primarily in terms of social or economic democracy, but rather in philosophical and theological terms. Or, to put it differently, the problems of Puritan thought on which Miller concentrated were not concerned with political or economic power but with theology and philosophy. Miller's several volumes were devoted to analyzing the body of Puritan thought which was brought to New England, the way it faced its intellectual problems, and the alteration of that body of thought by the 1700's. Democratic aspects of Puritan thought were not ignored, but they were not the focus of Miller's inquiries about Puritanism as they had been of Parrington's, Beard's, and Curti's.

The New England Mind: The Seventeenth Century (1939) was an exceedingly detailed study of the content and structure of ideas, with almost no attention given to the environment from which the ideas came. It was this volume, above all others, which exemplified in its purest form Miller's nonenvironmental technique of describing ideas, as well as his detailed analysis. He wrote of Puritan thought at its point of full development in the 1600's; he was not concerned in this volume with showing the rise or fall of Puritan ideas, but with showing what they consisted of at full fruition.

Miller opened *The New England Mind: The Seventeenth Century* by emphasizing the importance of his subject. When "considered in the broad perspective of Christian history," he wrote, Puritanism "appears no longer as a unique phenomenon, peculiar to England of the seventeenth century, but as one more instance of a recurrent spiritual answer to interrogations eternally posed by human existence." Miller continued, "Inside the shell of its theology and beneath the surface coloring of its political theory, Puritanism was yet another manifestation of a piety to which some men are probably always inclined and which in certain conjunctions appeals irresistibly to large numbers of exceptionally vigorous spirits."[41]

It was this strain of piety, piety labeled Augustinian by Miller, which was the "subjective mood" he attempted to recapture in the volume, while at the same time he described formal thought. Formal Puritan thought was an expression of this piety, according to Miller:

> the great structure of the Puritan creed, ostensibly erected upon the foundation of logic, will have meaning to most students today only when they perceive that it rested upon a deep-lying conviction that the universe conformed to a definite, ascertainable truth, and that human existence was to be had only upon the terms imposed by this truth.[42]

By presenting Puritan doctrines as specific expressions of an important and recurring spiritual mood, Miller subtly minimized what was odd or unique about Puritanism and maximized what was more universally relevant. The difference in emphasis amounted to a greater sympathy, respect, and sense of relevance for Puritanism in Miller's scholarship than would have been possible otherwise.

Miller also, in his opening pages, explicitly defended the Puritans against charges of hypocrisy, otherworldli-

[41] *The New England Mind: The Seventeenth Century*, p. 4.
[42] *Ibid.*, p. 5.

ness, and inconsistency. Answering criticisms that there was an unusually wide deviation between professions and practices of piety, Miller admitted that the "divorce between conduct and belief was probably as wide in Puritan society as in any other," but, he asserted, it was "certainly no wider." To the charge of Puritan otherworldliness, Miller answered that only worldly excess, not worldly living itself, was criticized by Puritan doctrine. "No seventeenth-century Puritan ever said that food, love, and music were intrinsically bad," he commented, "or that recreation was inherently sinful." Miller wrote that

> what is generally characterized as "other-worldliness" in Puritan theology was in fact a recognition of the world, an awareness of a trait in human nature, a witness to the devious ways in which men can pervert the fruits of the earth and the creatures of the world and cause them to minister to their vices. Puritanism found the natural man invariably running into excess or intemperance, and saw in such abuses an affront to God, who had made all things to be used according to their natures. Puritanism condemned not natural passions but inordinate passions, not man's desires but his enslavement to them, not the pleasures found in satisfaction of appetites, but the tricks devised to prod satiated appetites into further concupiscence.[43]

As for the charge that Puritans were inconsistently energetic in the face of their theology, Miller answered that Puritanism's concept of original sin was activist rather than gloomily defeatist. "It is not accurate," he wrote, "to call the Puritan sense of life 'tragic,' or to find the bustling energy which Puritans exhibited in war

[43] *Ibid.*, pp. 36, 41, 42.

and commerce inconsistent with their theology of pre-destination."[44]

Miller, in addition to bringing an appreciative point of view toward Puritan piety, brought in his scholarship an emphasis upon Puritan intellect itself. "The usual connotations attached to the word 'Puritanism,' " wrote Miller, "refer almost entirely to its piety." Even if the piety were more justly and sympathetically understood, he argued, Puritanism would not be fully comprehended unless the importance and activity of the Puritan intellect apart from piety were appreciated. "Neither the friends nor the foes of the Puritans have shown much interest in their intellects," Miller wrote, "for it has been assumed that the Puritan mind was too weighted down by the load of dogma to be worth considering in and for itself." He concluded that "when the whole range of Puritan thought and writing is passed in review, the impression grows undeniably that though Puritanism was a piety, it was at the same time an intellectual system, highly elaborated and meticulously worked out."

> Piety, therefore, is only a half of Puritanism. It is the essential part, no doubt; yet unless we consider the machinery of theory and demonstration which accompanied it, we can give no full account of Puritan thought and expression.[45]

Miller's emphasis upon Puritan intellect as well as piety opened up a new field, or rather one never before so thoroughly cultivated, in American histories of ideas.

The bulk of *The New England Mind: The Seventeenth Century* was devoted to detailed analysis of various expressions of the Puritan mind. Like Morison's *The Founding of Harvard College*, this volume of Miller's drew him into the history of European thought,

[44] *Ibid.*, p. 37.   [45] *Ibid.*, pp. 64, 67, 69.

for Puritan ideas were developed out of European Protestantism of the sixteenth and seventeenth centuries, Renaissance humanism, and medieval scholasticism. He declared the logic of Petrus Ramus to be as great an influence on Puritanism as either Augustine or Calvin, and Miller analyzed Puritan logic at length. In similar detail he described Puritan epistemology, natural philosophy, rhetoric, literary style, ideas of government, and theory of human nature, as well as theology.

Miller's analysis of Puritan ideas in this volume was ordinarily without reference to environmental conditions. Only rarely did he mention social and economic background information as being relevant in any way to a fuller understanding of Puritan thought. He commented that sectarian objections to formal Puritan education and learning "sprang from social causes as well as from piety," and he pointed out that the Puritan leaders admitted their class interests "were protected by the cultivation of learning."[46] But these remarks were made in passing and nothing more was made of them. Symptomatic was Miller's statement that "there can be no denying that in Puritanism as in all Protestantism there was an economic motive, that the creed had its origins in society as well as in the Augustinian temperament, and that its ethic was adapted to such considerations. He added,

> Nevertheless, it is eminently worth pointing out for the moment that though some Puritan doctrines may appear to us marvellously suited for the needs of adolescent capitalism, to Puritans they were all logically consistent with the cosmology. Furthermore, in this cosmology were certain dogmas which proved obstacles rather than helps to the bourgeois economy.[47]

[46] *Ibid.*, pp. 79, 84.   [47] *Ibid.*, p. 43.

Similarly, when summarizing in this 1939 volume the reasons for the decline of Puritan thought after the seventeenth century, Miller briefly mentioned "economic and social forces," but he stressed the ideas themselves. As part of the new scientific and humanitarian reform ideas which undercut Puritan thought, there was, he said, a change in the intellectual mood:

> When the belief and the temper which the first settlers brought to America is examined, when the piety is estimated on the emotional and non-theological level, it seems obvious that the reason later generations ceased marching to the Puritan beat was simply that they could no longer stand the pace.[48]

The ideas described in *The New England Mind: The Seventeenth Century* were presented without particular regard to chronological change; the chronological development of ideas received treatment in *Orthodoxy in Massachusetts, 1630-1650* (1933), and in *The New England Mind: From Colony to Province* (1953). The 1933 volume on *Orthodoxy* was written without regard for the social and economic conditions which might have affected Puritan thought, but Miller departed from his nonenvironmental approach in *The New England Mind: From Colony to Province* in 1953. To put it more precisely, he combined with his usual intensive analysis of the "interior" of thought, an accompanying concern in his later volume for social and economic conditions related to the changes in Puritan ideas as the eighteenth century approached. The fact that *From Colony to Province* represented no change in Miller's interest in, and respect for, Puritan thought, is clear. But it is also clear that his frequent disclaimers of interest in an environmental interpretation of thought—disclaimers made particularly during the 1930's—were contradicted when

[48] *Ibid.*, p. 59.

he treated the declining years of Puritan thought in *From Colony to Province*.

In the Foreword to his 1953 volume Miller remarked not on the grandeur and autonomy of human thought, but instead pointed out that colonial New England was a "laboratory" for seeing the relation between ideas and their environment. Indeed, he believed "profoundly that the story herein recounted is chiefly valuable for its *representative* quality" as a "case history of the accommodation to the American landscape of an imported and highly articulated system of ideas."[49] This expression of concern with interaction between thought and its environmental context was a new one in Miller's writings.

From Colony to Province showed Miller's usual preoccupation with the detailed investigation of ideas, and the volume opened with a discussion of Puritan thought. "The major events of the first decades in the history of these plantations," he wrote, "were not the developments which now interest our historians: such mechanical adjustments as the land system or the bicameral legislature." "For the leaders themselves," Miller continued, "the important episodes were those in which they acted out their consciousness of filling roles in the over-all strategy of Protestantism." He cited such Puritan activities as the suppression of

Anne Hutchinson and the Antinomians; banishment of Roger Williams; tricky diplomacy with King, Parliament, Presbyterians and Oliver Cromwell; adroit maneuvers to defeat the "Remonstrance of Dr. Child"; formulating *The Cambridge Platform*: these actions were guided not by domestic considerations but by their sense of New England's part in the Holy War. Learned books contributed to the fundamental issue

[49] *The New England Mind: From Colony to Province*, p. x.

of the age: Hooker's *Survey*, Cotton's *The Way of Congregational Churches Cleared*, Shepard's *A Defence of the Answer*, and Richard Mather's *Church-Government* were not written for home consumption but for an audience stretched across half Europe.[50]

The interaction between these ideas of the Puritan orthodoxy imported from Europe and the new American environment, was the theme of the volume. The theme told a story "of a society which was founded by men dedicated, in unity and simplicity, to realizing on earth eternal and immutable principles," but which, according to Miller, "progressively became involved with fishing, trade, and settlement." The story of Puritan New England constituted, he said, "a chapter in the emergence of the capitalist mentality, showing how intelligence copes with—or more cogently, how it fails to cope with—a change it simultaneously desires and abhors." The tone of these remarks contrasted markedly with Miller's earlier comments belittling the importance of social and economic studies in history. He wrote in *From Colony to Province* that "New Englanders had to learn commerce or perish." They learned it so well that the " 'sacred cod' became a symbol second only, if that, to the Bible."[51] Miller noted that as soon as "God made clear the market value of the cod, pious citizens, acting from both necessity and freedom, bought up the fishing fleet, and by the end of the century a few rich men dominated the industry." He continued, "By then, New England merchants had taken hold of their opportunities with such diligence, expedition, and perseverance that they succeeded the Dutch as the principal competitors of merchants in London and Bristol"; and

at the same time, they were steadily draining the backcountry and Newfoundland of specie, bringing

[50] *Ibid.*, p. 6.   [51] *Ibid.*, pp. 40, 44.

in cargoes from southern Europe, diverting the coinage of the Caribbean into their pockets, earning freight-charges on everything they handled, and then —to cap the climax—selling their very ships at immense profit![52]

Miller discussed economic conditions because he was convinced that they effected changes in orthodox Puritanism as the 1600's advanced. "At every point," as he said, "economic life set up conflicts with ideology."[53]

The result of New World social and economic forces was that by the 1700's, the old Puritan intellectual system was transformed, according to Miller:

religion became the support, not of Winthrop's ideal city, but of property. Long before the conception of uniformity was shuffled off, that of economic regulation and the just price had been let go. Soon afterward, the philosophy of social status yielded to the ethic of success, and merchants who took advantage of the market learned to control congregations despite the clerics; the prestige of ministers still was great, but they would need every bit of it were they still to dominate.[54]

"Parties and alignments were not drawn, as in the Antinomian crisis, on doctrinal issues," he said of the early eighteenth century; "they arose out of social conflict."

Up to 1690, although the intellectuals had been learning from experience, they had been pouring their experience into literary forms—such as the jeremiad —originally devised to accord with the now vanishing cosmology. Henceforth, they would have to rescue what they could of religion and morality by modifying those forms, or by finding others more pertinent

[52] *Ibid.*, p. 45. [53] *Ibid.*, p. 51. [54] *Ibid.*, p. 171.

to the social reality. Loyalty to the Crown, toleration, and constitutional liberties—these were the preconditions of provincial culture.[55]

It is not obvious why Miller told only the story of the dissolution of Puritan thought in terms of interaction with an economic environment; he apparently thought, however, that the influence of social and economic conditions was crucially important only at this point. Nevertheless, it is worth remembering that it would have been possible to describe the decline of Puritan ideas without any reference to the social and economic context, just as Miller had done in his other volumes on the New England mind.

By emphasizing the environment in his explanation of the decline of Puritan thought, and of the corresponding rise of new eighteenth century ideas, Miller in a sense did just the opposite of Beard, Parrington, and Curti. They emphasized the environmental factors which contributed to the rise of Puritanism, and they tended to minimize environmental factors in the decline of Puritan ideas and the rise of Enlightenment thought. Miller argued, symptomatically, that the proper characterization of the late 1600's and early 1700's was not "a growth of toleration, but rather a shedding of the religious conception of the universe, a turning toward a way of life in which the secular state, even when embodied in a provincial corporation, has become central."[56] Thus Miller objected to historical portraits of early Puritan dissidents, such as Roger Williams, as being modern libertarians who intentionally contributed to a positive growth of modern liberty.[57]

[55] *Ibid.*, p. 172.   [56] *Ibid.*, p. 171.

[57] Speaking of Williams, Miller said: "We need to remember that he repudiated the persecuting power of the civil arm not because, like Jefferson, he was religiously indifferent, but be-

This glance at *The New England Mind: From Colony to Province* reveals that, despite Miller's lack of concern in his other works for socioeconomic interpretation, this volume frequently tried to relate changes in ideas to changes in society. But Miller in this volume, as in all his others, spent most of his pages describing the ideas themselves, regardless of how he "explained" their existence and development. He discussed at length the intellectual battles over church membership, political policy, covenant changes, and the "jeremiads" which harangued the Puritan population from the pulpit and in the press, warning them not to become sinful and forgetful of God in their earthly occupations. Miller's consistent interest was in the composition and interplay of ideas, irrespective of how he explained the formation of the ideas. Human thought clearly provided the excitement in history for Miller. He remarked in *From Colony to Province* that from the standpoint of "financial problems" and "political contests" alone, the eighteenth century appears "dull" and "uneventful." But when "examined more closely, and from the inside," by a historian of ideas, "the period becomes a complex of tensions and anxieties." Miller saw "an intricate system of interacting stresses and strains which not only foretell explosions, but predict the manifold directions in which the fragments will fly." New England had by

---

cause he took Congregational purity with dreadful literalness." (*Ibid.*, p. 120.)

Similarly, in discussing Solomon Stoddard's (Presbyterian) Northampton revolt during the late 1600's against the early (Congregational) theory that only a select minority of visible saints could be church members: "Since historians have incautiously saluted Stoddard's revolt as an assertion of democracy —on the grounds that it did away with restrictive membership —we should observe that by his explicit declaration the aim was to put dictatorial powers into the hands of ministers and elders." (*Ibid.*, p. 258.)

the 1700's "become a time-bomb," he wrote "packed with dynamite, the fuse burning close."

It was a parched land, crying for deliverance from the hold of ideas that had served their purpose and died. It had more than the rudiments of new conceptions, an abundance of abilities demanding expression. It was a part of Protestant civilization, and, as everywhere in that kingdom, the weight of the past had become stifling. For the revivification of great principles, religious or civil, an awakening was necessary. It was a problem not only for thought but even more for language. The covenant had accurately described reality for John Winthrop, and Richard Mather had framed enduring counsel within its confines; but now reality—all the complex, jostling reality of this anxious society—demanded new descriptions. Ideas relative to these facts had to be propounded, and in words that could make the relation overwhelmingly felt.

"By the end of 1730," Miller continued, "it was evident that everybody had spoken from whom ideas or words were apt to come." "Or rather," he added, "all except one." "The next spring it was known that Jonathan Edwards would come to the Harvard Commencement, and he was pressed to give the Thursday lecture."[58]

Miller continued his story of New England Puritanism on into the mid-eighteenth century in the biography of *Jonathan Edwards*.[59] An examination of Miller's treatment of Edwards' thought—when compared with Vernon Louis Parrington's handling of Edwards' ideas—may delineate more precisely the nature of the challenge offered by Perry Miller's histories of ideas.

[58] *Ibid.*, pp. 484-485.
[59] Miller published *Jonathan Edwards* in 1949, but it actually followed *From Colony to Province* (1953) chronologically.

Parrington, in *Main Currents*, entitled his rather long sixteen-page sketch, "The Anachronism of Jonathan Edwards" and emphasized that Edwards "was the unconscious victim of a decadent ideal and a petty environment."[60] Parrington saw Edwards as a potentially great thinker who wasted his powers trying to rejuvenate Puritanism.

> In his early years, before his conversion turned him aside from his true path, setting the apologetics of the theologian above the speculations of the philosopher, Edwards gave promise of becoming a strikingly creative thinker.[61]

Unfortunately, according to Parrington, Edwards' "strong bias toward theology had tended to warp his interest in the purely metaphysical," and Edwards "followed a path that led back to an absolutist past, rather than forward to a more liberal future. He had broken wholly with the social tendencies of his age and world." Edwards supported "the doctrine of predetermined election by the sovereign will of God," and thus contributed to "the conservatism that was stifling the intellectual life of New England."[62] New England thought and society were becoming by the eighteenth century more secular, liberal, egalitarian, tolerant, rationalistic, and even religiously indifferent—in short, enlightened, said Parrington. The tragedy of Edwards' life was that he opposed these progressive forces and instead supported reaction.

Edwards as a youth showed signs of subscribing to a more optimistic concept of human nature, according to Parrington. Indeed, he was a philosophical transcendentalist, "rediscovering the doctrine of the inner light." Edwards thus, as a young man, came close to

[60] Parrington, *Main Currents*, Vol. 1, pp. 162-163.
[61] *Ibid.*, p. 153.   [62] *Ibid.*, pp. 155, 156, 157.

espousing Quaker doctrine, "a train of thought that threatened to disrupt the entire Calvinistic system." Edwards had to choose, said Parrington, whether to develop his thought along forward-looking transcendentalist lines or reactionary Puritan lines of "the dogma of total depravity." Instead of choosing transcendentalism, unfortunately, Edwards

> sought refuge in compromise, endeavoring to reconcile what was incompatible. Herein lay the tragedy of Edwards's intellectual life; the theologian triumphed over the philosopher, circumscribing his powers to ignoble ends. The field of efficiency allotted by the later theologian to this "in-dwelling vital principle," was no longer coextensive with the universe, but was narrowed to the little world of the elect. In the primal state of man, Edwards argued, before the sin of Adam had destroyed the harmony between creature and creator, the light which flowed from God as from a sun shone freely upon His universe, filling its remotest parts with the divine plenitude; but with the fall the harmony was destroyed, the sun was hidden, and only stray beams broke through the rifts to shine upon those whom God willed them to shine upon; all else in creation was given over to eternal darkness.[63]

Edwards thus became for Parrington an anachronistic Puritan in Jefferson's and Franklin's eighteenth century world. Parrington characterized Edwards' "logic" as "grotesque, abortive, unseasoned by any saving knowledge of human nature," and devoted "to an assiduous stoking of the fires of hell." Edwards' sermons, said Parrington, provided "a sanction for other men to terrify the imaginations of ill-balanced persons," but at least they were so offensive that they "thrust into naked

[63] *Ibid.*, p. 158.

relief the brutal grotesqueries of those dogmas that professed thus to explain the dark mysteries which lie upon the horizons of life." The final fall of Puritanism was guaranteed, concluded Parrington, as soon as "the horrors that lay in the background of Calvinism were disclosed to common view."[64]

Whereas Parrington pictured Jonathan Edwards as an anachronism, Perry Miller sketched Edwards as a figure "so much ahead of his time that our own can hardly be said to have caught up with him." Miller argued that Edwards' message was not simply a cruel, inhumane, unsympathetic, gloomy waste, but that instead

> he is a reminder that, although our civilization has chosen to wander in the more genial meadows to which Franklin beckoned it, there come periods, either through disaster or through self-knowledge, when applied science and Benjamin Franklin's *The Way to Wealth* seem not a sufficient philosophy of national life.

Miller's admiration for Edwards stemmed not from sympathy for any explicit doctrine, but rather from sympathy for Edwards' concerns and questions as a probing thinker. "The student of Edwards," wrote Miller, "must seek to ascertain not so much the peculiar doctrines in which he expressed his meaning as the meaning itself."

> In terms of what he strove toward rather than of his creed, Edwards is a spokesman, almost the first, for

[64] *Ibid.*, p. 159. The brief references to Edwards by Charles Beard and Carl Becker, written before Parrington's *Main Currents* was published, contained roughly the same attitude toward Edwards. See Becker, *Beginnings of the American People*, Boston, 1915, reprinted by Cornell University Press, Great Seal Books, 1960, pp. 85-86, 123; Beard, *The Rise of American Civilization*, Vol. 1, pp. 145-159.

the deep, the most rooted, the really native tradition. His opponents, who are customarily called the liberals, often prove upon analysis to speak for limited and particular interests which, because of their circumscribed conception of the goal, were bound, upon gaining their private ends, to become vested interests.

"Edwards was a Puritan," Miller continued, "who would not permit mankind to evade the unending ordeal and the continuing agony of liberty."

As a Protestant, he protested against the tyranny of all formalism, especially of that which masquerades as sweet reasonableness. He preached a universe in which the nature of things will permit no interest to become vested. My contention is that no American succeeded better, even though his experience was set within narrow limits, in generalizing his experience into the meaning of America.[65]

Instead of viewing Edwards as an anachronism or as a doctrinal theologian, Miller saw him as a figure whose ideas had special relevance for modern man. Miller described at length Edwards' theology, theory of history, psychology, epistemology, and other aspects of his philosophy, and Miller consistently emphasized the perennial philosophical implications—rather than the specific doctrinal aspects—of Edwards' thought. Edwards' "mind was so constituted," wrote Miller, "that he went directly to the issues of his age, defined them, and asserted the historic Protestant doctrine in full cognizance of the latest disclosures in both psychology and natural science." By so doing, Miller asserted, Edwards was in an essentially modern predicament:

That the psychology he accepted was an oversimplified sensationalism, and that his science was unaware

[65] *Jonathan Edwards*, Foreword, pp. xiii-xiv.

of evolution and relativity, should not obscure the fact that in both quarters he dealt with the primary intellectual achievements of modernism, with the assumptions upon which our psychology and physics still prosper: that man is conditioned and that the universe is uniform law.

Edwards "asked in all cogency why," according to Miller, "if the human organism is a protoplasm molded by environment, and if its environment is a system of unalterable operations, need mankind any longer agonize, as they had for seventeen hundred years, over the burden of sin?" Miller continued, "By defining the meaning of terms derived from Locke and Newton in the light of this question, Edwards established certain readings so profound that only from the perspective of today can they be fully appreciated."[66] It was in this sense that Miller insisted the importance of Edwards derived not from his doctrinal statements but from the questions he asked.

An example of Edwards' profundity which, according to Miller, can be better understood by the twentieth century than by the eighteenth, was Edwards' early realization of the insecurity of man as a consequence of Lockean "sensationalist" psychology and Newtonian physics. Miller interpreted Edwards' Enfield sermon, "Sinners in the Hands of an Angry God," as an expression of Edwards' prescient understanding of the terror of human insecurity in a universe which, according to science, is indifferent. The Enfield sermon contained the famous spider imagery:

> The God that holds you over the pit of hell, much as one holds a spider, or some loathsome insect, over the fire, abhors you, and is dreadfully provoked; his wrath towards you burns like fire; he looks upon

[66] *Ibid.*, pp. 72-73.

you as worthy of nothing else, but to be cast into the fire.[67]

Instead of interpreting this sermon as the weird product of a wasted mind, Miller characterized it as one of Edwards' profound intellectual achievements. Locke had confirmed for Edwards what the example of the spider suggested, "that the life of the soul is the life of the senses."

Edwards scientifically, deliberately, committed Puritanism, which had been a fervent rationalism of the covenant, to a pure passion of the senses, and the terror he imparted was the terror of modern man, the terror of insecurity. He overthrew the kind of religious philosophy that had dominated Western Europe since the fall of Rome, the system wherein there was always—whether in terms of the City of God, or of the Mass and absolution, or of final causes and substantial forms or, at the last, in terms of the Puritan covenant—an ascertainable basis for human safety.

"Edwards brought mankind," said Miller, "as Protestantism must always bring them, without mitigation, protection, or indulgence, face to face with a cosmos fundamentally inhuman." This is what Miller meant by saying that "Edwards' preaching was America's sudden leap into modernity."[68] Miller argued that at mid-twentieth century, "the terms forced upon us, albeit more complex, are essentially those that confronted him: a behavioristic psychology and a universe of a-moral forces."[69]

Thus, Miller's sketch of Jonathan Edwards was almost totally unlike Parrington's, both in description and evaluation. Miller's portrait of Edwards, when com-

---

[67] *Ibid.*, pp. 145-146. Quoted from Edwards.
[68] *Ibid.*, p. 147. [69] *Ibid.*, p. 148.

pared with Parrington's, was more sympathetic and admiring, less political in implication and more philosophical. Miller saw Edwards trying to come to terms with science and religion, that is, to come to terms with an indifferent universe and ethically conscious human beings. Parrington viewed Edwards as one trying to resist modern, humane, progressive movements of thought, that is, trying to turn back the calendar to a more cruel age. Edwards was, for Parrington, "the unconscious victim of a decadent ideal and a petty environment," whereas for Miller, Edwards was "so much ahead of his time that our own can hardly be said to have caught up with him."

Miller's presentation of Edwards was representative of his Puritan scholarship generally—he analyzed thought at length and in detail. With *From Colony to Province* being the significant exception, Miller usually paid little attention to the influence of social and economic forces on ideas, and most of his general statements on the role of ideas in history emphasized the virtual autonomy of thought in human affairs.[70] Spe-

[70] Despite Miller's remark in the Foreword to *Jonathan Edwards* that "no writer ever emerged more directly out of the passions, the feuds, and the anxieties of his society," the study was not an exception to the generalization that Miller ordinarily paid little attention to social and economic environmental influences on ideas. In the *Edwards* volume, Miller separated what he called "external biography" into short background sections, and he devoted most of the pages to analysis of Edwards' thought.

During the 1950's and early 1960's, Miller moved out of the colonial period and into nineteenth century intellectual life in the United States. But he published no large-scale work comparable to his Puritan studies. He published smaller studies, including *The Raven and the Whale*, New York, 1956, and introductions to anthologies (such as *American Thought: Civil War to World War I*, New York, 1954; *The Transcendentalists*, Cambridge, 1950). Segments of his last work were published posthumously as *The Life of the Mind in America: From the Revolution to the Civil War*, New York, 1965. These writings

cifically, this comparison of the treatment given to Jonathan Edwards by Miller and Parrington indicates the kind of challenge Miller offered to progressive histories of ideas. It was a challenge to take ideas more seriously, to analyze them in more depth and at greater length, and it was a challenge to social and economic interpretations of thought. It was a call to make ideas, and not simply political and economic ones, the center of written histories. And Miller's histories of ideas made a case for the proposition that the meaning of American experience could be best located, not through uncovering the hidden economic and political aspects of life, but through uncovering the hidden meaning of ideas.

Miller's writings were characterized, negatively, by his lack of adherence to social reform ideology. Positively, they were marked, as were the publications of Samuel Eliot Morison, by admiration for Puritanism. Morison's and Miller's reinterpretation of Puritanism (a reinterpretation which included both a new description and a different evaluation) played an important part in the development of a tradition in the writing of American intellectual histories during and after the 1920's. This tradition challenged the dominant one expressed by Beard, Becker, Parrington, and Curti. During the 1920's and 1930's it would perhaps have been less obvious than later that arguments over Puritanism amounted to anything more than any other difference of opinion among historians as to the proper description and estimation of one particular historical phenomenon. But it can be seen in retrospect that these differences over Puritanism were accompanied by parallel differences among historians about other aspects of the American past and present. As previous discussions of

---

were characterized, above all, by Miller's conviction that ideas are fascinating to study, regardless of their social, political, or economic origins and implications.

individual historians have indicated, the particular treatment (or lack of treatment) of Puritanism by Eggleston, Beard, Becker, Parrington, and Curti was an integral part of their histories, as was the extended treatment of Puritanism by Morison and Miller.

Morison's and Miller's sympathy and respect for
Puritanism was only part of their sympathy and respect for certain aspects of the American past and
certain American traditions which were not cherished
by Eggleston, Robinson, Beard, Becker, Parrington,
and Curti. These reform-minded historians were not
indiscriminately critical of the past, of course, for they
celebrated scientific and reform thought in their histories. But these reform-minded scholars did share in
some of the debunking of traditional beliefs expressed
mainly by young, alienated intellectuals during the
1920's. By contrast, Morison and Miller contributed,
on a scholarly level in their Puritan histories, to the
popular re-embracement of America by intellectuals
during and after the 1930's.[71]

RALPH GABRIEL

Ralph Gabriel (1890—) raised many of the same
questions concerning intellectual progressivism which
were raised by Morison and Miller, and he shared their
emphasis on the power and dignity of ideas in history.
Gabriel's writings were, however, concerned primarily
with the history of ideas in the United States of the

---

[71] Harvard took the lead in the re-vitalization of Puritanism
as a foundation for the history of ideas in America not only
through the scholarship of Murdock, Morison, and Miller, but
also through the work of their students during and after the
1930's. Foremost has been Edmund S. Morgan (see, for example, *The Puritan Family*, Boston, 1944; *Puritan Dilemma:
The Story of John Winthrop*, Boston, 1958; *The Gentle Puritan: A Life of Ezra Stiles, 1727-1795*, New Haven, 1962; *Visible Saints: The History of a Puritan Idea*, New York, 1963).

nineteenth and twentieth centuries. As Morison and Miller had long associations with Harvard, Gabriel was long connected with Yale, beginning with his going to Yale College intending to become a minister.[72] Following Army service in France during World War One, Gabriel pursued graduate studies at Yale and taught American history there until his retirement in 1958. He taught at American University in Washington, D.C., after his retirement. During the 1920's and 1930's Gabriel expressed ideas about various aspects of society, as well as ideas concerning the writing of the history of ideas, which implicitly and explicitly differed from the ideas expressed by Robinson, Beard, Becker, Parrington, and Curti. Gabriel had fully revealed his own intellectual position when his full-scale history of ideas, *The Course of American Democratic Thought*, was published in 1940.

The extent to which Gabriel's ideas concerning society contrasted with those of progressive historians can be seen by examining several aspects of Gabriel's social thought. Gabriel's attitude toward religion, for example, revealed the same sympathy as did Morison's, and the same respect as did the attitudes of both Morison and Miller. Speaking of the role of religion in the modern world as well as of its role in history, Gabriel asserted its basic importance. "It is the problem of religion," he wrote in 1924, "to deal with the adjustments of human life to the infinite mysteries."[73] Gabriel chided

[72] This intent to enter the ministry is mentioned in a letter from Gabriel to John Higham, cited by Higham, "The Rise of American Intellectual History," p. 470.

[73] From Gabriel's Foreword to a collection of essays, edited by Gabriel, *Christianity and Modern Thought*, New Haven, 1924, p. xi. Gabriel's writings reveal a closer personal identification with organized religion than do the writings of even Morison. In Gabriel's Foreword to *Christianity and Modern Thought*, he expressed the hope for unity among Protestant churches. In the 1950's, the Church of Christ in New Haven

modern scholars, just as Morison and Miller did, for ignoring religion. Reviewing the *Encyclopaedia of the Social Sciences*, Gabriel commented that "there is no place in the scheme for religion which appears to be clearly beyond the pale." Playfully, yet with obvious seriousness, he continued:

> The reviewer, running through its columns, chanced upon the name of Philo Judaeus and found an excellent brief statement of his philosophical positions. A search was begun for Philo's contemporary, Paul, who wrote some letters in the first century which dealt, among other things, with social ideas and problems. It did not appear. Nor did that of the Palestinian teacher, Jesus, who is reputed to have made some contributions to social thought.[74]

Thus Gabriel emphasized, as did Morison and Miller, the contributions made by religious ideas and religious figures.

Gabriel, like Morison, argued that war had been an important and frequently noble and purposeful part of American experience. In the late 1920's, when Curti was publishing his first history of American peace movements, and when antiwar sentiment was at a high point in the United States, Gabriel was the joint author of two pictorial histories of American wars, one significantly entitled *In Defense of Liberty*.[75] The theme of

---

asked him to write its history, which he published in 1958: *Religion and Learning at Yale: The Church of Christ in the College and University, 1757-1957*, New Haven.

[74] Review of *Encyclopaedia of the Social Sciences*, Vols. 14, 15 in *American Historical Review*, XLI (October 1935), 113, 114.

[75] William Wood and Gabriel put together Volume 6, *The Winning of Freedom* (1927), and Volume 7, *In Defense of Liberty* (1929), in *The Pageant of America*, 15 vols., New Haven, 1925-1929.

the introduction which Gabriel wrote for this volume was that Americans had consistently failed to understand the importance of military affairs and of being prepared for war. Speaking of the First World War, Gabriel stated that

again, as in the War of 1812 and the Civil War, the people of the United States escaped by the narrowest margin paying the extreme penalty for lack of adequate preparedness. This time they were saved by the blood of their allied comrades in arms who were fighting on land and sea in the Old World.[76]

The presence of war was almost an inevitable factor in history, according to Gabriel, because human conflict was rooted in human nature.

War, almost as ancient as man himself, still persists. Its roots lie deep in human life. From the beginning of social organizations larger than the family group all men, save those living like the Esquimaux in extreme isolation, have been compelled to adjust themselves to the fact of human conflict. The military aspects of the folkways of a people are, at times, as fundamental to their well being as the getting of food and raiment or the maintaining of government.[77]

Gabriel suggested in 1928 that pacifists, insofar as they believed that wars were unnecessary, had an extremely optimistic conception of human nature which they had inherited from the Enlightenment—and it was clear that Gabriel thought such a conception was unwarranted.[78]

Another respect in which Gabriel's views disagreed with those of the progressive historians was in his more

[76] *In Defense of Liberty*, p. 6.
[77] *The Winning of Freedom*, p. 1.
[78] *In Defense of Liberty*, p. 8.

cautious appraisal of the developing social sciences and of modern scholarship generally. Gabriel's scholarship showed much more interest in, and indebtedness to, the social sciences than did the histories of Morison and Miller, but Gabriel's interest was accompanied by continual questions and criticisms directed at the social sciences. In scholarly reviews during the 1930's, Gabriel recognized the increasing wealth of knowledge in the new sciences of man and society, but he continually stressed the uncertainty of modern knowledge and the differences of opinion among scholars. He lacked the confidence in the social sciences which progressive scholars more often felt. Reviewing a collection of analyses of the scholarship of modern social scientists, Gabriel commented:

> The Social Science Research Council in a volume of eight hundred odd pages has discovered (what we have long suspected) that the image of society which filters through the casements of the social sciences is as blurred and distorted as is that of history. The discovery is, no doubt, a useful labor. The historian has sometimes noted an ominous cocksureness among practitioners of the social sciences which only recently have disentangled themselves from theology, philosophy, and history. Perhaps the book will have a chastening effect on naive young men in different disciplines whose minds are filled by what they deem to be a great light. We recommend the volume to devotees of all cults, be they disciples of *Gestalt*, of economic determinism, or of the "new history."[79]

These comments may have been rooted in irritation at enthusiastic disciples of the social sciences or of

[79] Review of Stuart Rice's *Methods in Social Science*, *American Historical Review*, xxxvi (July 1931), 786.

Robinson's New History, but they also stemmed from Gabriel's concern that contemporary man had no secure base of certainty from which to think and live—and the newest scholarship, despite its hopes, had not significantly lessened the uncertainty. Gabriel remarked, in one of his reviews of the *Encyclopaedia of the Social Sciences*, that "the *Encyclopaedia* mirrors the intellectual confusion of a generation that has lost its moorings and has failed to find a guiding principle in a cosmos wherein all appears to be flux."[80] It seemed to Gabriel that the traditional certainties in scholarship, religion, and ethics had increasingly collapsed, due largely to developments in the natural and social sciences. This was in itself an intellectual crisis for thoughtful men, but the rise of European totalitarianism tragically brought the crisis into practical affairs. For the existence of totalitarianism as a powerful attraction and force in the modern world meant that each individual (or community) had to know which principles or institutions he wished to defend. Yet, Gabriel pointed out, modern scholarship was interpreted by many—because of its environmental emphasis on the origin of values and ideas—as implying that ideas or principles could be only of relative and transitory worth:

> the rise of the biological and social sciences had made it extremely difficult for the mid-twentieth century man to define the good save in terms of a particular culture, while at the same time the emphasis on the relativity of standards of values had lowered the prestige of all ideals and ethical principles. Among these was the idea of human dignity and the importance of the individual.[81]

[80] Review of Vols. 11-13, *American Historical Review*, XL (January 1935), 307.
[81] "Democracy: Retrospect and Prospect," *American Journal of Sociology*, XLVIII (November 1942), 416.

The new knowledge had not filled the moral void which it created by challenging the old certainties, and Gabriel argued, in the spirit of Tyler or Morison, that the most fundamental of the old certainties were in fact as valid as ever. It was these values which Americans should defend in their opposition to totalitarianism of any variety. The dignity of man and the existence of a free society in which man could realize that dignity were values assumed even by the very sciences which seemed to threaten the existence of these "eternal" values. For Gabriel argued that science was itself dependent upon the existence of a free society which granted integrity of the individual:

> the hope of the present world is to be found in the fact that science itself, which is the ultimate source of power in the modern age, is by a strange paradox founded on an ethical code that is absolute and universal. Science requires freedom for the investigator.

It seemed to Gabriel moreover that the values which could be inferred from science, such as dependence upon reason, individual freedom, individual honesty, and mutual cooperation, were really traditional values. "They are a twentieth-century statement in naturalistic terms of the standards of value that were the core of the democratic pattern as it was established in America at the end of the eighteenth century."[82]

It was against this background of rising totalitarianism and the questioning of old traditions that Gabriel published *The Course of American Democratic Thought* in 1940.[83] He attempted to locate the fundamental beliefs and values which had earlier sustained nineteenth century Americans and he tried to trace the fate of

[82] *Ibid.*, pp. 417, 418.
[83] New York, revised and reissued in 1956. Quotations cited here refer to 1940 edition, unless specified otherwise.

these ideas in the twentieth century. The traditional "democratic faith" which Gabriel found was not identical with the "eternal" humane values of a free society and of a dignified individual within a free society about which Gabriel was so concerned at mid-twentieth century. The traditional "democratic faith," however, contained these humane values within it. The ideas included in the "democratic faith" were: belief in the free individual human being, confidence in continued human progress, faith in a universal moral law, and conviction that America was fulfilling a special mission. Gabriel manifested a distinct sympathy, if not nostalgia, for mid-nineteenth century America which had "that mental peace and that sense of security which comes to the man who feels that he has planted his feet upon the eternal rock." Gabriel unfavorably contrasted the intellectual uncertainty of the mid-twentieth century with the certainty of a hundred years earlier. "The absolutism of the nineteenth century which expressed itself in the theory of the moral law is out of fashion in our America," he wrote. "Faith in the eternal character of right and wrong is in retreat before the advance of the pragmatic ethics of expediency." "But," he said, "the retreat has not yet ended, and while it continues, modern Americans are confused. The bitter fruit of their confusion is a sense of intellectual and of social insecurity."[84] It was not clear to Gabriel, in 1940, whether the "democratic faith" could survive challenges of new knowledge, on the one hand, and totalitarianism on the other:

> Tradition in carrying the American democratic faith into the twentieth century has brought it into a strange and hostile world. One of its doctrines, nationalism, is magnified almost beyond recognition. All of the others, those of the fundamental law, of the

[84] *Ibid.*, pp. 18-19.

free individual, and the philosophy of progress, are challenged. It may be that they are on the way out. Only the future can answer that question.[85]

Because of Gabriel's concern for the traditional ideas or beliefs which had sustained Americans during the 1800's and which were threatened in the 1900's, *The Course of American Democratic Thought* expressed a spirit or tone which was noticeably, if subtly, different from the works of Beard and Curti. The twentieth century pages of Gabriel seemed to be looking back to their nineteenth century forerunners, whereas the early pages of Beard and Curti seemed to be saying excitedly that the best was yet to come in the twentieth century pages.

Gabriel's characteristic tone or spirit, emanating from his search for the location of key traditional American ideas, was expressed in his method of describing ideas as well as in his explicit evaluation of them. Although he did not analyze thought in great depth as Perry Miller did, Gabriel investigated the content of ideas and values in more detail than Morison or most of the progressive historians did. Gabriel selected for treatment comparatively few men, and probed the ideas of each with relative fullness.[86] The kinds of men that

[85] *Ibid.*, p. 417.

[86] A comparison with Merle Curti may be made in the allotment of space by Gabriel: for the period between the Civil War and World War One Gabriel devoted two to fourteen pages to each of two dozen outstanding intellectual figures, an average treatment of almost five pages per figure, whereas Curti devoted more than a single page to no intellectual figure except William James, John Dewey, and Henry George. Both Gabriel and Curti allotted approximately two hundred pages to the period between the Civil War and World War One. The thinkers whose ideas Gabriel described for two or more pages were Sumner, James, Royce, Henry Adams, Judge Field, Rauschenbusch, Henry George, Morgan, Lester Ward, Turner, Washington Gladden, Ingersoll, John Wesley Powell, Octavius Brooks Frothingham, Bellamy, Brooks Adams, Simon Patten,

Gabriel selected were those whose ideas had relevance for the traditional American ideas embodied in what he called the "democratic faith": beliefs in absolute morality, in progress, in the free individual, and in the mission of America. These figures were thus social thinkers, in a broad sense, or at least thinkers whose ideas had important implications for society. Gabriel investigated thought which had social importance either in the sense of referring to relations between the individual and the group, or in the sense of referring to the place and meaning of all individuals in the cosmos. Gabriel's method was, in one respect, an execution of his concern for the answers Americans gave to these questions of relations between individual members and the group, and to the meaning of individual human life in the universe. The thinkers Gabriel selected gave answers relevant to these questions. The following examples of Gabriel's treatment of specific ideas and individuals will show how he continually came back to the same questions, and to the traditional answers given by Americans. In Gabriel's concern for these questions and answers, relatively little attention was paid the economic and social environment, although it was mentioned in the sketch of each thinker.

Gabriel's analysis of Supreme Court Justice Stephen J. Field revealed, especially when compared to Merle Curti's sketch of Field, Gabriel's approach to ideas. Gabriel's eleven pages on Field (compared to Curti's one paragraph) were part of a chapter on the contribution of American constitutional law to late nineteenth century social thought. Gabriel noted that as "the cen-

---

John Bates Clark, Bliss, Herron, Sheldon, Albertson, Noah Porter and Carnegie. For an interesting statement by Gabriel on his own method of *teaching* the history of ideas, see "Ideas in History," *History of Education Journal*, ii (Summer 1951), 97-106. The statement minimizes what is distinctive in Gabriel's method, at least in his written histories.

tury drew to a close, conflicts among economic groups increased in intensity." But Gabriel's emphasis was not on the economic conflict, nor on the ideas which were mere reflex reactions to the economic conflict. Instead, his emphasis was on the philosophic base and theoretical implications of the social debates. Justice Field, according to Gabriel, "had long recognized the potential power of numbers in a representative democracy. He sensed the vulnerability of the small minority who possessed vast accumulations of capital." Justice Field "sought to defend these men of property," said Gabriel, "not because he was himself rich, for he was not, but because he believed in that upstanding individualism, controlled by a sense of stewardship, which was the social creed of the gospel of wealth." Field held, said Gabriel, that the

> principal weapon for such defense was the Constitution of the United States interpreted by the courts. The judicial tribunal, when need should arise, must be set against the usurping legislature. Only by such balance could the rights of the minority be protected against the tyranny of the majority and those fundamental principles upon which orderly and progressive society depends, be preserved.

As Gabriel described Field's ideas, the Justice's devotion to principle, rather than to self-interest, was emphasized. Gabriel presented him as an "absolutist" who believed that the basic principles of the law were fixed. From this fixity, men derived confidence and stability in both public and private matters.

Because Field recognized "flux in the affairs of individuals and of communities," said Gabriel, "Field sought the security of changeless and eternal principles. In this respect his point of view was that of Story and of Kant—a blend of absolutism and empiricism—absolutism as to the fundamental law, empiricism in the application of changeless principles to changing situations." Gabriel thus stressed Field's belief in universal social principles as well as his belief in the dangers of unrestricted majority will. "In Field's thought, Carnegie's code for the individual was blended with the American political belief in a government of law." These ideas were the foundation on which Field built his judicial opinions.

Gabriel described the effect upon Field of post-Appomattox political events. Field watched apprehensively as Congressional power increased at the expense not only of the Presidency but also of the Supreme Court. Congress even removed from the jurisdiction of the Court a case which involved the constitutionality of the Radical Republican reconstruction policy. "Field's subsequent record," according to Gabriel, "suggests that he never forgot this humiliating episode." This Congressional highhandedness

> taught him the revolutionary potentialities of uncontrolled legislative majorities. In frontier California he had argued that the legislature must be restrained by the electorate. In Washington during the reconstruction era his faith in so simple a democratic procedure declined. In 1873 he boldly declared his conviction that legislatures, state or national, which threatened the rights of men must be restrained by the courts.[87]

Justice Field announced his views in the Slaughter House cases, which arose from Louisiana carpetbag legislation ostensibly designed as a preventive health measure, but which had taken away the means of livelihood of many butchers. The injured butchers argued, through their attorney, that the new Fourteenth Amend-

[87] *The Course of American Democratic Thought*, pp. 217-221.

ment made it illegal for Louisiana and other states to deprive individuals of their employment. A man's right to employment was one of those natural rights, Field argued along with the butchers, which included life, liberty, and the pursuit of happiness, and which the Fourteenth Amendment had written into the Constitution. Field's opinion was a dissenting one in the first series of Slaughter House cases—the majority of the Court rejected the arguments of the butchers.

Later, when the cases came back to the Supreme Court during the 1880's, Field's dissent was accepted as the majority decision. Gabriel presented Field's opinion as stemming from a belief in the free individual and not from an apology for business privileges. As Gabriel pointed out, Field believed in certain ethical values as absolutes which were necessary for civilized living and argued that only by honoring them could free institutions survive. One of these crucial moral values was the pursuit of happiness, and Field interpreted this pursuit to include the right to pursue lawful employment. Thus, Gabriel emphasized the philosophical nature of Field's thought which led him to adopt judicial doctrines of individual laissez-faire.

Merle Curti's one-paragraph depiction of Justice Field's thought differed markedly from Gabriel's. Curti emphasized the social and economic environment from which Field's ideas came, and the relevance of Field's ideas was, for Curti, almost entirely in immediate social and economic matters. In other words, Curti treated Field's thought as a function of pressing economic matters more than, as did Gabriel, a function of pressing social theory. Curti discussed Field in a chapter entitled, "The Conservative Defense," and pictured Field as a supporter of the status quo. Curti opened the chapter by citing with approval E. A. Ross' statement that "those who have the sunny rooms in the social edifice have . . . a powerful ally in the suggestion of Things-as-they-are."[88]

Curti introduced the discussion of Justice Field by reciting the argument which was offered by those in the "sunny rooms in the social edifice." "The inequality of riches in American society," wrote Curti, "was justified by the argument that riches rested on natural laws no less than on God's revelation. In the earlier part of the period," Curti continued, "the law of nature was often interpreted in terms of the eighteenth-century doctrine that every man had, among other natural rights, that of acquiring and keeping property."

> As a dissenter in Munn vs. Illinois and in the slaughter-house cases, Mr. Justice Field pioneered in developing the substantive interpretation of due process. In his famous minority opinion in the slaughter-house cases he maintained that the right to profit from butchering livestock in Louisiana was an inalienable right which the state could not annihilate. "I cannot believe," he wrote, "that what is termed in the Declaration of Independence a God-given and an inalienable right can be thus ruthlessly taken from the citizen, or that there can be any abridgement of that right except by regulations alike affecting all persons of the same age, sex, and condition."[89]

Curti's description of Field placed the Justice's thought as part of the "conservative defense" of the economic "haves" against the threatening "have-nots." The roots of the Justice's "conservative defense" were not specifically located in his own economic interest, but Curti did imply that Field was part of the ruling social class which acted out of a material environment (inequality of wealth) favorable to the class and which the class

---

[88] Curti, *The Growth of American Thought*, p. 633.
[89] *Ibid.*, pp. 637-638.

tried to perpetuate. In other words, Curti related Field's ideas to the immediate economic environment of late nineteenth century America. Curti presented Field's thought as directed primarily to the matter of protecting "the right to profit from butchering livestock in Louisiana" as a part of "the right to profit" generally without interference from the state. Field was pictured by Curti as engaged in an intellectual battle between those who were defenders of the economic environment as it was in the late 1800's, and those who wanted to change it: the economic environment provoked the intellectual issue and Curti presented Field's thought insofar as it was directly relevant to that issue. It was not necessary for Curti, because of his method, to dwell on Field's thought in detail as Gabriel did. Gabriel's contrasting method in treating Justice Field was to minimize the relation between Field's thought and the immediate economic environment, and to maximize the roots and implications of his ideas with regard to such problems as absolute ethics and relativism, as well as problems of social order and the freedom of the individual. Gabriel related Field's thought to those traditional ideas which he traced throughout his volume.

The preceding comparison of Gabriel's treatment of Field with that of Curti has indicated and emphasized differences in method rather than differences in ideological position or sympathy. The differences in method resulted in differences in description—Curti's Field was not Gabriel's Field. But differences in sympathy accompanied those of method, as a reading of the quoted passages from the two historians clearly shows. Though differences in sympathy are crucial, it is less necessary to dwell on them than on those of method since they are much more obvious. Curti's treatment of Field suggested that the Justice was so apologetic a defender of the capitalists, so firmly set against democratic social progress, that he glorified the right to profit from a slaughterhouse into an inalienable, God-given right of man. Gabriel's dissimilar treatment of Field suggested that the Justice contemplated, in a thoughtful and humane way without forgetting the public interest, the perennially worrisome problems of communal living.

The contrast between Gabriel's and Curti's methods of treating historical figures and their ideas can also be seen in their treatments of John C. Calhoun. Curti's discussion of Calhoun's thought presented the Southern politician as primarily a defender of sectional, particularly slaveowning, interests. Curti wrote that Calhoun "tore to pieces Jefferson's castle built on the ideas of humanitarianism, natural rights, and an educated democracy of small landowners." Calhoun destroyed Jeffersonian dreams, according to Curti, in "the interest of the planting aristocracy and, as he thought, in the interest of the whole South." The South Carolinian erected a body of political thought "to justify slavery and the aristocratic domination in the South on the one hand, and, on the other, to insure the protection of the southern minority in the federal scheme." Calhoun was fearful that the plantation South would be subjugated by the faster growing North and West, Curti wrote. "Calhoun rationalized his devotion to the interest of the plantation aristocracy and his devotion to the Union by devising a system designed to safeguard both." Curti's emphasis was thus upon Calhoun's defensive rationalization of his local interests, although Curti remarked in the last sentence of his Calhoun sketch that "he did make a bold and original effort to come to grips with one of the great problems of democracy—the protection of minorities." It was no surprise to find this evaluation of Calhoun by Curti: "if democracy be regarded as multiple leadership, multiple participation, and the sharing of values deemed good, Calhoun's conception was indeed limited."[90]

Gabriel's discussion of Calhoun differed with Curti's in much the same way as his discussion of Justice Field had. Gabriel, who devoted eight pages to a fairly detailed discussion of Calhoun's thought (compared with Curti's two pages), paid only passing attention to the practical threat "of a democratic numerical majority seeking to use a strong central government as an instrument to destroy the institution of slavery." In this same manner, Gabriel acknowledged that Calhoun's "warfare on this front led to his formulation of the famous theory of nullification." After briefly making these acknowledgments, Gabriel emphasized, not the practical exigencies which led to Calhoun's political ideas on nullification, but instead the philosophy which supported the political theory. For, back "of this aspect of his political theory was an analysis of the doctrine of the free individual whose cogency was unrivaled in his generation." Clearly, Gabriel's evaluation, as well as his description of Calhoun's thought, was different from Curti's.

In describing Calhoun's ideas, Gabriel placed stress upon his Calvinistic reservations concerning human potentiality. "Calhoun, in his assumptions concerning human nature, was under an unconscious, but nonetheless heavy, debt to Calvin. Man, thought the South Carolinian, was created to live in society but, paradoxically, his egoistic tendencies outweigh the altruism in his nature." Because of this wary view of man's nature, said Gabriel, Calhoun expressed the "doctrine that no public official can be trusted unless he knows that he is being watched by citizens who have the power to check usurpations."

Calhoun, said Gabriel, "looked deeper than the super-

[90] *Ibid.*, pp. 442-444.

ficial ties of Independence Day orations," because he realized that nationalism depends upon security. Calhoun saw, that is, that national loyalty was based upon the conviction that individual and local loyalties are fostered, not threatened, by simultaneous national loyalty. Gabriel argued that from this philosophical perspective, Calhoun believed "that the numerical majority offered no security to endangered Southern civilization." "He proposed, therefore, the political doctrine of the concurrent majority." Gabriel's conclusion was that

> Calhoun's chief contribution to American thought was his emphasis upon the fact that the sentiment of nationalism cannot be taken for granted even in the United States, and that it must be nourished by wise and tolerant governmental policy and encouraged by giving to individuals and to interest groups power to make war upon what they, in honesty, consider to be evils.[91]

Gabriel's and Curti's discussions of Calhoun differed in method as well as in evaluation. Gabriel's treatment looked to Calhoun's ideas whereas Curti's looked to Calhoun's political situation. The contrasting evaluations made by the two historians were related to the contrasting methods of studying Calhoun's thought. Curti found the Old South, whose interest Calhoun was advancing, deficient in its lack of democracy, and since Calhoun's ideas were to be understood largely according to the interests they served, Curti was mainly critical of Calhoun's thought. Gabriel, on the contrary, minimized the specific situation in which Calhoun's thought was expressed. After examining the thought to ascertain its profundity without sole regard for the pre-Civil War situation (ignoring the question of whose

[91] *The Course of American Democratic Thought*, pp. 106-110.

ox was being gored), Gabriel found Calhoun's theories wise. Thus were methods of describing ideas related to historians' evaluations of ideas.

Yet another comparison between Gabriel's and Curti's discussions of a man and his philosophy—William James' pragmatism—reveals further differences in the writings of the two historians. These are differences stemming partly from contrasting descriptions of James' pragmatism, and deriving in large part from differing evaluations of modern American thought.

Curti's description of William James' philosophy of pragmatism focused on its "scientific" nature, and pragmatism's role in the history of American ideas was characterized as one of fortunate liberation from old "absolutisms." He stressed the influence of James the psychologist upon James the philosopher. James was presented as having absorbed from Darwin the conviction that human thought was merely another part of adaptation to environment. "Mind," said Curti of James' view, "became a function of living. The conception of mind as an instrument which enabled the organism to adjust to its environment or even to transform it was novel and far-reaching in its implications." One of the implications was that the meaning and validity of ideas are relative to the circumstances which provoke them. Curti characterized James' relativism as "naturalistic":

> James' conception of "the open universe," his emphasis on the "unfinished experiment," his opposition to any and all dogmatisms, including scientific dogmatisms, and his view of all life, of the whole universe, as an effect of progressive selection, all these meant that he operated within the evolutionary, naturalistic framework.

Thus, James developed Darwinian theories and helped

shift American thought from supernaturalism to naturalism.

Curti did not mention James' values, except to note his emphasis on individualism, on risk, freedom, and progress, and Curti minimized generally the strain of mysticism in James' thought. The influence of James' Swedenborgian father was alluded to, as was James' "emotional dissatisfaction" with the materialism of "traditional empiricism which rested on sense experience alone." But Curti's emphasis was on "the pragmatist and experimentalist" spirit in which James "tried to push empiricism to more radical lengths by giving the *connections* between sense experience a psychological status on a par with whatever was actually data, in themselves." Instead of stressing the nonscientific elements in James' ideas, Curti emphasized the scientific. He wrote:

> in thinking of any idea, even of any supernatural idea, as true if it enabled the individual to deal satisfactorily with the concrete experiences at which it aims, James did not at all go back on the scientific and evolutionary character of his philosophy; any idea "true" at any given time for a given person might not be true for others, or even for that person under different circumstances.[92]

Curti raised no questions, nor suggested the existence of any problems, resulting from James' relativistic theories. Modern American thought was characterized by Curti as a movement toward experimentalism, relativism, functionalism or instrumentalism or pragmatism, skepticism, and realism, and away from supernaturalism, absolutism, and formalism. James was described as part of this overall movement of thought.

Ralph Gabriel, like Curti, presented William James

[92] *The Growth of American Thought*, pp. 558, 562.

as an individualist and a relativist in reaction against materialistic determinism. "Were Americans," asked Gabriel for James, "freed after many years from Calvinistic foreordination, to become slaves to scientific determinism?" But, unlike Curti, Gabriel said that, to James, the greatest danger "lurked in the growing prestige of Darwinism." James had indeed begun "his thinking with an acceptance of the validity of science in its proper realm," but, wrote Gabriel, he had "fewer illusions than some of his contemporaries concerning the extent of the usefulness of science to man."

Gabriel explained James' reservations about science on the basis of his conviction of the importance of faith in human life, a conviction to which he was predisposed by his religious background. Faith was, to James, "the necessity to believe," "the willingness to take risks when the issue is not sure." James' views undercut religious absolutisms as well as nonreligious ones, of course, and Gabriel was left with a plural universe, in which "creation is constantly going on." "In such fashion," Gabriel wrote, "James tossed on the rubbish heap all the absolutisms of the nineteenth century: Deism, Transcendentalism, orthodox Christianity, and classical physics."[93] In their place, he submitted pragmatism, which judged beliefs by their results in practice.

Although Gabriel personally thought that James' pragmatism contained within it certain implicit values —for the pragmatic method of experimentation and discourse could only be carried out with free, honest, and creative minds—Gabriel expressed concern about pragmatism's relativism. James had not emphasized the implicit moral values to which he subscribed, rather, he had emphasized only the relativism and individualism of pragmatism. To Gabriel, in 1940 when totali-

[93] *The Course of American Democratic Thought*, pp. 282, 283, 285-286.

tarianism was rising throughout the world, statements of relativism posed crucial problems, problems which Americans ignored. James, commented Gabriel, had contributed significantly to "the post-Versailles American ethics of pragmatic expediency," and he "rejected the traditional ethics of the nineteenth century." The importance of the philosophical clash between traditional value systems and pragmatic relativism was paramount to Gabriel: Did Americans mean to express no traditional values? "The central problem in post-Versailles America," asserted Gabriel in 1940, "is to achieve a definition of the good."[94] Gabriel, in contrast to Curti, was worried about the relativistic implications of pragmatism.

Thus, Gabriel's description of James' ideas differed from Curti's, for Gabriel emphasized nonscientific elements, and Gabriel raised questions about pragmatism which reflected a contrasting interpretation of the course of modern American thought.

Gabriel's selection of subject matter generally contrasted with Curti's, and it contributed to, or reflected, the methodological as well as the ideological differences between the two historians. Curti's broad sweep of popular attitudes—emphasizing changing moods in technology, politics, communications industries, business, labor, and science—moved with the enthusiasm of his subject matter on the waves of the popular thought which he recorded. Gabriel, who moved much more narrowly, raising the same few questions of each of the relatively select group of men and ideas which he treated, used different criteria for selection. Gabriel did not directly focus on ideas of democratization or egalitarianism, but instead on such ideas as that of a universal moral law. Gabriel's "democratic faith" was not Curti's egalitarian faith—though the two were not con-

[94] *Ibid.*, pp. 289, 288, 384.

tradictory. Gabriel's idea of the free individual was not Curti's idea of the increasingly skeptical, liberated individual who had escaped religious authority. Nor was the material Gabriel drew on to examine the idea of the free individual in a time of capitalistic individualism (such as the late nineteenth century) the same material Curti used to investigate his concern with the idea of the individual free from capitalistic exploitation. These contrasts in the selection of subject matter can be illustrated by the extent to which religion was featured in the histories of ideas by Gabriel and by Curti.

Curti's treatment of religious ideas was exemplified in his chapter on "The Delimitation of Supernaturalism" during the late 1800's. Religious thought was characterized as "supernatural," and the history of American intellectual life was a story of movement away from supernaturalism. When Curti discussed religion, he tended to speak of specific doctrinal beliefs. Thus, supernaturalism was the doctrine which "assumes that a divine Creator not only stands above the laws of nature but directly intervenes in natural events and the affairs of men through miracles and the granting of grace." Supernaturalism was continually in retreat, because each "scientific advance imperceptibly reduced the range of the unknown and, as men had supposed, unknowable mysteries."[95]

Curti described as part of "supernaturalism": censorship based upon "a narrow concept of Christian morals"; popular writings such as General Lew Wallace's *Ben Hur*, which "succeeded in dramatizing Christ as a hero without in the least lessening reverence for Him as a supernatural force";[96] and spiritualism, such as mesmerism. Religious thought meant to Curti, in other words, specific beliefs which were characteristi-

[95] *The Growth of American Thought*, p. 531.
[96] *Ibid.*, p. 535.

cally threatened by the increase of scientific knowledge. Ordinarily, in Curti's pages there was implicit or explicit opposition between religious thought and secular thought, and the story of human betterment which he related meant in general a delimitation of religious thought. In a sense, religious ideas represented a failure of knowledge which modern learning remedied. Religion was not tremendously important, one may say with only slight exaggeration, except as an obstacle to modern, "progressive" ideas.

Gabriel, by contrast, placed immense emphasis upon the role of religion in American thought, and he indicated that the importance of religious ideas remained great, even in the twentieth century. Gabriel did not limit religious ideas to specific supernatural doctrines, as did Curti. Gabriel instead emphasized religious thought and maintained that it was concerned with values or ethical questions in addition to narrow doctrinal issues. It was obvious that Gabriel felt religion had been crucial to the development of American ideas in the past, and that religion still had an important role to play in determining the future character of American ideas and therefore of American life.

Some of the questions Gabriel asked repeatedly, especially concerning the existence of a universal moral law, were intimately connected with religious thought. *The Course of American Democratic Thought* therefore devoted a great deal of space to religious ideas, and great causal significance was attributed to them. John Calvin's thought, for example, was given credit for contributing to constitutionalism in the United States:

American constitutionalism, which seeks by means of a written document to restrain from wrong doing individuals, majorities, and even governments, owes a heavy debt to that young Frenchman who, in the summer of 1536, made his home in Geneva and began to expound the epistles of St. Paul.

Religion was even more crucial on the frontier, as Americans moved westward. "The frontier was crude, turbulent, and godless. Evangelical Protestantism," according to Gabriel, "more than any other single force, tamed it." In fact, "American social thought" throughout the years prior to the Civil War "was founded largely on religious postulates," he said. "Religion was the most powerful drive behind the humanitarian movements of the age."[97]

Even more important than specific instances of religious influence in the nineteenth century, according to Gabriel, was the fundamental relationship between religious ideas and American social thought. He pointed out the numerous parallels "between the doctrine of the democratic faith and Protestant Christianity." "These parallels become more significant," he wrote, "when it is recalled that certain disparities between religious and social beliefs tended to disappear in the nineteenth century." "Supernaturalism remained dominant in the American climate of opinion" until the later 1800's, according to Gabriel, and "the secular faith of democracy and the religious faith of evangelicism were not only closely interrelated but were mutually interdependent." "They complemented each other," he wrote:

> Together they provided the American with a theory of the cosmos which gave significance and direction to human life, and with a theory of society which gave a meaning not only to the relation of the individual to the group, but of the United States to the congregation of nations.[98]

[97] *The Course of American Democratic Thought*, pp. 30, 33, 161.
[98] *Ibid.*, pp. 37, 38.

Gabriel's focus on religious thought persisted in his discussion of the late nineteenth and the twentieth centuries, despite the usual view that religious ideas decreased in importance. What Gabriel emphasized in his discussion of the late 1800's and the 1900's was the basically religious nature of much nonreligious, and even irreligious, modern thought. Following a description of the modern, skeptical, "scientific" ideas of Lester Ward, Henry George, Bellamy, and labor reformers, Gabriel stressed the basically religious nature of their secular thought. "The religion of humanity and the new rationalism were negative and positive aspects of the same late nineteenth century humanism," he said. "But this new humanism, although its disciples would have denied it, was, in fact, a parade of ancient beliefs tricked out in new costumes."

Man, the creator, replaced God, the creator. The Holy Spirit became the spirit of humanity, the basis of natural religion. The aspiration of the religious heart and worship of divine perfection was discovered to be merely man's age-old effort to perfect himself. The mystic's feeling of the presence of God was, in the eyes of the new humanists, an old-fashioned way of describing the sentiment of human brotherhood. For the salvation of the soul by divine grace was substituted the concept of the liberation and expression of the basic goodness of human nature made possible by the increase of knowledge and the renovation of the environment. The ancient belief in the providence of God became the doctrine of progress by scientific advance. For the Christian technique of saving the individual by conversion was substituted the program of saving society by social inventions. The old Christian concept of a hell to be avoided beyond the grave was replaced by emphasis upon that degrading poverty to be avoided on the earth. The vision of paradise in another world became that of a golden age in the world we know.[99]

Gabriel's casting of secular reform thought in a religious imagery had far-reaching implications for his entire volume. Whereas, in Beard's and Curti's pages, there was a progressive movement in time from early ignorance to modern enlightenment and reform, Gabriel's volume minimized the progressive change and maximized the stability of fundamental beliefs. This continuity of ideas and values was argued through emphasizing the similarities, rather than the differences, between religious and nonreligious outlooks. In other words, by equating traditional religious thought and modern nonreligious thought, Gabriel undercut the view that great progress had been made by moving from the former to the latter. This also resulted in a clear implication by Gabriel that many of the same human problems persisted under either world-view. Gabriel explicitly focused on problems of Americans in a world of apotheosized science and denigrated religion. Gabriel wondered, in 1940, if twentieth century problems would not lead Americans back to a set of beliefs similar to the traditional democratic faith in the free individual and the absolute moral law. Gabriel suggested "the possibility that the cult of science has waned." During the late 1800's "the great hope" was preached "that science would enable man to create the golden day." "But," remarked Gabriel in 1940, "the age of science has been marked by economic and international disaster. The golden day, in spite of intellectual advances as great as those of Plato and Aristotle, has turned out to be a time of fear." As Gabriel interpreted the history of American ideas, therefore, the modern

[99] *Ibid.*, p. 214.

world's demolition of traditional bodies of "nonscientific" faith presented an unhappy picture. Revered science, including social science, had undercut absolute morality as well as undercutting the doctrine of the free individual. Even social affairs reflected the same developments: "In the twentieth century the ethics of expedience and force dominate in the realm of international affairs. To a greater or less degree expediency and force have controlled the course of domestic affairs in every great nation."

Nevertheless, despite Gabriel's lengthy discussion of the apparent undermining of traditional beliefs effected by science, Gabriel was not convinced that science actually did erode the essentials of traditional values. It was apparent that large numbers of Americans felt science to be a great destroyer of old truths, for much modern thought was testimony to the dissolution of the verities which were formerly held to be eternal. But Gabriel was strongly of the view that the fundamental validity of the traditional American beliefs remained basically unimpaired, despite new scientific knowledge. Ideals were not only necessary to make life meaningful, but, as Gabriel said in discussing William Graham Sumner, the pursuit of science itself rested upon certain universal moral beliefs:

Sumner in emphasizing ethical relativism was seeking emancipation from that code of his childhood in New England whose precepts were prefaced by the phrase, "Thus saith the Lord." A curious paradox, however, is associated with Sumner's discovery that the mores can make any type of behavior right. He used the methods of science. He gathered evidence from the cultures of the world. He let the facts lead to what conclusions they would. He announced courageously what he knew would be in 1906 an unpopular doctrine. In all this process his behavior implied acceptance on his part of absolute ethical standards. Without freedom to investigate and to announce the results of his labors, his conclusions would either have been impossible or would have had no social significance.

"In other words," he continued, "without liberty, honesty, and courage science is impossible. Sumner's behavior implied that these standards of value are universally good—that, in short, they are absolutes." Gabriel granted the paradox that Sumner, following an absolute code of scientific investigation, nevertheless concluded as a result of specific anthropological investigations that "mores can make any mode of conduct right or wrong." "Out of absolutism," Sumner "got relativism." To Gabriel, the "absolutism" of Sumner's method was even more significant than the "relativism" of his specific conclusions. Because of this absolutism of science's demand for honesty, truthfulness, and freedom, Gabriel concluded that morality had not been undermined. He expressed the hope, in 1940, that Americans would realize this, for he suggested that a proper consciousness and articulation of these values would mean that the codes of mid-twentieth century Americans would "not vary materially from the codes of Emerson or of William Ellery Channing." "The democratic faith," wrote Gabriel,

has from the beginning been a cluster of ideals which would serve as standards with which to measure conduct. Imbedded in the doctrine of the fundamental law has been the ideal that it is possible for men to govern their lives by stable ethical principles. It is the opposite of an ethic of mere expediency or of force.

Gabriel suggested that Americans in 1940 were more sympathetic to traditional Calvinistic reservations concerning human nature than they had been during the earlier twentieth century, because of the revelations about totalitarian behavior in the 1930's. "The rape of Ethiopia, the air raids over Barcelona, the sack of Nanking, and the Nazi war upon the Jews raised up doubts in the minds of many Americans," said Gabriel, "of the efficacy of the law of love to which Rauschenbusch pinned his faith." Gabriel noted that American Protestants looked back more favorably upon certain intellectual ancestors:

> In their new doctrine of man they have not gone all the way back to Calvin's belief in the corruption of the human soul. The philosophy of Reinhold Niebuhr and of the rest of the neo-Calvinist group resembles more the common sense of John C. Calhoun, who thought that men were both good and bad but that the drive toward egoism outweighs that toward altrium [*sic*]. The neo-Calvinists postulate a perpetual struggle between good and evil in the heart of the individual.

A practical political result of the return to a more reserved view of human nature was, according to Gabriel, a greater acceptance of the necessity of conflict and of war. More Americans during the late 1930's, he said, were "abandoning absolute pacifism," being "convinced with Mahan that force, even war, is necessary at times to combat the evil in the world." American sentiment expressing rejection of mere "humanism" seemed to Gabriel to be increasing in 1940. The result was, he concluded, that the "half-forgotten doctrines of orthodox Christianity are heard again amidst the roar of the modern world."[100]

100 *Ibid.*, pp. 382, 384-386.

After World War Two, Gabriel became even more explicit and emphatic concerning his conviction that Americans needed to adhere to traditional values. And, as a result of the American response to totalitarianism after *The Course of American Democratic Thought* was published in 1940, he was further convinced that Americans were themselves coming to realize the necessity for dedication to "absolute" humane values. Gabriel was encouraged when Americans questioned overly optimistic views of human nature and the validity of theories of relativism in areas of belief, and he was particularly encouraged when they fought for a humane way of life in World War II. He concluded, from the postwar perspective of 1950, that the "idea of fundamental human rights applicable to all men everywhere had begun to take form" during the war years. Instead of "agnosticism," "realism," "skepticism," and "relativism," which characterized American ideas between the two wars, Gabriel wrote that totalitarianism had forced Americans to realize "that only ideals and values, tenaciously held, can control power." "Americans who had insisted that relativism provides the only realistic approach to ethics discovered," according to Gabriel, "that a philosophy of ethical relativism made American criticism of genocide as practiced by the Nazis within their jurisdiction irrelevant."[101] In other words, for Americans to criticize the Nazis, implied a nonrelativistic standard of judgment which had validity whether or not it was recognized in Germany. It seemed to Gabriel in 1950 that Americans had come to realize that their society was based upon certain traditional, humane values or ideals which had a validity or truth of virtually universal applicability. The Second World War had forced Americans to re-

[101] "Thomas Jefferson and Twentieth-Century Rationalism," *Virginia Quarterly Review*, XXVI (Summer 1950), 332, 330, 334, 331.

alize the strength of their devotion to these traditional principles, and the lengths to which they would go to defend them.

In 1960, Gabriel summed up the challenge and repudiation of ethical relativism by Americans when he discussed the anthropological theory of cultural relativism. He commented that the discovery and exploration of the differences of behavior and beliefs among peoples of various cultures was "one of the more important achievements of the science of cultural anthropology in the 20th century." But, continued Gabriel, the theory of ethical relativity which resulted from the discovery of different behavior patterns among different societies, "seemed to an increasing number of persons to fail to probe to the depths of life. The mid-20th century generations saw and experienced in more than one culture conspicuous evil acts, too dark to be justified." Consequently, these evil acts were opposed unalterably in the United States, and "condemned throughout the world." Increasing numbers of people arrived at "the conviction that in human affairs some forms of behavior are always wrong." In this 1960 essay, entitled *Traditional Values in American Life*, Gabriel concluded his prefatory remarks by expressing the hope that his discussion of traditional American values

> may bring a little more clearly into view the shape of those universal values which our awareness of the evil in human life and our knowledge of the capacity for nobility of the human heart compel us to believe exist for the guidance of men.[102]

[102] Gabriel, *Traditional Values in American Life*, rev. 2nd edn., Washington, D.C., 1960, pp. vi-vii. Gabriel also expressed satisfaction in the 1960's that historians had, in his judgment, modified or withdrawn earlier support for a relativistic theory of written histories: "Their guild has now rejected Charles A. Beard's doctrine of relativity. Recognizing that complete objectivity represents a perfection impossible of attainment, they

Lengthy discussions of his ideological position occupied a large part of the total content of Gabriel's published writings. Like Samuel Eliot Morison, he called for a resurrection and new appreciation of traditional beliefs. But Gabriel's method of studying the history of ideas, though less analytical than Perry Miller's, offered a greater methodological challenge than did Morison's to the progressive historians. Gabriel attempted to locate central values which had governed the transitory opinions and actions of Americans throughout their past. His importance to the story of the writing of American intellectual histories derived both from his concern for the significance of ideas and from his ideological position. Relatively neglected by fellow scholars until after World War Two, Gabriel received increased postwar attention along with the rising influence of Miller and the other challengers of the progressive tradition.

OTHER WRITERS

The preceding discussions of the writings of Morison, Gabriel, and even Miller have made it clear that ideological aspects played an important part in the challenges offered to the progressive histories. Quite apart from disagreements over evidence or how histories of thought should be written, disagreements over ideological position emerged. During the period between, roughly, 1910 and the late 1930's, a scholarly dialogue was carried on between a dominant group of progressive scholars (who issued most of the proclamations

---

insist, however, that their awareness of the problem, plus their critical methods, makes possible a practicable objectivity out of which can come dependable conclusions concerning the past." Gabriel, "History and the American Past," in Robert Spiller and Eric Larrabee, eds., *American Perspectives: The National Self-Image in the Twentieth Century*, Cambridge, 1961, p. 16.

and wrote most of the popular books) and a smaller group of doubters and dissenters. While the dialogue continued, during the later 1930's and after, a transformation took place in intellectual progressivism. The progressive historians modified certain of their views during the era of the Second World War and the cold war, and thereafter found themselves closer to the views of their critics. The dialogue did not cease between say, a Merle Curti and a Samuel Eliot Morison, but the area of agreement broadened and the initiative passed from the former to the latter. Furthermore, the intensity of the dialogue diminished as the leading scholars of the 1920's, 1930's, and 1940's gave way to their juniors.

The clusters of values and opinions expressed by historians concerning society's past and present—here called their ideological positions—were, of course, part of the climates of opinion of their times. The rise, great popularity, and then after 1940 the diminishing prestige of progressive histories were all related to currents of thought which extended beyond the offices of academic historians. For that reason, certain ideological currents during and after the late 1930's can properly be said to have constituted a challenge to progressive histories. Foremost among these currents of the later 1930's was the pattern of attitudes sometimes referred to as "the re-embracement of America." Morison's, Miller's, and Gabriel's scholarship revealed, of course, an embracement of America, but the phrase customarily refers to the re-embracement by those intellectuals who were formerly hostile to their native country. Rebellious literary intellectuals preceding and following the Great War, such as those described in Malcolm Cowley's *Exile's Return*, as well as in Daniel Aaron's politically minded *Writers on the Left*, who expressed their discontent on into the 1930's, were

examples of figures who set the tone of avowed estrange-
ment from America by many intellectuals between the
wars. The alienated intellectuals were during these
years characteristically contemptuous of America's past,
its repressive Puritanism, its hypocritical moralizing
and materialistic acquisitiveness, and its barrenness in
the arts.[103] But as the Second World War approached,
many intellectuals expressed a new regard for their
country, an appreciation which featured a celebration
of America's past.

Van Wyck Brooks, for instance, turned away during the depression decade from his earlier indictment
of national literary sterility to write a multivolume history of American writers which was saturated with
affirmation.[104] The novelist, John Dos Passos, who had
been critical of the disparity between American ideals
of freedom and democracy and American violations in
practice, applauded his country's democratic and libertarian traditions in a book of popular history, *The
Ground We Stand On* (1941). European totalitarianism provoked Dos Passos to make a less hostile assessment of life in the United States. "I think there is enough
real democracy in the very mixed American tradition
to enable us, with courage and luck, to weather the
social transformations that are now going on without
losing all our liberties or the humane outlook that is

[103] For various manifestations of avowed alienation among
American intellectuals between, roughly, 1912 and 1941, see
the following: Henry May, *The End of American Innocence*,
New York, 1959; Malcolm Cowley, *Exile's Return*, New York,
1934, rev. edn., 1951; Daniel Aaron, *Writers on the Left*, New
York, 1961; Christopher Lasch, *The New Radicalism in America*, New York, 1965.

[104] Brooks' first depiction of the writer's fruitful and har-
monious position in America was *The Life of Emerson*, New
York, 1932. His most famous volume of "positive" reinterpretation was *The Flowering of New England*, New York, 1936.

the medium in which civilizations grow," he wrote in 1939.[105]

The attitude of re-embracement was so pervasive by the end of the decade that the editors of the left-wing literary journal, *Partisan Review*, submitted a questionnaire in 1939 to leading writers which included the following questions: "Are you conscious, in your own writing, of the existence of a 'usable past'? Is this mostly American?"; "Are you sympathetic to the current tendency toward what may be called 'literary nationalism'—a renewed emphasis, largely uncritical, on the specifically 'American' elements in our culture?" The writers' answers differed in many respects, but most agreed that a re-embracement of American traditions had occurred.[106]

Because the attitude of re-embracement included a new appreciation of the validity of various traditional values, or beliefs, or ideas in the American experience, this attitude constituted an ideological challenge to the prestige of progressive histories. The nature of the challenge was complex and not entirely logical. The progressive historians had always championed certain traditional American beliefs, so why should they have been threatened by the neo-Americanism of the 1930's and later? Why should the progressive historians not

---

[105] Dos Passos, in response to a list of questions concerning "The Situation in American Writing," in *Partisan Review*, VI (Summer 1939), 27.

[106] The questions and responses appeared in VI (Summer 1939), 25-51, and (Fall 1939), 103-123. Writers canvassed were: John Dos Passos, Allen Tate, James T. Farrell, Kenneth Fearing, Katherine Anne Porter, Wallace Stevens, Gertrude Stein, William Carlos Williams, John Peale Bishop, Harold Rosenberg, Henry Miller (Summer); Sherwood Anderson, Louise Bogan, Lionel Trilling, Robert Penn Warren, Robert Fitzgerald, R. P. Blackmur, Horace Gregory (Fall).

Alfred Kazin described the literary intellectuals' re-embracement in his concluding chapter, "America! America!," in *On Native Grounds*, New York, 1942.

have benefited, as historians, by the new concern for the nation's past? The answer is, of course, that the American past depicted in progressive histories was not quite the same American past being discovered and applauded during the era of totalitarianism. Even the same historic figures had different faces, and the same historic ideas were viewed differently. The later interpretations of American thought tended to emphasize continuity and stability in fundamental intellectual traditions rather than progressive change from darkness to light. The appeal of the emphasis upon the morality and stability of American traditions can be seen most dramatically perhaps by recalling the effect that it had on the writings of some of the older progressive scholars themselves. Both Charles Beard and Carl Becker implicitly and explicitly qualified certain aspects of their earlier progressive interpretations in the face of European totalitariansm.[107] Stability and the continuity of democratic constitutional government in the United States were emphasized as facts of American life when they became virtues of American life. Intellectual change occurred according to either interpretation, but whereas progressive histories featured economic conflict as a cause of change, along with the inherent force of good ideas, the later interpretations ordinarily lacked a formula to indicate how change occurred. The foundation for these later interpretations had, of course, already been laid by 1940 in the writings of Samuel Eliot Morison, Perry Miller, and Ralph Gabriel.

A new interest in American religious thought was one component of the embracement of America's past which contributed a subject suitable for histories of ideas, as well as presenting ideological opposition to progressive interpretations. Morison's, Miller's, and Gabriel's great concern with religious ideas and the con-

---

[107] See discussions of Beard and Becker, Chapter Two.

trast between their treatment of religion and that of the progressive scholars have already been discussed at length. Moreover, this new interest in the history of religious belief in America can be singled out as a challenge to the prestige of progressive histories—they seldom took religious thought seriously except to criticize it. "The recovery of American religious history really began in the 1930's," according to the most recent survey of the subject.[108] A "recovery" occurred in the sense that there was a new interest in the history of religion and histories of religion evinced newly sympathetic attitudes toward their topic as well. The sources and expressions of the "recovery" were numerous. They included inquiries into the relationship between religious beliefs, practices, and groups, on one side, and social groups on the other. This social analysis was the least challenging to the progressive histories, but few progressive historians undertook the inquiry, and most of the studies allowed for some causal influence on the part of religious belief as well as some social environmental influence.[109] More threatening to the dominance

[108] Henry May, "The Recovery of American Religious History," *American Historical Review*, LXX (October 1964), 79-92. I am indebted to this article for the paragraphs which follow concerning recent interest in the history of religion in the United States.

[109] The leading social interpretations came from seminaries: H. Richard Niebuhr, *Social Sources of Denominationalism*, New York, 1929; Will Herberg, *Protestant-Catholic-Jew*, Garden City, N.Y., 1955. But it is true that among the most significant pioneering attempts at social interpretations of religion by secular academic historians were those by scholars who were intellectually related to the progressive historians: Arthur Schlesinger (senior), "A Critical Period in American Religion, 1875-1900," *Proceedings of the Massachusetts Historical Society*, LXIV (June 1932), 523-547; Lee Benson, *The Concept of Jacksonian Democracy: New York as a Test Case*, Princeton, 1961, especially pp. 186-207. These environmental interpretations included religious belief itself as one causal element in the total environment.

of progressive histories were the studies of American religious thought which assumed that the ideas themselves were interesting and of intellectual worth, in addition to possessing certain causal power in the environment.

The variety implied in these assumptions concerning religious thought has already been suggested by the discussions of Morison, Miller, and Gabriel. Morison showed the effect on worldly life of Puritan beliefs, Miller demonstrated the intellectual richness of Puritan theology, and Gabriel traced the central values expressed by religion during more than a century of American history. The number of scholarly volumes concerning specific individuals, themes, and events in American religious history had become considerable by the mid-1960's.[110] And even more challenging to the prestige of progressive histories was the relatively pes-

[110] Studies published through the middle of the 1950's can be found in Nelson R. Burr, *Critical Bibliography of Religion in America*, 2 vols., Princeton, 1957. Books of particular interest to historians of ideas published since that bibliography include: Edwin Scott Gaustad, *The Great Awakening in New England*, New York, 1957; Thomas F. O'Dea, *The Mormons*, Chicago, 1957; Timothy Smith, *Revivalism and Social Reform*, New York, 1957; Barbara Cross, *Horace Bushnell: Minister to a Changing America*, Chicago, 1958; Robert Cross, *The Emergence of Liberal Catholicism in America*, Cambridge, 1958; Robert Moats Miller, *American Protestantism and Social Issues, 1919-1939*, Chapel Hill, 1958; Edmund Morgan, *Puritan Dilemma: The Story of John Winthrop*, Boston, 1958; Bernard Weisberger, *They Gathered at the River*, Boston, 1958; William G. McLoughlin, Jr., *Modern Revivalism: Charles Grandison Finney to Billy Sunday*, New York, 1959; Donald B. Meyer, *The Protestant Search for Political Realism, 1919-1941*, Berkeley and Los Angeles, 1960; C. C. Goen, *Revivalism and Separatism in New England, 1740-1800*, New Haven, 1962; Edmund Morgan, *The Gentle Puritan: A Life of Ezra Stiles, 1727-1795*, New Haven, 1962; Louis Leonard Tucker, *Puritan Protagonist: President Thomas Clap of Yale College*, Chapel Hill, 1962; Edmund Morgan, *Visible Saints: The History of a Puritan Idea*, New York, 1963.

simistic conception of human nature and of the human situation which, during and after the 1930's, accompanied the increasing influence of neo-orthodox theology in the United States and which stood in contrast to the relatively optimistic conceptions expressed earlier by the progressives.

The newer outlook has been phrased in different ways, depending upon who has done the phrasing. Sympathetic scholars, particularly those in sympathy with the neo-orthodox theologians Reinhold Niebuhr and Paul Tillich, have preferred to say that the progressives were too optimistic and too simplistic in their view of man. The progressives, according to the indictment, failed to perceive the perennial selfishness of the individual, the inherent complexity of group relations, and the continual irony of man's past; the Judaic-Christian tradition taught more wisdom than the secular rationalism of intellectual progressivism. Specifically, the Calvinist portrait of man was symbolically, if not literally, true. The characteristic progressive weakness, therefore, was to assume too much plasticity in men, to equate change with betterment, and to risk loss of what was traditionally good through futile attempts at utopia.

Scholars sympathetic to the indictment of progressivism, but wishing to minimize any dependence upon theology, have simply omitted the theological aspect and based their critique on what they have argued to be the disparity between the progressive assumptions concerning man and the way man has behaved in history. Furthermore, there have been very few attempts by historians to resurrect the progressive view of man and society since 1930 and the beginnings of the era of totalitarianism. Instead, those scholars most sympathetic to the older progressivism have merely insisted that the indictment of progressivism has exaggerated the innocence and simplicity of the progressives and has contributed to complacency and acceptance of the status quo.[111] It was generally accepted by 1960, whether or not the indictment of the progressives was justified, that man's potential for radical improvement in personal and social relations was severely limited, and that traditional religious inquiry, whether stated in theological terms or not, was again respectable among serious scholars and intellectuals.[112]

Each of these challenges to the popularity of progressive histories during and after the 1930's, including the ideological embracement of America and the interest in religion, was manifested in the publications of Morison, Miller, and Gabriel as well as in those of others. So it was too with a third challenge, namely, intensive "internal" analysis of ideas. Gabriel to some

[111] Studies of the American past which since 1945 have expressed the criticisms of intellectual progressivism indicated include the following, written by political scientists and literary critics as well as historians. Leslie Fiedler, *An End to Innocence*, Boston, 1955; Louis Hartz, *The Liberal Tradition in America*, New York, 1955; George Kennan, *American Diplomacy, 1900-1950*, New York, 1951; Kennan, *Russia and the West under Lenin and Stalin*, Boston, 1961; Henry May, *The End of American Innocence*, New York, 1959; David Noble, *The Paradox of Progressive Thought*, Minneapolis, 1958; Robert Osgood, *Ideals and Self-Interest in America's Foreign Policy*, Chicago, 1953; Arthur Schlesinger, Jr., *The Vital Center*, Boston, 1949; Cushing Strout, "The Twentieth-Century Enlightenment," *The Political Science Review*, XLIX (June 1955), 321-339; C. Vann Woodward, "The Irony of Southern History," *Journal of Southern History*, XIX (February 1953), 3-19. Except for Kennan, born 1904, and Woodward, born 1908, all these scholars were born between 1915 and 1925, and they reached maturity in the era of the Second World War. (For a brief essay which discusses most of these scholars, from the standpoint of their attribution of "innocence" to earlier Americans and their own attempt to escape "beyond innocence," see Skotheim, " 'Innocence' and 'Beyond Innocence' in Recent American Scholarship," *American Quarterly*, XIII [Spring 1961], 93-99.)

[112] See, for example, the *Partisan Review* symposium, "Religion and the Intellectuals," New York, 1950.

extent, but especially Miller analyzed the content of ideas at greater length and in more detail than did most progressive historians. Primarily methodological in its challenge to the "external," environmental analysis of thought offered by progressive historians such as Beard and Curti, internal analysis was not free from ideological suggestions. To stress the content and structure of thought was to emphasize the human mind, and even perhaps to suggest the mind's creativity or autonomy. In a period of American ideological conflict with totalitarianism, it was easy (however illogical) to interpret environmental and relativistic theories of ideas as undercutting belief in the dignity of the free mind. The appeal of such reasoning was not confined to critics of progressivism, as Beard's and Becker's modifications of their earlier relativism made apparent.[113]

Perry Miller's methodological challenge to the way most progressive histories treated ideas resembled the philosophers' internal analysis of ideas; the essential differences were ones of purpose and of source materials. Miller was attempting to locate the roots of a national mind, not the logic of a philosophical system, and he surveyed the ephemera of pulpit sermons as well as the weightier tomes of philosophy and theology. But Miller's analytic approach to thought was sufficiently unlike that of most historians to cause many of them to wonder privately whether his analysis was perhaps too philosophical, too inclined to treat ideas solely as they appeared on the printed page—without enough

[113] See discussions of Beard and Becker, Chapter Two. For examples of c. 1940 criticisms of environmental-relativist interpretations of ideas, and assertions of the importance of granting greater autonomy to the role of the mind, see C. H. McIlwain's review of Sabine's *A History of Political Theory*, *American Historical Review*, XLIII (April 1938), 567-569; Carl Friedrich's review of three books, *American Historical Review*, XLVI (July 1941), 863-866.

regard for what happened to them in the world. Or, to put the question differently, many historians wondered whether only a few expressions of American thought— even if Puritanism were admittedly one of them—might profitably be subjected to such analytical scrutiny. Whatever reservations American historians privately felt about Miller's methods (expressed through their failure to emulate him), one distinguished philosopher, Arthur O. Lovejoy, explicitly issued to historians a general challenge to study the history of thought by intensive analysis of the content of ideas.

Since his own prolific studies in esthetics and philosophy during the first half of the twentieth century concerned European thought, Lovejoy had no great impact upon the actual writing of American intellectual histories. But as the originator of the History of Ideas Club at Johns Hopkins in the 1920's, as the leader in the founding of the *Journal of the History of Ideas* in 1940, and as the author of innumerable analyses of ideas in history, Lovejoy was the most articulate spokesman for the internal analysis of the content of thought in history without regard to the social and economic environmental factors. In studies such as "The Thirteen Pragmatisms," "On the Discrimination of Romanticisms," and *The Great Chain of Being: A Study of the History of an Idea*, Lovejoy dissected ideas with unmatched care and rigor.[114]

Lovejoy's challenge to environmental analyses of thought was, like Perry Miller's, an important one, and its acceptance would have altered the character of American histories of ideas. But in Lovejoy's case, even more than in Miller's, admiration rather than emula-

[114] Lovejoy, "The Thirteen Pragmatisms," *Journal of Philosophy*, v (1908), 5-12, 29-39; "On the Discrimination of Romanticisms," *Publications of the Modern Language Association (PMLA)*, xxxix (1924), 229-253; *The Great Chain of Being*, Cambridge, 1936.

tion was the reward extended by American historians.

Lovejoy's intensive analysis of ideas without regard to their environmental background was not, at least in the pure form practiced by Lovejoy, a successful challenge to environmental interpretations of thought. Nevertheless, Lovejoy's approach was one of the challenges offered during and after the 1930's, which also included: Perry Miller's writings, the studies of Puritanism generally, the scholarship of Morison and Gabriel, the recovery of religious history, and such purely ideological currents as the embracement of American traditions and the national response to European totalitarianism. The total effect of these developments was by the time of the Second World War a serious challenge to the prestige and popularity of the progressive histories of American ideas. By 1940 the challenges were in full force and by the 1950's progressive histories were no longer dominant in America.

DISCUSSIONS of progressive legacies and of continuing challenges to progressive histories have already indicated that the historians' dialogue did not altogether cease after the Second World War. Studies which expressed the ideological position and employed the methods of earlier progressive histories continued to be written. Similarly, criticisms of those interpretations and techniques continued to be voiced. At the same time, however, the form of the prewar dialogue has been so altered by scholarship since the war that convergence in both interpretation and method has become as marked as divergence. Signs of convergence have appeared in the later works of the older intellectual historians whose writings formerly followed one of the divergent paths, as well as in the works of the younger historians. And there has been convergence in method as well as in ideological position.

An initial example of this convergence in both interpretation and method may be seen by comparing the writings of two scholars, Henry Steele Commager (1902——) and Stow Persons (1913——). Commager, though a self-styled Parringtonian, has minimized the economic environmental interpretation of ideas in practice and has severely qualified its significance in theory, while modifying after World War Two certain features of his earlier progressive outlook. Persons, a student and follower of Gabriel, has been less critical of American reform thought than his former mentor, and by the 1960's came to place more emphasis than he had formerly on environmental influences upon thought. Despite their divergent intellectual backgrounds, the histories of ideas published by Commager and Persons in the 1950's revealed surprising similarities in addition to certain obvious differences.

Commager's writings, prior to the Second World War, supported a "revisionist" interpretation of American entry into the First World War;[1] during the early 1940's he pleaded for greater governmental responsiveness to the will of the majority;[2] and, at least as late as the middle 1950's, he expressed marked sympathy for Dewey's progressive education.[3] Throughout these years, he wrote prolifically in defense of historic American reform. From a sympathetic biography in 1936 of the pre-Civil War reformer Theodore Parker, he moved to *The American Mind* (1950), which picked up the intellectual threads of the 1880's, where Parrington's incomplete third volume had left them dangling. "My greatest intellectual debt is to Vernon Louis Parrington," Commager wrote at the beginning of the volume, "whose great study of American thought has long been

[1] See Commager's review of Charles Tansill's *America Goes to War*, in *The Yale Review*, XXVII (Summer 1938), 855-857. The tenor of this 1938 review strongly suggests an isolationist view toward European affairs at that time. Later, however, Commager became a defender of American intervention in World War Two. See his statement in *The American Mind* (New Haven, 1950) that "only a generation ignorant or contemptuous of history could have been guilty of the reckless errors that characterized American foreign policy from 1919 to 1938." (pp. 277-278)

[2] *Majority Rule and Minority Rights*, New York, 1943; reprinted by Peter Smith, New York, 1950.

[3] See "The Necessity of Experimentation," in *Freedom, Loyalty and Dissent*, New York, 1954, pp. 60-63.

an inspiration and whose disciple I gladly acknowledge myself."[4]

Despite his identification with Parrington, Commager by the 1950's expressed views which suggested other loyalties as well. He no longer indicated sympathy for a "revisionist" interpretation of American entry into World War One; he implied criticism of American "isolationist" foreign policy between the two wars; and his volume on public affairs, published in the 1950's, consisted of a plea for minority rights and civil liberties rather than, as in the early 1940's, a plea for more efficient implementation of the majority will.[5] Because of these later developments in Commager's thinking, as the period of totalitarianism advanced into the cold war, it is illuminating to see which aspects of Parrington's writings Commager found most attractive in 1950. In the discussion of Parrington in *The American Mind*, Commager admiringly emphasized one trait above any other: Parrington's celebration of certain beliefs in American history. Commager wrote that Parrington "was sure there were American ideals and, what is more, he was zealous to champion them." Parrington knew, said Commager, that ideas cannot be stopped, that "ideas are carried with the wind."[6] In other words, Commager placed stress on that part of *Main Currents* which maximized the importance of thought, and he did not emphasize those aspects of Parrington's writings which minimized the influence of ideas.[7] The specific aspect of *Main Currents* which Commager cited

[4] *The American Mind*, p. ix.

[5] *Freedom, Loyalty and Dissent*. Both this volume and *Majority Rule and Minority Rights* (1943) were collections of speeches and essays.

[6] *The American Mind*, pp. 298, 299.

[7] Commager mentioned, but only mentioned once, in a five-page discussion, that Parrington "understood the economic bases of politics," and that "he was able to place American thought in its economic context." (*Ibid.*, p. 302.)

as exemplifying Parrington's celebration of ideas was, of course, his treatment of reformist currents of thought. "Parrington insisted" that the "great tradition of American thought" was "the tradition of liberalism and revolt," Commager noted. "Parrington did not regard his task as a judicial one or pretend to be objective, impartial, or aloof. He interpreted American intellectual history as a struggle between the forces of freedom and of privilege, and he deliberately took sides in that struggle." Sympathetically, Commager concluded his section on Parrington by writing that *Main Currents* was "a monument to all that had been pledged and sacrificed that America might continue to mean liberty and democracy; it was a magnificent tract calling upon Americans to be true to their past and worthy of their destiny."[8] Light is shed on Commager's *The American Mind* by his portrayal of *Main Currents*. He minimized Parrington's socioeconomic interpretation with its resultant depreciation of the role of thought in history. He instead emphasized Parrington's glorification of certain ideas as powerful historical forces. *The American Mind* was characterized—just as Commager characterized *Main Currents*—by celebration of the importance of ideas in human affairs.

Commager's celebration of ideas as important factors in history did not mean, however, that he failed altogether to adhere to a view of ideas as instruments. He repeatedly presented beliefs and institutions as being best understood if considered as pragmatic tools or instruments. In part, the philosophy of pragmatism was, to Commager, this way of analyzing beliefs functionally. The nineteenth century American was "incurably utilitarian," said Commager approvingly, "and it was appropriate that the one philosophy which might be called original with him was that of instrumentalism."

[8] *Ibid.*, pp. 300-301, 303.

The American judged doctrines and practices by their usefulness. "To the charge that he had no political philosophy he was cheerfully indifferent, for he regarded his freedom from the exactions of political theory as good fortune rather than misfortune." Twentieth century triumphs were largely due, according to Commager, to the fact that pragmatic analysis was used on ideas and institutions. "Sociological jurisprudence," for example, "was pragmatism. . . . It was a legal philosophy fitted to the realities of social life in an urban order, of economic life in an industrial order, and of political life in an egalitarian order." In the study of politics, to take another example, "the pragmatists did not so much constitute a school as a whole educational system." Frank Goodnow, Charles Merriam, J. Allen Smith, A. Lawrence Lowell, and Brooks Adams, in place of trying to "fit men to some preconceived pattern of political conduct," "turned instead to the analysis of government as it actually operated, addressing themselves not to the original blueprint but to the living structure."[9] These remarks of Commager implied that the nature of ideas and institutions was best understood as being man's instruments for dealing pragmatically with his environment. Thus Commager's implied theory of the development of ideas was similar to the views of Robinson, Beard, Becker, Parrington, and Curti.

Despite Commager's apparent acceptance of a view of ideas as instruments serving practical needs, he devoted little space in the *American Mind* to a discussion of the needs themselves. In other words, environmental circumstances were assumed to be important to the ideas which emerged, but he did not describe the environment in any detail. Commager instead described ideas at work. Regardless of the origin of ideas, Com-

[9] *Ibid.*, pp. 8, 9, 380, 327, 326.

mager's concern was to examine what the ideas had done in the world.

Commager's concern with what ideas achieved instrumentally, was associated with his theory of the truth of ideas. He did not draw relativistic conclusions as to the truth or morality of thought despite the fact that thought was a tool serving practical needs. Theories of the origin of ideas were dissociated by Commager from theories of the validity of ideas.

His discussion, in *The American Mind*, of Beard's *An Economic Interpretation of the Constitution* and *Economic Origins of Jeffersonian Democracy* exemplified Commager's tendency to accept environmental interpretations of beliefs, but to minimize the relativistic conclusions which might be drawn from them. In these studies Beard had focused on economic components in the environment and suggested that they best explained the resultant political doctrines. What Commager emphasized about Beard's economic interpretation was not its relativistic implications (How can beliefs be evaluated if they are economically determined and hence have a meaning and "truth" relative only to their environment?), but instead Commager stressed the fact that Beard had ignored the whole question of whether worthwhile doctrines had come from the economic environment. That is, Commager dissociated the origin of ideas from the validity of ideas. Beard's studies, said Commager,

> were more concerned with cause than consequence. They might be accepted as definitive but could not be regarded as conclusive, for economic motivation was not a conclusion but a point of departure. What was primarily important was not, after all, the motivation of the men who made the Constitution and formulated the policies of Jeffersonian democracy but

the consequences of their work. The search for the recondite led, as it so often does, to the neglect of the obvious, and a generation familiar with the economic influences at work in the Federal Convention was inclined to ignore the fact that the Convention had created a Federal Constitution.[10]

Commager thus made the same point in 1950 that Beard himself had come to in *The Republic* in 1943: whatever forces were responsible for the political beliefs which were expressed in the Constitution, the beliefs themselves were the important thing in an era of totalitarianism.

Beard and Becker, who prior to the late 1930's emphasized the environmental backgrounds of ideas and who pioneered among American historians in statements of relativism, later modified their positions in the face of what seemed to them the immorality of totalitarianism. Commager, a generation younger than Beard, Becker, and Parrington, and at the height of his powers during the period of totalitarianism, was more concerned with whether ideas were moral or immoral, humane or inhumane, than he was with relating ideas to their environmental origins. Having lived in a world more lawless and amoral than that of his master Parrington, Commager did not make as much of relativism and environmental determinants of thought, though he did not deny their theoretical validity.

Commager's treatment of James' pragmatism in *The American Mind* revealed the book's sympathy for reform, the contrasts with a treatment such as Gabriel's, and yet revealed a typical postwar concern with the problem of values. Although Commager described James' skepticism at length ("James confronted all dogma with skepticism and made skepticism itself a dogma"), the

[10] *Ibid.*, p. 306.

absolute morality and humanity of James' thought was equally stressed. James had a desire, said Commager, for "empiricism without inhumanity," due to his "compelling consciousness of moral obligation." Pragmatism was a "democratic philosophy," and it was also "a humane and optimistic philosophy." Pragmatism held, wrote Commager, "that man's fate was not determined by mechanical powers but by man himself, and it insisted that man could create as well as succumb to environment."[11] Thus he did not discuss James' skepticism as possibly leading to relativism or amorality, as did Gabriel, but instead Commager emphasized James' morality, humaneness, and commitment to democracy. Just as Commager minimized the relativistic implications of Parrington's writings, so he minimized the relativistic implications in James' thought. When Commager evaluated pragmatism he quite obviously had in mind its humane values:

> pragmatism was affluent, magnanimous, heroic; it enlisted all those sentiments we have come to consider generous and noble in the battle for salvation. That it should have been equated with a success philosophy, watered down to an acquiescence in cash values or a justification of business efficiency, associated with a series of shabby compromises and concessions, translated into a cunning technique for outwitting Providence, was discreditable.

The test which Commager used in evaluating pragmatism was the same one he applied to Beard's Constitutional fathers, namely, the pragmatic one of how the beliefs worked out in practice. Again, Commager stressed the ethical humaneness of pragmatism, and the test of ethical humaneness was opposition to totalitarianism:

[11] *Ibid.*, pp. 94, 93, 91, 95, 96.

It is perhaps fair to ask whether, in the great crisis of the twentieth century which tested the efficacy of all philosophies, that people who most fully subscribed to pragmatism or that people who clung to the traditions of Hegelian idealism conducted themselves more rationally. It would be a bold student who, comparing America and Germany in the generation after James' death, could have concluded that it was the pragmatists who had abandoned themselves to emotionalism and their souls to anarchy, who had displayed contempt for reason or for law or for morality. It has been noted, to be sure, that the tyrant Mussolini counted himself an early convert to pragmatism; it is relevant to remark that it was Santayana, not John Dewey, who found it convenient to take up residence in Italy.[12]

Commager applied this workability test to most of the ideas he described in *The American Mind*, and the standard of judgment, which he took for granted, and with which he judged workability, was what might be called the humane dignity of the individual. Commager's underlying question was whether each idea pragmatically contributed to greater or less humanity and dignity for Americans.

In the background, and clearly contributing to Commager's search for the location of humane American values, was European totalitarianism. The same background was apparent in the scholarship of Stow Persons (1913——). Born in Connecticut and a student of Ralph Gabriel at Yale during the 1930's, Persons extended Gabriel's method and outlook into the seventeenth and eighteenth centuries and covered as well the nineteenth and twentieth centuries. Persons' *American Minds* (1958), the most recent full-scale history of

[12] *Ibid.*, pp. 101, 102.

American ideas published in the United States, was in several respects a synthesis of the writings of Morison, Miller, and Gabriel.

Persons' first published volume, originally his doctoral dissertation under Gabriel, was a study of late nineteenth century religious ideas, *Free Religion: An American Faith*.[13] First treated by a twentieth century historian in Gabriel's *The Course of American Democratic Thought*, "free religion" was a movement of religious thought which, influenced by contemporary scientific currents, attempted to rid religion of superstition, outdated dogma, and sectarianism.[14] Persons examined in detail the religious controversies during the late 1800's, taking the arguments seriously, and showing sympathy not only with the "modernist" ideas but the antimodernist ideas as well. For example, in discussing the "anti-religious animus" of the modernist thinkers, Persons noted that "the anti-religious animus of the rationalists was due in part, at least, to the firm stand of orthodox Christianity upon an uncompromising formula of ancient dogmas." But, added Persons in an attempt to sympathetically understand why orthodox Christians were firmly opposed to the rationalists, the "historian cannot do justice to the spirit of the Christian opposition to the new science unless he recognizes the anti-Christian moral and religious overtones accompanying the deification of science by the rationalists." For, continued Persons, the modernist rationalists transformed "the new science," which was itself "neutral as far as moral or ethical values were concerned, into an optimistic cosmology where science was made to provide seemingly conclusive evidence of progressive mundane existence."[15] Persons thus sounded the Gabriel

[13] New Haven, 1947.
[14] Gabriel, *The Course of American Democratic Thought*, 1940 edn., pp. 175-179.
[15] Persons, *Free Religion*, New Haven, 1947, pp. 105-106.

note, ringing the characteristic theme—many modern thinkers had erroneously assumed that science demonstrated the human condition to be progressively improving.

Free Religion: An American Faith explored religious ideas without reference to the social and economic background from which they emerged, but the discussion was in constant relation to the nonreligious ideas which affected religious thought in the nineteenth century. Similarly in *American Minds* (1958), Persons' large-scale history of ideas, ideas were not closely nor consistently related to the socioeconomic environment. Persons selected relatively few figures and their ideas for discussion, and each intellectual sketch was in relative detail. Persons identified five American "minds," including "The Colonial Religious Mind," the "Enlightenment," "The Mind of Nineteenth-Century Democracy," "The Naturalistic Mind" and "The Contemporary Neodemocratic Mind." These systems of ideas were investigated not only without consistent relation to the material environment, but also without much attention to how they developed. The spotlight was placed on fully formed bodies of ideas as they were at their time of greatest vitality. "No effort is made," Persons commented in the Preface to *American Minds*, "to explore the formation or dissolution of these systems of ideas or to trace the transitions between them." These systems of ideas were called "social minds," by which Persons meant that each

> social mind is the cluster of ideas and attitudes that gives to a society whatever uniqueness or individuality it may have as an epoch in the history of thought. It binds together in an intellectual community those who share its beliefs. This book is con-

cerned principally with the intellectual functions of the social mind.[16]

Thus, Persons focused on several different sets of ideas which he held to be foundation structures for the thought of each period.

Persons' careful sketch of "The Colonial Religious Mind: 1620-1660" followed Perry Miller's large and detailed portrait. Persons summarized early colonial ideas with a minimum of reference to social and economic circumstances, and he repeated Morison's and Miller's emphasis upon the positive contribution of the Puritan respect for learning. He applauded too the thought of the Puritan orthodoxy rather than that of the Antinomian and sectarian opposition.[17] Like Morison and Miller, he sympathized with the Puritan leaders in their view that individualist, subjectivist sectarians might fragment society socially as well as intellectually.

Persons emphasized the communal nature of Puritan doctrine, and he interpreted the Puritan sense of community as stemming not from mere rationalization of the self-interest of the governing group, but stemming instead from a proper realization of the need for community. Persons suggested that even in theological matters, Puritans placed most stress "upon the corporate element": "It was extremely important that God's covenant people should be united in a social community. We may even say that the early American Puritans were

[16] *American Minds*, New York, 1958, p. vii.

[17] Persons commented that the "emphasis upon learning furnished one of the most convincing indications of the essentially moderate and practical spirit" of early Puritanism in contrast to the "sectarians with their contempt for mere knowledge." (*Ibid.*, pp. 23-24.) Speaking of the sectarian demand that the Puritan orthodoxy define regeneracy in purely spiritual terms, and not at all in visible conduct, Persons wrote that "It was, of course, impossible for the Congregationalist system to operate upon any such elusive and subjective criterion as this without inviting chaos." (*Ibid.*, p. 28.)

incapable of conceiving of a purely individualistic relationship of man to God." Similarly, according to Persons, Puritan thought insisted upon the great importance of government or social organization. Government had to be taken seriously because, the Puritans said, it was necessary to restrain "selfish and sinful men." And the Puritans assumed that the restraint would be directed toward the fulfillment of shared communal values. The minority sectarians, by contrast, were not interested either in shared communal values or in governmental affairs. Stow Persons, like the orthodox Puritans, assumed the significance of social organization, and he, like they, thought that there had to be "recognition of the necessity for implicit agreement upon certain positive if minimal affirmations before any political system can function in practice."[18] Persons thus summarized sympathetically, without particular emphasis upon nonintellectual environmental factors, the ideas of the Puritans which gave meaning and viability to the community.

Since Persons set out to survey the whole course of American thought in one volume of less than five hundred pages—approximately one hundred pages were devoted to colonial ideas—and since Persons' method was to treat ideas in considerable detail, he described the ideas of only a few individuals by name. Only the ideas of John Cotton, Roger Williams, and Anne Hutchinson were specifically discussed in the seventy pages on seventeenth century thought, the bulk of the space being devoted to ideas without reference to which individuals expressed the ideas. The organization in terms of "minds" contributed to this type of analysis.

Persons' discussion of the eighteenth century "enlightenment mind," which was treated at the same length as the thought of the seventeenth century, men

[18] *Ibid.*, pp. 16, 36, 67.

tioned such thinkers as Jefferson, Adams, Paine, Franklin, Edwards, Charles Chauncy, Ethan Allen, and the
Bartrams, but the analysis was by segments of the
"mind": its religion, science, history, and politics. Despite mention that Enlightenment thought "expressed
the ideology of a social and governing elite,"[19] Persons
paid little attention to environmental factors and he consistently concentrated on the content of the ideas he described. This technique of treating ideas accompanied
a conception of thought which assumed its causal importance and historic significance.

Persons' ideological position was further revealed in
his discussion of eighteenth century ideas. His admiration for the Enlightenment mentality was more restrained
than that manifested by Eggleston, Robinson, Beard,
Becker, Parrington, and Curti. Persons never praised it
as enthusiastically as did these progressive historians,
and he sometimes questioned its wisdom. Persons, like
Gabriel, turned on its head the environmental technique
of suggesting how much religious doctrines and practices were drawn from, and were rooted in, secular or
material doctrines and practices. The effect of the environmental technique was to minimize the religious or
intellectual element in intrinsic dignity and to maximize the importance of the secular or material which was
suggested to be the more fundamental element. Persons, on the contrary, noted that Enlightenment secular
thought remained, in several respects, within the confines of Puritan religious thought. "Enlightened ideas,"
he commented, were principally the possession of an
elite group which was "in some respects comparable to
the regenerate Puritans."[20] Despite the pretensions of

[19] *Ibid.*, p. 92. This statement followed a discussion of the
fact that social background was relevant to positions taken by
proponents and opponents of the Great Awakening.
[20] *Ibid.*, p. 129. Leslie Stephen in the nineteenth century and
Carl Becker in the early twentieth century had, of course,

originality expressed by the Enlightenment—the word itself was created to distinguish a new age—"enlightened ideas" in religion comprised a "relatively superficial deviation" from Puritan thought, according to Persons, and he cited specifically Jefferson's completely traditional ideas of geological history. Finally, insofar as enlightened thought was different from Puritanism, Persons characterized it as "complacent." It was the function of eighteenth century Americans, "as the enlightened thinker saw it," "to exploit nature and thus achieve happiness," a view which Persons obviously thought was superficial.[21]

Persons' description of "The Mind of Nineteenth-Century Democracy: 1800-1860" stressed above all the relation of religious ideas to the democratic mind. Democratic thought accompanied the disintegration of certain earlier social class distinctions, and at the same time there occurred the development of Protestant denominationalism. These denominations "effectively Christianized" the West in "the transfer of culture from the coastal region to the watershed of the Mississippi." Religion was even more generally important, according to Persons, in furnishing the foundation for prevalent "ways of apprehending the most important truths of life." Of the three major approaches to truth prior to the 1800's, said Persons,

> it was noteworthy that in American intellectual history each of these ways to the truth was closely associated with a religious tradition. Even the secular-

stressed the subtle continuities between earlier religious thought and later rationalist thought. But the theme was central to Persons' entire interpretation of American history, as it was also to Gabriel's.

[21] *Ibid.*, pp. 117, 71, 94, 106, 76. Persons also criticized the shallow view of history held by the Enlightenment. (p. 121)

minded thinkers of the Enlightenment subscribed at least formally to the principles of deism.[22]

In the book's longest section, "The Naturalistic Mind: 1865-1929," Persons dwelled on the impact of naturalistic ideas in undermining traditional American beliefs. Writing almost two decades after the first edition of Gabriel's *The Course of American Democratic Thought*, Persons expressed, as emphatically as had Gabriel, the view that naturalistic thought posed many of the same problems for traditional American values as did totalitarianism. "Because of its traditional affiliations and commitments, the democratic mind inevitably resisted certain propositions of naturalism," Persons remarked, "especially those that bore upon the conditions of human freedom." He continued by saying that with

the rise of totalitarianism on the international scene during the second quarter of the twentieth century, Americans confronted in practical form issues that they had been debating in the intellectual realm for over half a century. It was inevitable, therefore, that a majority of them should react strongly to totalitarianism on ideological grounds, and that, consequently, certain of the naturalistic ideas should acquire a patriotic as well as a moral stigma.[23]

Although some naturalistic ideas were held by Persons to have posed threats to traditional American values, he placed great stress upon the extent to which naturalistic thinkers were intellectually committed to the traditional scheme of beliefs. "This commitment," said Persons, "compelled the naturalists to discharge their social responsibilities by attempting to understand and systematize" the conflict between old and new thought; in addition, this same commitment found ex-

[22] *Ibid.*, pp. 167, 208, 209.   [23] *Ibid.*, pp. 217-218.

pression in the "paradoxical mixture of scientific objectivity and passionate moral preachment which their thought characteristically displayed," and which "revealed ambiguous commitments that they were unable to resolve."[24] When a resolution of intellectual commitments by American thinkers ultimately occurred in the twentieth century during an era of depression and totalitarianism, the resolution was, according to Persons, in favor of traditional American values and took the form of what he called the "neodemocratic revival." Thus Persons emphasized not only the threatening amoral implications of naturalistic thought, but he stressed also the strain of traditional humane values which remained alive within it.

Persons' interpretation of the threatening aspects of naturalistic thought emphasized traditional values, such as that of an absolute morality, which risked being undercut by naturalism. He did not particularly emphasize, as did Beard, Parrington, and Curti, that naturalistic thought was threatening because it hampered social reform, but because it undercut traditional values. Thus, Persons was not thinking specifically of social reform, nor for that matter of opposition to reform, when he commented that naturalistic thought developed a determinism which comprised "a thoroughgoing repudiation of the traditional doctrine of the free individual."[25] Persons was thinking simply of the value of the free individual, which Americans had traditionally cherished. He repeatedly queried whether naturalistic thinkers were conscious of the need for developing criteria for judging value.

In his description of Watson's behavioristic psychology, for instance, Persons noted that Watson said there could eventually be devised "an experimental ethics that would tell men what behavior would be advisable in

[24] *Ibid.*, p. 221. [25] *Ibid.*, p. 224.

order to achieve desirable adjustments." But Persons added, in criticism, that Watson did not "provide the criteria for determining what a 'desirable adjustment' would be." Persons suspected that the "criteria of evaluation would probably prove to be hedonistic and intensely individualistic," although Persons added, the "ethical ends to which control would be applied did not greatly concern him [Watson]."[26]

Similarly, Persons wrote of evolutionist Minot Savage that he argued the inapplicability of all ethical standards inherited from the past. Savage believed that rather than follow traditional ethical standards, man should simply try to understand evolutionary development and place value on "that which tended to promote life." According to Savage, Persons wrote, "virtue was that which made for life or which was advantageous to men. Vice or evil was that which made for disintegration or death." Persons clearly was doubtful that Savage was facing up to the difficulty of defining standards of judgment. "The nature of the good," in Savage's eyes, was adjustment to the 'real facts' of life," which were "presumably, the material conditions and institutional circumstances in which the individual might find himself." Savage thought that such an adjustment would bring, Persons wrote, "health, happiness, and peace of mind." "Moral good was defined by Savage as consisting of equitable adjustment between man and man." Persons' customary question was asked of Savage, but there was no answer: "How the principle of equity was related to the adjustment declared to be the essence of natural good, Savage did not explain."[27] For Persons, as for Gabriel, the question of values was always present. It seemed to them impossible to minimize the importance of the question by appeals to workability, adaptation, or utility. According to Gabriel and Persons,

[26] *Ibid.*, pp. 263, 264.   [27] *Ibid.*, pp. 338-339.

even these supposedly practical tests of value left open the difficult and necessary question of determining standards for judging "workability," "adaptation," or "utility."

The concluding section of *American Minds* was devoted to "The Contemporary Neodemocratic Mind" which triumphed during and after the 1930's. "The reaction to naturalism," Persons wrote, "was controlled by the continuing appeal of the traditional American democratic ideals. It took the form of a reaffirmation of these ideals, modified somewhat in the light of modern conditions."[28]

In Persons' presentation the neodemocratic mind absorbed from naturalism certain characteristics, such as support of science and the scientific method. But despite some common beliefs, the neodemocratic mind was fundamentally in conflict with the naturalistic mind. After a long conflict during the late nineteenth and early twentieth centuries, when traditional American ideals were constantly threatened by naturalistic thought, neodemocratic ideas triumphed, due largely to events in Europe and Asia. "The rise of totalitarianism in the middle third of the twentieth century," wrote Persons, "presented Americans with the spectacle of naturalism in action." The disregard for values expressed by totalitarianism was anticipated by naturalism's lack of concern for values.

The preceding summary of Stow Persons' *American Minds* has suggested its indebtedness to the writings of Gabriel, as well as to those of Miller and even Morison. But Persons' scholarship, when compared with Commager's *The American Mind*, did not constitute simply a perpetuation of the prewar dialogue over progressive histories. The contrasts between Persons' and Commager's books were accompanied by similarities. Commager's Parringtonian zeal for social reform was per-

[28] *Ibid.*, p. 349.

meated with concern for traditional humane values, and
Commager minimized the social and economic environmental interpretation of thought expressed by Parrington and other progressive historians. If Commager had
pulled the progressive tradition into the totalitarian era
along a line which tended to converge with the writing
of a Gabriel follower like Stow Persons, Persons too
had contributed to the convergence. He expressed less
nostalgia for nineteenth century America than did Gabriel, and more unreserved praise for twentieth century
reform thought. Persons, writing in the late 1950's
after the New Deal's pragmatic reforms seemed to be
accepted into the traditional American system, did not
raise doubts, as Gabriel had earlier, concerning the
awareness of ethical considerations on the part of pragmatic philosophers. "Democracy was the central social
ideal of pragmatism," wrote Persons in his sketch of
pragmatism, which was particularly sympathetic toward Dewey. It was clear that Persons thought Dewey
consciously subscribed to, and helped perpetuate, traditional humane values in the United States. Dewey, said
Persons, was committed to a view of individuals with
"uniquely distinctive qualities," and at the same time,
"Dewey's sense of the importance of the social was also
very great."[29] The suggestion of convergence in the
interpretations of Persons and Commager was further
reinforced by Persons' concluding chapter, which emphasized the significance of civil liberties to Americans
in a totalitarian world—a topic of equal concern to Commager in the postwar years.

Finally, there was more than a hint of convergence
between Persons' and Commager's methods of writing
about ideas. Commager adopted Parrington's emphasis
upon the power of ideas, but minimized Parrington's
equal emphasis upon the socioeconomic determinism

[29] *Ibid.*, p. 402.

over ideas, and Commager described ideas with only passing attention to the environment from which they came. Persons attributed great power to thought, and he devoted almost all of his pages to descriptions of the ideas themselves. Yet, though he did not explore environmental relationships, he like Commager frequently noted the relevance of social conditions to the history of the reception and development of ideas.[30] By the 1960's, Persons placed additional emphasis upon the importance of environmental conditions, for, he wrote, "conditions modify ideas, and it is the job of the historian to find out how."[31] Thus, despite their contrasting backgrounds, Persons' and Commager's writings revealed signs of convergence.

A second sign of convergence can be seen in the postwar histories which combine an outspoken environmental interpretation of ideas with an ideological affirmation that the greatness of traditional American thought and life has been caused primarily by the American environment. These histories take the former progressive emphasis upon environmental conditioning of those ideas which they liked least, and apply an environmental interpretation to all ideas, especially to the ideas which are most admired. The role of the environment has moved, in these histories, from that of an explanation for bad ideas, as it was in progressive histories, to that of an explanation for good ideas and for the greatness of America.

Daniel Boorstin (1914—) has published the most fully developed interpretation combining an environmental explanation of American thought with a celebration of those ideas which were most responsive to environmental conditions. Boorstin, who moved ideo-

[30] See *ibid.*, pp. 88, 92, 154, 164, 171, 197, 221, 241, 277, 349-350, 400, 430.

[31] Letter from Persons to author, June 4, 1964.

logically from the political far left in the 1930's to a postwar position which applauded the course of American politics and society, emphasized the importance of the nonintellectual environment upon ideas in his histories which first appeared after the Second World War. But the nature of Boorstin's environmental interpretation of American beliefs was as different from earlier environmental interpretations as his glorification of America's past was different from the views of earlier progressive scholars. Boorstin described the American mind as a product of the New World environment; a virgin land, innocent of European history, decisively influenced American beliefs. The heart of Boorstin's environmental interpretation was thus "The Influence of America on the Mind," as he titled the first chapter of *The Lost World of Thomas Jefferson* in 1948.[32]

The vast continent presented continual problems and opportunities which structured the necessary response. "When the intellectually and spiritually mature man of Europe first settled in America," Boorstin wrote, "he was forced to relive the childhood of the race, to confront once again the primitive and intractable wilderness of his cave-dwelling ancestors." The only successful response possible was a pragmatic one. Success demanded "not thought but action, not ideas but things."[33] From this first sketch based upon the Jeffersonian mind,

[32] New York, 1948, reprinted Boston, 1960. In this introductory chapter in 1948 Boorstin echoed Frederick Jackson Turner and anticipated Louis Hartz's *The Liberal Tradition in America*, New York, 1955. The emphasis upon returning to primitive living conditions was Turnerian, but the emphasis upon the lack of European history was Hartzian. Boorstin wrote in the same chapter that America "had never even experienced the Middle Ages." The American Revolution, he continued, was unlike the French: "On this continent there was no Bastille and no Versailles Palace to symbolize the enemy; nor was there a mature and outspoken conservative philosophy to require an outspoken enemy." (pp. 6, 7)

[33] *The Lost World of Thomas Jefferson*, pp. 3, 7.

Boorstin went on to a projected three-volume history of the unfolding of pragmatic American responses to immediate challenges. Consistent with this pragmatic view Boorstin, like Commager, stressed the consequences of ideas in behavior. In the first volume of the planned trilogy, *The Americans: The Colonial Experience*, published in 1958, he made clear that not only were American ideas best understood by relating them to immediate environmental conditions, but that the best ideas emerged in this fashion. Boorstin's method of analysis thus merged with his ideological position. The making of a great modern nation was the perspective from which he judged colonial thought. Ideas which successfully coped with pressing problems were implicitly or explicitly praised; abstract, rigid, doctrinaire, otherworldly, and utopian ideas imported from Europe and usually less useful in solving immediate colonial problems were criticized. The pragmatic test was applied by Boorstin. His assumed standard of workability was the making of a nation.

New England Puritans were freshly viewed as untheoretical and un-contemplative. "Theirs was not a philosophic enterprise; they were, first and foremost, community-builders," said Boorstin. The very fact of theological orthodoxy allowed them freedom from theological enquiry. "American Puritans were hardly more distracted from their practical tasks by theology and metaphysics than we are today." Puritanism was practical, and it earned Boorstin's commendation. "The failure of New England Puritans to develop a theory of toleration, or even freely to examine the question," he wrote, "was not in all ways a weakness":

Had they spent as much of their energy in debating with each other as did their English contemporaries, they might have lacked the single mindedness needed to overcome the dark, unpredictable perils of a wilderness. They might have merited praise as precursors of modern liberalism, but they might never have helped found a nation.[34]

Boorstin applied the same stern test of practical worldly success to Pennsylvania's colonial Quakers, but they failed to pass the test because of their unflinching adherence to a body of beliefs which were held irrespective of environmental conditions. "Never has there been a better example of the futility of trying to govern by absolutes, and of the price of self-deception paid by those who try to do so," he wrote. By contrast, colonial Virginians "possessed a sense of full-bodied economic and political reality," he continued, and it was one of "their greatest strengths" that they had "no particular genius for the abstractions of closet-philosophy": "How irrelevant to look to the bookish prospectuses of English or French political theorists—of Locke, Montesquieu, or Rousseau—to explain Virginia's political enthusiasms!"[35] The earlier progressive historians would have applauded Boorstin's emphasis upon the environmental influences over thought, and applauded too his judgment of ideas on the basis of their consequences. But Boorstin's resulting histories were radically unlike Beard's, Parrington's, and Curti's. The environmental approach was not used by Boorstin as a weapon to locate and, perhaps, to undercut ideas inimical to reform, but instead to explain American development irrespective of reform considerations. Reform was no longer the central subject matter, and the progressive scheme of values no more supplied the yardstick by which the practical efficacy of thought was measured. The progressive accent upon ideas as instruments to

[34] Boorstin, *The Americans: The Colonial Experience*, New York, 1958. Vintage edn., 1964, p. 9. The second volume, *The Americans: The National Experience*, New York, was published in 1965.

[35] *Ibid.*, pp. 47, 122.

solve immediate problems was joined with a mid-twentieth century concern for national strength at a time of international conflict.

Boorstin's writings have shown a convergence of formerly divergent strains in intellectual histories in the sense that he has assimilated environmental interpretation into an un-progressive ideological position. This is not to deny that each strain was transformed by Boorstin. The environmental interpretation featuring the influence of a virgin but wealthy land became an explanation for consensus among almost all Americans, rather than an explanation of social conflict between "haves" and "have-nots." The traditionalism of an un-progressive ideological position became the traditionalism of a pragmatic past.

Another example of convergence among formerly divergent strains, as well as an example of an important new direction in the writing of histories of ideas, can be seen in each of several studies which link politics and ideas. The writings of Arthur Schlesinger, Jr. (1917–), Richard Hofstadter (1916–), and Eric Goldman (1915–) have criticized various aspects of the progressive ideological position, but they have related ideas closely to the political, social, and economic contexts in which the ideas appeared. They have critically questioned how values are derived from a purely relativistic pragmatism, but they have described ideas in terms of pragmatic political consequences. Each has written of modern American reform thought and action from a perspective provided in large part by mid-twentieth century European totalitarianism, but each has expressed a loyalty to the reform tradition.

Arthur Schlesinger, Jr., has perpetuated many characteristics of progressive histories. He has written of ideas in their social contexts, and he has not written detailed internal analyses of ideas; he has preferred to

study reformers, reform thought, and reform movements; as citizen and scholar, he has consistently expressed partisan reform sympathies. But despite these
similarities with earlier progressive histories, Schlesinger's writings have not been the same as those of his
reform predecessors. He related ideas closely to their
social contexts not to "explain" how the ideas arose but,
like Commager, in order to explore their consequences
in behavior. Schlesinger emphasized the pragmatic cast
of the American mind but, again like Commager, emphasized equally the traditional values underneath American utilitarianism.

The central theme of Schlesinger's major work, *Age
of Roosevelt*,[36] still incomplete, has been the New Deal's
willingness to experiment *within* the constitutional,
democratic traditions of the United States. In the background of the volumes has been the lawlessness and immorality of European totalitarianism. In the foreground
Schlesinger has placed the Rooseveltian forces in conflict with extremists on Right and Left, as well as more
moderate opponents to the New Deal. Roosevelt's greatest success consequently was not the degree to which
he coped with economic depression, but rather the degree to which he coped with economic depression within
the limits of traditional American values.

American politics and politicians assumed a significance in Schlesinger's scholarship exceeding that of
public decision-making. The imperfection of politics, its
give-and-take, as well as its peaceful discourse within
established rules, represented both the limitations and
the accomplishments of man in society. The failings of
human nature prevented utopia on earth and rendered
unwise attempts at radical reform. Schlesinger criticized
intellectual progressivism insofar as it expressed overly

[36] Arthur Schlesinger, Jr., *Age of Roosevelt*, 3 vols., Boston,
1957-1960.

optimistic conceptions of human nature, or uncritical faith in progress, or otherworldly pacifism. On the other hand, moderate reform led by an Abraham Lincoln, a Theodore Roosevelt, and a Franklin Roosevelt, with the support of consensus, received Schlesinger's approbation. The "vital center" he championed after World War Two drew upon historic reform deeds for a usable past, but drew its understanding of present prospects from a Niebuhrian view of man.[37]

Richard Hofstadter's writings featured ideas more centrally than did Schlesinger's, but Hofstadter too usually linked states of mind to behavior. And, like Schlesinger, Hofstadter wrote out of sympathy for American reform but raised serious questions concerning its intellectual temper.

In *The American Political Tradition*, published in 1948, Hofstadter emphasized the social and economic environment behind political thought as much as any progressive history had ever done, but he did not repeat the characteristic progressive emphasis upon conflict between "haves" and "have-nots," nor between "backward-looking" and "forward-looking" ideas. Instead, he emphasized the extent of consensus on fundamental questions by participants in the American political tradition, a consensus "bounded by the horizons of property and enterprise": "However much at odds on specific issues, the major political traditions have shared a belief in the rights of property, the philosophy of individualism, the value of competition; they have accepted the economic virtues of capitalist culture as necessary qualities of man."[38] It was possible for progressives to miss the chal-

[37] Schlesinger's ideological position was elaborated most fully in *The Vital Center*, Boston, 1949. His major works included *Orestes A. Brownson*, Boston, 1939; *The Age of Jackson*, Boston, 1945.

[38] *The American Political Tradition*, New York, 1948, Vintage edn., 1954, p. viii.

lenge of this interpretation to older progressive views by overemphasizing the fact that Hofstadter remained unfriendly to the capitalistic environment and had merely moved his perspective from the "left" of the political system to a position outside it. Nevertheless, the challenge was real and Hofstadter was closer to Boorstin than to Beard. It is true that all Hofstadter did was to alter the progressive emphasis upon conflict between two traditions to an emphasis upon the unity of one. But this descriptive statement of consensus, despite its origin in a vantage point outside the American economic order, and obviously unfriendly to it, became peculiarly susceptible to new evaluations under the pressure of the postwar climate of opinion. By 1955, in *Age of Reform*, Hofstadter studied the modern political reform mentality with markedly more sympathy for the political temper which had accommodated itself to social and economic realities. Hofstadter seemed by the 1950's almost to have backed his way into considerable approval for the pragmatic American mind which he had first approached in a spirit of criticism in the 1940's. However he got there, Hofstadter had reached a position which at least faintly resembled Boorstin's celebration of pragmatic American thought, and which was critical of American thought that seemed utopian and visionary.[39]

Eric Goldman's *Rendezvous with Destiny* also surveyed modern political reform with sympathy, yet raised fundamental questions concerning aspects of reform thought. Goldman asked whether the relativism used by intellectual progressives in their attack upon the foundations of "conservative" principles (as in their economic interpretations) was not perhaps too successful

---

[39] Hofstadter's major histories included *Social Darwinism in American Thought*, Philadelphia, 1944; *The American Political Tradition*, New York, 1948; *Age of Reform*, 1955; *Anti-Intellectualism in American Life*, New York, 1963.

in undermining foundations of belief. That, in short, absolute belief in reform principles fell along with absolute belief in nonreform principles, and that no principles remained except those held on purely pragmatic grounds. Goldman's specific criticism, namely, that intellectual progressives were too relativistic, was different from Hofstadter's criticism. But despite the difference in substantive interpretation of progressivism, Goldman, as much as Hofstadter and Schlesinger, was a reformer in an age of totalitarianism, when the reformer's more customary fear of not enough change was matched by the fear of too much change.[40]

The signs of convergence in contemporary writings, insofar as they are related to the postwar climate of opinion, are continuing examples of the involvement by American historians in the world outside that of "pure" scholarship. From the first colonial chroniclers to the professional historians today, most scholars who have treated ideas in American histories have been "of the world" and have described ideas mainly by looking at their consequences in human affairs. Whether or not consciously pragmatic in their interpretation of ideas, most American historians have not chosen to analyze the content and structure of ideas intensively as would, say, a philosopher. This predilection for approaching thought through its effect upon the world of action may sometimes have reflected an assumption that American ideas lacked sufficient complexity for sustained philosophical analysis. But more important, surely, has been the assumption of most American historians that *all* ideas are most meaningful when viewed with reference to their worldly consequences.

Most of the disagreements between progressive historians and their critics during the first half of the twentieth century, except for those over general ideo-

[40] Eric Goldman, *Rendezvous with Destiny*, New York, 1952.

logical position, were over the alleged environmental origin of ideas and the ideological inferences to be drawn from the environmental interpretation of the origin of ideas. There was little disagreement that ideas had consequences and could be studied with reference to their impact upon the worldly environment. Critics of environmental interpretation of the origin of ideas and of the intellectual progressivism which ordinarily accompanied it, joined with the progressive scholars in emphasizing the pragmatic consequences of thought.[41] Because American historians have been more common-sensical than rigorously analytic, however, their interest in the practical effect of thought upon society has been more often asserted than demonstrated. Their craft has been more "humanistic" than "scientific," and they have most characteristically shied away from intensive analyses of the influence of ideas in society, just as they have refrained from intensive analyses of the content and structure of ideas as abstractions.

The pragmatic, common-sense, unsystematic approach

[41] Among recent historians discussed above, only Boorstin and Hofstadter emphasized the environmental origins of ideas as well as the other side of the pragmatic emphasis, the effect upon the environment of the ideas. Hofstadter's work most clearly resembles the "rigid" environmental interpretations of the progressive historians, and he adopts a psychological rather than an economic formula. See Hofstadter's "status revolution" explanation of progressive ideas in *Age of Reform;* see his "psychic crisis" explanation of imperialist ideas in "Manifest Destiny and the Philippines," in Daniel Aaron, ed., *America in Crisis,* New York, 1952, pp. 173-200.

Another prominent historian of ideas who has perpetuated both sides of the pragmatic interpretation is John Higham, in *Strangers in the Land,* New Brunswick, 1955. He, like Hofstadter, has emphasized the psychological environment of ideas. Higham's (1920————) scholarship constitutes a good example of convergence. His writings blend environmental interpretations with analyses of the content of ideas; in substantive interpretation, he has been a friendly critic of progressivism. See Higham, "The Cult of the 'American Consensus,'" *Commentary,* XXVII (February 1959), 93-100.

of American historians of thought, expressed in panoramic surveys of ideas in the United States, brought the prestige of the study of the history of ideas to an apparent high point by the middle years of the twentieth century. But signs of new directions have appeared in postwar histories which suggest that historians no longer feel comfortable attempting to cover all, or even a large part, of America's past. The present hesitation, however, is not solely a matter of shrunken scope. It is a matter of reduced terrain plus some new avenues by which to approach ideas. Goldman, Hofstadter, and Schlesinger have joined ideas and modern political reform movements, which is to say that they have selected topics and then studied the ideas which emerged in relation to those topics. Such an approach suggests, from the standpoint of intellectual history, topic specialization and a rejection of the panoramic sweep. It may also suggest a rejection of a panoramic sweep *which is organized around ideas*. The historian who moved over the course of American thought with the inclusive net of a Beard, a Parrington or a Curti, no longer dominates the scene. The historian of the specialized topic, one part of which includes ideas, is becoming characteristic. In other words, lack of a systematic discipline of the study of the history of ideas is at the present time accompanied by many historical investigations of ideas which are carried out in piecemeal fashion by scholars of diverse interests. In this sense, American historians today seem to attach more importance to ideas in history than to histories of ideas.

The two most important new interdisciplinary directions charted in the study of American ideas during the last quarter-century have also contributed to the movement away from classic large-scale histories of ideas. One interdisciplinary influence, the least significant one to date, has come from the postwar social sciences, and can be summarized as a concern with quantification. The influence of the social sciences can be seen in the charge that historians describe ideas, the people who hold ideas, and the causal importance of ideas, in too impressionistic and unsystematic a manner. Of particular relevance to studies of public opinion and less complex patterns of thought, the concern with quantification has been expressed in pleas for "content analysis," for ascertaining what constitutes "representative" ideas at a given time and place, and for approaching states of mind through groups or collective biography.[42] It is too early to tell how much of an impact upon the writing of intellectual histories this concern with quantification will ultimately have.

The second and much more immediately important recent interdisciplinary influence has been the American Studies movement. Generally interdisciplinary in theory, but mainly literary in practice, the American Studies movement has made its most obvious impact in formal academic programs of American Studies, and in American literature courses taught in English departments. The books which have emerged from American Studies programs to date have been characterized by sophisticated literary analysis and most have focused mainly on writers of imaginative literature.[43]

[42] For an example of the "content analysis" of ideas in American history, see Louis Schneider and Sanford Dornbusch, *Popular Religion*, Chicago, 1958. For a discussion of the need to erect criteria to determine "representative" ideas, see Lee Benson, "Causation and the Civil War," *History and Theory*, I (No. 2, 1961), 172-175. For a study of a group mind, by use of the concept of "social role," see Thomas Cochran, *Railroad Leaders, 1845-1890: The Business Mind in Action*, Cambridge, 1953.

[43] The outstanding books which have emerged from the program include: Henry Nash Smith, *Virgin Land: The American West as Symbol and Myth*, Cambridge, 1950; R. W. B. Lewis, *The American Adam*, Chicago, 1955; John William Ward, *Andrew Jackson: Symbol for an Age*, New York, 1955; David

Convergence and New Directions

As might be expected, the influence of these books has varied depending on the extent to which scholars base their study of the history of ideas upon imaginative literature. Historians of ideas outside of English and American Studies departments have tended to value most highly those "American Studies" books based least upon imaginative literature. The future influence of the American Studies movement upon historians generally, and therefore upon American intellectual histories, will probably increase if the social science content of American Studies programs increases. Despite the humanistic bias of historians and their tendency to reinterpret humanistically the knowledge which they acquire from the social sciences, historians nevertheless remain at least as much a part of the social sciences as of the literary humanities. Most American historians, even those interested in the history of ideas, have revealed a tendency to lean in the direction of a synthesis provided either by politics or by broad social movements.

Whatever the eventual influence of the American Studies movement or of the concern with quantification on the study of ideas in history, it appears that for the present the history of ideas in America will be approached by scholars through relatively specialized studies, some of which closely link politics and ideas. One can only conjecture whether the ultimate result will be new panoramic histories of ideas which synthesize specialized scholarship or simply a vast collection of specialized and fragmentary studies of ideas in history.

Brion Davis, *Homicide in American Fiction, 1798-1860: A Study in Social Values*, Ithaca, 1957; William R. Taylor, *Cavalier and Yankee: The Old South and American National Character*, New York, 1961; Leo Marx, *The Machine in the Garden: Technology and the Pastoral Idea in America*, New York, 1964. See also the articles in the official journal of American Studies, *American Quarterly*, 1949–.

Appendixes

APPENDIX A

The Increase in Concern during the
Twentieth Century with the History of Ideas

American historians have commonly remarked that the study of the history of ideas has increased in popularity during the 1900's to the point of general academic acceptance and prestige. "By the time World War II began, historians of the American past were no longer so suspicious of the academic standing of intellectual history," wrote Harvey Wish in 1960. In fact, he continued, "they were often quite willing to give enthusiastic praise to the intellectual historian."[1] Another scholar, Thomas Cochran, surveying in 1949 the historical writings of the 1940's, singled out "the historian's invasion of the field of American intellectual history" as comprising "perhaps the outstanding cumulative achievement of the last decade."[2] By 1961, John Higham, when discussing "the increasing popularity of intellectual history," noted that "the pioneering is over": "the historical guild has accepted the intellectual historian and respects his work. The old fogeyism that used to breathe distrust of ideas, unless they were treated as so many inert facts, no longer weighs heavily upon us."[3]

[1] Harvey Wish, *The American Historian*, New York, 1960, p. 293.
[2] Thomas Cochran, "A Decade of American Histories," *Pennsylvania Magazine of History and Biography*, LXXIII (April 1949), 153.
[3] John Higham, "American Intellectual History: A Critical Appraisal," *American Quarterly*, XIII (Summer Supplement 1961), 230.

Another historian, John Caughey, writing after World War Two, asserted that his survey of the complete file of the *Mississippi Valley Historical Review* from 1914 to 1957 had revealed to him the appearance in that journal's pages of the

Concern with the History of Ideas

These statements by historians asserting the increased practice, acceptance, and prestige of the study of the history of ideas among professional historians present impressive evidence because they are based upon first-hand observations. The statements presumably derive from impressions not only of what is being published, but also of what is being taught and talked about. As such they are undoubtedly accurate.

Out of curiosity to determine whether these statements by historians could be corroborated quantitatively in various areas of historical activity, I have made crude attempts to measure the relative decrease, stability, or increase of attention paid to ideas between the late nineteenth and the mid-twentieth century.

To take a first area of historical activity, and one not filled entirely by professional historians, two dictionaries of American biography were surveyed. It was ascertained that there was an appreciable increase, between the dictionary published in the late 1890's and the one published as late as the 1930's, in the number of biographical entries devoted to historical personages whose lives have traditionally been grist for the intellectual historian's mill, rather than that of, say, the military or political or economic historian. That is, a comparison of the index of the *National Cyclopaedia of American Biography*, covering its volumes published from 1891 to 1894, with the index of the *Dictionary of American Biography*, covering its volumes published between 1928 and 1937, reveals that there were approximately 50 per cent more biographical sketches in the *DAB* designated as "scholars," "philosophers," "authors," "reformers," "scientists," "educators," "journal-

---

"discovery of intellectual history" during the twentieth century by contributors. See "Under Our Strange Device: A Review of the Review," *Mississippi Valley Historical Review*, XLIV (December 1957), 521.

ists," "editors," "clergy," and "jurists," rather than "soldiers," "politicians," "lawyers," "doctors," "merchants," and others. These "intellectual" categories climbed from slightly more than one-third of the total number of entries in the *Cyclopaedia* of the 1890's, to somewhat over one-half of the total in the later *DAB*.[4]

A second and quite different area of historical activity, this one populated solely by academic historians, is the teaching of college history courses. The evidence here is overwhelming that college courses in American intellectual history have become commonplace by mid-century. From James Harvey Robinson's sole course in intellectual history in (and not *of*) the United States at Columbia in 1904 (entitled "Intellectual History of Western Europe"),[5] the situation has changed by mid-

[4] The sample used in the comparison of the two multivolumed dictionaries consisted of every seventh letter: A, G, M, S, Y. This meant that over 6,000 names from the new *DAB* were compared with slightly under 1,500 names from the old *National Cyclopaedia*, which was a smaller compendium covering the period up to 1894. The percentage distribution between "intellectual" and "nonintellectual" entries was quite consistent for each letter sampled: the range in the letters from the old *National Cyclopaedia* was only 35% to 36% "intellectuals"; from the new *DAB*, the percentage of "intellectual" entries ranged among the letters sampled from 54% to 49%. Out of a total sample of 6,033 from the new *DAB*, 3,138 or 52% were in "intellectual" categories; out of 1,426 sampled from the old *National Cyclopaedia*, 503 or 35% were in "intellectual" groups.

A question may legitimately be raised as to whether the indicated classification changes in biographical dictionaries can be equated with a change in interest concerning the history of ideas. It may be, for example, that the biographical entries in the two dictionaries are in some cases the same individuals but merely entered under different classifications. If this occurred often enough, the comparative evidence summarized above would suggest changes in editors' classifications, as much or more than increased interest in the history of ideas on the part of the scholars who wrote the biographical sketches. But even editors' changes are suggestive.

[5] Luther Hendricks traces the course evolution year by year in his *James Harvey Robinson: Teacher of History*, New York, 1946, pp. 13-15.

century so that almost all large colleges and universities offer courses on the history of American ideas.[6] Presumably there has continued to be an increase in American "intellectual history" courses since World War Two, judging from the increased offerings in the "cultural-intellectual" history of all areas.[7]

[6] This statement is based upon a survey of the following rather diverse group of college catalogues for the years 1959-1963: Antioch, American University, Boston University, Bucknell, California at Berkeley, Cornell, Dartmouth, Denver, Florida, Georgetown, Harvard, Johns Hopkins, State University of Iowa, Kansas State College of Pittsburg, Michigan, Michigan State, New Mexico at Albuquerque, New York University (Washington Square College), North Carolina, Oklahoma, Oregon State, Pennsylvania, Pittsburgh, Princeton, Sacramento State, San Jose State, San Diego State, Smith, Syracuse, University of Southern California, Tennessee, Texas, Vanderbilt, Vassar, Vermont, Washington (Seattle), Washington State (Pullman), Wayne State, Wisconsin. Of this list, more than three dozen, only Georgetown, Vermont, and New York University (Washington Square College) offered no courses described as the history of American ideas or intellectual history. Judging from this list of schools, however, courses are still almost as likely to be entitled "*Social and* Intellectual" as to be called solely intellectual history or the history of ideas. California at Berkeley, Harvard, Johns Hopkins, State University of Iowa, Michigan, Michigan State, North Carolina, Princeton, Smith, Texas, Washington, and Wayne State, for example, call their course solely "Intellectual History," or "American Ideas," or "American Thought." But "Social and Intellectual" history is the name given to the course at Dartmouth, Oklahoma, Ohio State, Pennsylvania, Syracuse, and "Thought and Culture" at Wisconsin.

[7] In a survey of 77 American universities (all of which grant Ph.D.'s in the field of history) which has recently been published, 30 added courses between 1948 and 1958 to their offerings in the area of "cultural-intellectual" history. This is not restricted to American history, of course. (See Dexter Perkins and John Snell, *The Education of Historians in the United States*, New York, 1962, p. 124.) The only field revealing a greater number of additional courses was Asian history generally. In a parallel survey of 502 four-year colleges during the same decade, 1948-1958, 11% added courses in "cultural-intellectual" history whereas only .2% dropped courses in "cultural-intellectual" history. (*Ibid.*, p. 74.)

A third area in which one might expect to ascertain comparison in the amount of attention paid to the history of ideas is that of multivolumed histories of the United States. The recent beginning (in the 1950's) of the publication of the New American Nation Series by Harpers affords an opportunity to compare it with the original series published a half-century ago. Such an examination reveals the addition of volumes devoted to "intellectual" topics and thus offers another example of the increased concern during the 1900's with intellectual activity in the American past.[8]

A fourth area of possible comparison is that of guides to primary and secondary historical literature. In 1912 Frederick Jackson Turner joined with Albert Bushnell

[8] Volumes added to the New American Nation Series (with no counterpart in the original series), which focused in large part on intellectual life, were: Louis B. Wright, *The Cultural Life of the American Colonies, 1607-1763*, New York, 1957, (see Chapters 4, "Diversity of Religions," 5, "Zeal for Education," 6, "Books, Libraries, and Learning," 7, "Literary Production: North and South," 8, "Scientific Interest and Observation"); Russel B. Nye, *The Cultural Life of the New Nation, 1776-1830*, New York, 1960 (see Chapters 1, "The Foundations of American Thought," 2, "The Roots of an American Faith," 3, "The New World of American Science," 7, "The Training of Free Minds," 8, "The Idea of an American University," 9, "The Building of an American Church," 10, "The Great Revival of American Faith," 11, "The Quest for a National Literature," 12, "The American Style in Architecture and Art"). These volumes did not mainly trace ideas, but rather sketched the nature of intellectual life. The following volume of the new series placed a noticeably greater emphasis on ideas and intellectual life than did its (roughly) parallel volume in the original series: Clement Eaton, *The Growth of Southern Civilization, 1790-1860*, New York, 1961. (See Chapter 13, "The Southern Mind in 1860." Eaton wrote in his Preface that his original manuscript included two additional chapters on "education, literature, and the fine arts" which were omitted because of space limitations. Treatment of the Old South was dispersed among several pre-Civil War volumes in the original series, but there was nowhere a separate chapter on the "Southern mind.")

Hart and Edward Channing to bring up to date their 1896 *Guide to the Study of American History*. The 1912 *Guide to the Study and Reading of American History*,[9] like its predecessor, had no category specifically for "intellectual life," or "ideas." Under the category, "Development of American Society, 1820-1860," and "American Society in the Twentieth Century," "intellectual" entries (references to scholarly or primary works) were given in certain areas: "Intellectual Organization," "Educational Progress," "Literature," "Religious Movement," and "Reforms" for a total of approximately 4 pages out of a total of approximately 350 pages of references to scholarly works. The 1955 *Harvard Guide to American History* revised and expanded the old guide, avowedly making room "for such new interests as social and intellectual history."[10] Consistent with this plan, the new *Harvard Guide* demarcated specific "intellectual life" categories for most chronological periods, and continuously throughout the nineteenth and twentieth centuries. Of a total of approximately 300 pages, approximately 18 pages were devoted to references explicitly titled "intellectual life." This was more than five times the proportion of space allotted explicitly to "intellectual life" in the 1912 *Guide*.

A fifth piece of evidence suggesting increased interest in the history of ideas is the founding of scholarly journals. Several journals have published articles concerning the history of ideas, whether only in part American in focus, such as the *Western Humanities Review* (1947——), or solely American and even regional in focus, such as the *New England Quarterly* (1928——). The *American Quarterly* (1949——), has been exclusively interested in American Studies,

[9] Boston.
[10] Co-edited by Oscar Handlin, Arthur M. Schlesinger, Samuel Eliot Morison, Frederick Merk, Arthur M. Schlesinger, Jr., and Paul Buck. Cambridge.

and much of its content has contributed to the history of intellectual life in the United States. Although only in part focused on American subjects, the founding of the *Journal of the History of Ideas* (1940——) was a further example of the increased concern for the study of thought in the twentieth century.

Only one index of historical activity fails to yield the same conclusion. The American Historical Association's *Writings on American History*, collected almost every year since 1902, reveals no significant increase during the twentieth century in the number of writings listed under categories traditionally encompassed by "history of ideas" or "intellectual history." The volume of *Writings* for 1918 listed, according to my rough tabulations, approximately 15 per cent of its total books and articles on American history under the categories "religious," "educational," "fine arts," "literature," "music," and "science." The approximate percentages for 1923, 1928, 1936, 1939-40, 1948, 1949, 1950, 1951, 1952, and 1954 were, respectively, 13, 14, 17, 19, 9, 12, 14, 18, 16, and 17. There is a gradual increase in percentage before World War Two, but a surprising failure to maintain that increase afterwards. Over the whole period, if my tally of the books and articles is correct, there is no appreciable increase in the categories relevant to the history of American intellectual life.[11] It is true that after World War Two new subdivisions appeared, including "philosophy," "folklore," "theater," and "technology," which, together with the old subdivisions of "religious," "educational," "fine arts," "literature," "music," and "science," all appear now under the new major category of "cultural history." The creation of the separate category of "cultural history," including the specified subdivisions above, may indeed represent a cer-

[11] *Writings on American History*, 1902——, issued as a part of the annual reports of the American Historical Association.

tain coming-of-age and recognition by the Association bibliophiles, but it is noteworthy both that the new category was named "cultural" and not "intellectual" history and especially that there is no increase of items listed under the category.

Despite the failure of the *Writings on American History* to show any increased concern during the 1900's for ideas and intellectual life in historical study, it would appear that the other sources consulted—dictionaries of American biography, college course offerings, multivolume histories of the United States, scholarly journals, and historical guides—offer solid evidence in support of the previously quoted statements by historians themselves to the effect that the twentieth century has seen a dramatic increase in the concern for ideas and for intellectual life in the study of the American past.

APPENDIX B

Essay on Historiographical Scholarship

No formal bibliography is given because the text itself discusses the writings of historians. What is provided here is an additional brief commentary on writings concerning intellectual histories or histories of ideas, and a discussion of certain historiographical problems. Speaking generally, there are two kinds of historiography which may or may not be joined in the same piece of scholarship. One kind focuses on substantive and methodological questions in the writing of history, and usually stems from the author's desire to improve, or to show the improvement of, written histories. This type of historiography is, quite properly, by and for the guild. It serves a pragmatic function for a developing scholarly discipline. Howard K. Beale's well-known "What Historians Have Said About the Causes of the Civil War," *Social Science Research Council Bulletin 54, Theory and Practice in Historical Study*, New York, 1946, is representative of this approach. The emphasis is upon the increased knowledge of later historians, the new uses of evidence, and newly found source materials. Changing interpretations of historians are related to, and to this extent explained by, new evidence.

A second kind of historiography focuses on written histories as themselves documents in the history of ideas, just as other writings of a given period are used to reveal climates of opinion or the spirit of an age. These historiographical studies usually relate historians' interpretations to ideological positions rather than to uses of evidence, and they therefore suggest a "relativistic" instead of a "progressive" view of changing historical interpretations. Less useful to scholars who want to know how to write "better" histories, historiography conceived as the history of ideas is of most interest to nonspecialists, or to specialists who choose to take a more detached view of their specialty. Thomas J. Pressly's *Americans Interpret Their Civil War,* Princeton, 1954, represents this approach, as Beale's essay on the same subject exemplifies the "new evidence" approach.

Pressly, in a new introduction to the 1962 paperback edition of *Americans Interpret Their Civil War,* offers a clear and sympathetic statement of the two kinds of historiography, and he suggests the desirability of historiographical works which would combine the two approaches. Surveys of broad sweeps of historical writing, such as Harvey Wish's *The American Historian,* New York, 1960, sometimes summarize both kinds of historiography for which Pressly calls (studies of historians' evidence-methods, and of historians' climates of opinion), but such surveys are necessarily brief.

Scholars interested in the writing of American histories of ideas have been fortunate in having John Higham's learned and thoughtful articles on the subject. Higham has touched most often on problems of method, but he has also discussed the social thought of various historians of ideas in the past. See "The Rise of American Intellectual History," *American Historical Review,* LVI (April 1951), 453-471, for a survey of the topic. Higham dealt with certain problems of method in more detail in "Intellectual History and Its Neighbors," *Journal of the History of Ideas,* XV (June 1954), 339-347. In "American Intellectual History: A Critical Appraisal," *American Quarterly,* XIII (Summer Supplement 1961), 219-233, he related problems of method to climates of opinion. Although Higham concludes that in practice there is an anarchy of purposes and definitions among historians of ideas, he holds out hope for agreement upon a fundamental aim which justifies the history of ideas. He suggests that "the largest distinctive aim" of historians of ideas "is to describe and explain the spirit of an age," an aim which is distinguishable from general history and from any other single scholarly specialty. For various expressions of the same opinion that the definition of the history of ideas is an investigation of the spirit of an age or the climate of opinion, see the following statements by leading practitioners (who, however, work upon European subjects rather than American): Franklin L. Baumer, "Intellectual History and Its Problems," *Journal of Modern History*, XXI (September 1949), 191-203; John C. Greene, "Objectives and Methods in Intellectual History," *Mississippi Valley Historical Review*, XLIV (June 1957), 58-74; H. Stuart Hughes, *Consciousness and Society*, New York, 1958, p. 8. While this joint support for studying the history of ideas in a search for the spirit of an age represents a leading view among avowed historians of ideas, whether of American or of European subjects, it would be hazardous to attempt to describe more precisely what that view means to its adherents. I am not aware of any consensus among American historians, for instance, on such questions as whether "elite" or "popular" thought best reveals the climate of opinion; whether imaginative literature or advertising is a better source of evidence; whether "popular" thought is more or less susceptible to precise analysis than highly philosophical speculations; whether an explicit dialogue of opinion or an underlying base of assumption is the more "real" expression of a spirit of an age. With respect to such questions as these, scholars as a body are undecided, and moreover they are undecided over whether they ought to decide. For a recent statement of some of the existing disagreements among American historians of ideas, and an attempt to resolve them, see Rush Welter, "The History of Ideas in America: An Essay in Redefinition," *Journal of American History*, LI (March 1965), 599-614.

For other recent essays on the history of the writing of American histories of ideas see: Arthur Bestor, "Intellectual History to 1900," in William Cartwright and Richard Watson, Jr., eds., *Interpreting and Teaching American History*, 31st yearbook of the National Council for the Social Studies, Washington, 1961, pp. 133-155; Arthur Ekirch, *American Intellectual History*, publication of the American Historical Association's Service Center for Teachers of History, New York, 1963.

CHAPTER ONE:

Early American Chroniclers and Historians, 1600's-1800's

The first few pages mention a mere dozen or so of the chroniclers and historians from Bradford to Bancroft. The generalization offered—that the colonists assumed men's beliefs made an impact upon human affairs—is supported by quotations almost exclusively from those writers who discussed New England. By focusing upon New England writings, I am following a bias of historians honored by time, and rooted in the fact that most chronicles and histories come from the Northeast.

There is little scholarly comment on the colonial writers' treatment of ideas, but there are several items on the ideas of the chroniclers themselves, and on their histories. There are two surveys of American histories which cover all periods: Michael Kraus, *A History of American History*, New York, 1937, revised as *The Writing of American History*, Norman, 1953; a more recent and better survey is Harvey Wish, *The American Historian*, New York, 1960. Devoted mainly to the historians discussed in the text are: J. Franklin Jameson, *The History of Historical Writing in America*, Boston, 1891, Chapters 1-2; Samuel Eliot Morison, *The Puritan Pronaos: Studies in the Intellectual Life of New England*, New York, 1936 (reprinted as *The Intellectual Life of Colonial New England*, Ithaca, 1956), Chapter 8; Kenneth Murdock, *Literature and Theology in Colonial New England*, Cambridge, 1949, Chapter 3; Murdock, "William Hubbard and the Providential Interpretation of History," *Proceedings of the American Antiquarian Society*, Worcester, Mass., 1943, Vol. 52, Part I, pp. 15-37; Murdock, "Clio in the Wilderness: History and Biography in Puritan New England," *Church History*, xxiv (1955), 221-238; Richard Dunn, "Seventeenth-Century English Historians of America," in James Morton Smith, ed., *Seventeenth-Century America*, Chapel Hill, 1959, pp. 195-225.

Bancroft appears in the text as a latter-day colonial chronicler because of my narrow inquiry concerning his treatment of ideas—in this respect he was not different from his predecessors. In other respects outside the scope of this book, he was a more modern and a more important historian. See Russel B. Nye, *George Bancroft: Brahmin Rebel*, New York, 1944; John S. Bassett, *Middle-Group of American Historians*, New York, 1917; Watt Stewart, "George Bancroft," in *Marcus Jernegan Essays in American Historiography*, Chicago, 1937, pp. 1-24.

As the text indicates, the new European and American interest in the history of ideas during the later 1800's was one development among several simultaneous and related developments in historical scholarship. It was at the same time urged that histories should: tell of common men as well as great men; describe all aspects of life and not only the political; emulate modern science; tell the story of scientific thought; and contribute to the welfare of men in the present. Democracy and science thus joined to stimulate the study of the history of thought.

Under this covering summary, however, were many paths. Though they all fed the study of the history of ideas at some point, the paths were different and had various consequences for writing histories of thought. Social histories, for example, opened up new subject matter for exploration, including popular beliefs, and they gave a democratic rather than an elitist bias to those explorations. Because social history has been defined customarily as comprising virtually all man's activities except for matters of political and military policy, the history of opinion falls within the scope of social history. But social histories by necessity have catalogued or otherwise minimized beliefs in such a way that historians have ordinarily distinguished between inclusive social histories and relatively more exclusive histories of thought. (The rise and apparent decline of the writing of American social history have never been subjected to full historiographical treatment, perhaps because social histories have been even more amorphous than histories of thought, and perhaps also because the story is so integrally part of the writing of history generally.)

Whereas the names of social historians, from McMaster to Turner to the senior Schlesinger, are those of leading historians, most literary historians are known only to students of literature. Since Moses Tyler, studies in American literary history have generally been made by critics, members of English departments, or in any case by scholars not otherwise identified with the study of history. The obvious reason why scholars other than historians have written literary history is that special esthetic questions are involved. To the extent that esthetic themes are minimized, severely by a Parrington, less severely by an Alfred Kazin (*On Native Grounds*, 1942), to that extent literary history is appropriated by the history of ideas. It is thus only a matter of degree which makes most historians think of Parrington as a historian of ideas and Kazin as a literary historian. (Historians' judgments are so impressionistic in making such distinctions that one could reasonably suggest that Kazin's *On Native Grounds* might more likely be considered a history of ideas if Kazin's later work were not clearly literary criticism and if it were instead clearly intellectual history.) The line of literary historians who, chronologically between Tyler and Parrington, are not customarily considered to be engaged in the history of ideas, includes Charles Richardson (*American Literature, 1607-1885*, 2 vols., New York, 1886-1888); Barrett Wendell (*Literary History of America*, New York, 1900); George Woodberry (*America in Literature*, New York, 1903); John Macy (*The Spirit of American Literature*, New York, 1913); and Fred Lewis Pattee (*History of American Literature Since 1870*, New York, 1915).

The idea of modern science and the idea of scientific history influenced the writing of histories of ideas in Europe and in the United States, as it influenced the writing of all other kinds of histories during the later 1800's. I have suggested that admiration for "enlightened" scientific thought encouraged historians to write the success story of scientific or rational thought in conflict with traditional religion and irrationalism. Histories of ideas written from this viewpoint assumed the causal significance of human thought. This assumption was inconsistently joined with another, however, in writings stimulated by the dream of a scientific history of ideas.

For this dream was to locate scientifically the relationship between ideas and their environments, and the explicit emphasis was usually placed upon the determining nonintellectual environmental influences. Thus the idea of scientific history yielded an environmental interpretation of thought, as well as an inconsistent celebration of the autonomy of modern scientific thought.

CHAPTERS TWO AND THREE:

The Progressive Tradition in the Twentieth Century

In retrospect it appears that the progressive historians more nearly approximated a "school," or unified group with a coherent body of attitudes, than other historians in the United States before or since. This is said despite the individual qualities of the scholars discussed. Progressive historians, expressing what was in many respects a common viewpoint, seem to have been dominant throughout most of the first half of the twentieth century. This conclusion concerning their dominance is an impression based upon a reading of books, articles, and reviews during the period. The greatest prestige of progressive historians was reached between the two world wars.

Several excellent studies of individual progressive historians have been published (all are cited in the text). Questions which may still be profitably pursued concerning progressive historians are the same as those which should be pursued concerning intellectual progressivism generally: Can the change to progressive ideas be explained? Can the relationship between intellectual progressivism and political progressivism be described more precisely? What were the factors which were responsible for the transformation or decline of intellectual progressivism? (I am currently at work on a book which explores the impact of European totalitarianism upon American intellectuals during and after the 1930's.)

Questions of the success or failure of progressive ideas in coping with their early twentieth century world and in preparing for the mid-twentieth century world are controversial, and will continue to be so. Most recent studies of progressive thinkers, including historians, have been written by younger scholars, and have been critical of key progressive assumptions and viewpoints. It would be inaccurate, however, to interpret these criticisms as indications of deep hostility. These scholars are generally post-progressive rather than anti-progressive.

CHAPTER FOUR:

Challenges to the Progressive Tradition

In an earlier and briefer formulation of the themes presented in Chapters Two to Four, I suggested that Samuel Eliot Morison, Perry Miller, and Ralph Gabriel could be viewed as a "group" or "tradition" in opposition to the progressive historians. ("The Writing of American Histories of Ideas: Two Traditions in the XXth Century," *Journal of the History of Ideas*, xxv [April-June 1964], 257-278.) Chapter Four presents the writings of Morison, Miller, and Gabriel, as well as the publications of men who are not generally considered historians of American ideas; certain ideological currents in the climate of opinion are also presented as constituting a series of individual challenges to the one progressive tradition. Several readers of the earlier article, including John Higham, Henry May, and Robert Middlekauff, in different ways helped to persuade me that only the progressive historians were sufficiently similar to be called a school or tradition. Such labeling is, of course, hazardous at best. In my discussion of the writings of each scholar, I have tried to indicate the dissimilarities, as well as the similarities, to the writings of other scholars.

The most fundamental methodological challenge to the social and economic environmental interpretations of the progressive historians was the intensive analysis of the content and structure of ideas offered by a Perry Miller or an Arthur Lovejoy. And the most important fact concerning the Miller-Lovejoy challenge, viewed from the perspective of the history of the writing of histories of ideas, is that the reaction to the challenge has been ambivalent. Or, to put it more precisely, the "pure" intellectual analysis offered by Miller's *The New England Mind: The Seventeenth Century*, or by Lovejoy's *The Great Chain of Being*, has been received with mixed feelings by historians of ideas. Despite the praise frequently given by historians to these histories of thought, praise has seldom led to emulation. An example of the mixed feelings expressed by historians concerning Perry Miller's intensive analysis of thought can be found in Richard Schlatter's historiographical essay, "The Puritan Strain," in John Higham, ed., *The Reconstruction of American History*, New York, 1962, pp. 25-45. Schlatter praised Miller's two volumes of *The New England Mind* as being "unsurpassed in the whole corpus of American historical scholarship"— "models of what learned intellectual history should be." A greater compliment would hardly be possible. But Schlatter concluded his survey of Puritan histories by saying that they have been "too exclusively intellectual." Schlatter suggested that "the circumstances, the concrete times and places and social networks in which the thinkers lived" constituted "the American part of the story—the wilderness which produced the American modifications in the transplanted European intellectual system." Schlatter then endorsed the attempt of most contemporary Puritan scholars to escape "pure" histories of ideas.

Scholars who are most sympathetic to Miller's writings might say that the failure of historians to emulate his work can best be viewed as a revelation of the intellectual limitations of historians. For an eloquent statement of this view, see Edmund Morgan, "Perry Miller and the Historians," *The Harvard Review*, II (Winter-Spring 1964), 52-59. It is true of Perry Miller, as it is not true of any other historian I have discussed, that scholars most sympathetic to his books sometimes go so far as to say that Miller's scholarship is so superior to the work of others that it defies comparison. That is, Miller's writings are on these occasions said to be so superior as to be of a different order of scholarship. This was not said, to my knowledge, of Parrington or Beard or Curti even when the progressive historians' reputations were at their height between the two world wars.

American historians have tended to think that such intensive analyses of ideas as Miller's and Lovejoy's tend to leave the ideas too sterile and too removed from life. Thus, in their treatment of ideas, and in the choice of the ideas which they treat, American historians characteristically have related ideas to political, economic, and social life. The progressive historians commonly found the origin of ideas in the circumstances of daily life, but almost all American historians, whether or not they shared this progressive emphasis, have located the meaning and importance of ideas in their effect upon daily life.

CHAPTER FIVE:

*Signs of Convergence and New Directions
Since the 1940's*

The two most important histories of ideas written after
the Second World War conceived and executed in the
old style of "the grand sweep," were those of Commager and Persons, which are discussed at some length
in the text. Neither book has enjoyed the popularity of
earlier models. Exceeding all previous histories of ideas
in its all-inclusiveness, but restricted to the few years
immediately prior to American entry into the Great
War, is a recent book not discussed in the text, Henry
May's *The End of American Innocence*, New York,
1959. Symptomatic of most contemporary American
historians of ideas, May (born 1915) shortened the
time period under scrutiny to enable him to treat his
subject in more detail. The other historians discussed
in the final chapter, in addition to Commager and Persons, are treated only briefly. They are mentioned as
illustrations of certain (perhaps prematurely) suggested themes of contemporary scholarship. One suggested theme is the convergence of formerly divergent
characteristics in recent histories of ideas. Related to
this "convergence" is another theme—the treatment of
ideas as a part of political or topical histories. This
treatment is illustrated in the text only by the short discussions of the writings of Boorstin, Schlesinger, Jr.,
Hofstadter, and Goldman. The point is not that the
introduction of the interpretation of ideas into political
or topical histories is a brand-new phenomenon. But,
considering the pervasive interest in the study of ideas,
there have been since the war few old-style histories of
ideas. And, remembering Boorstin's, Schlesinger, Jr.'s,
and Hofstadter's first works (*The Lost World of*

Thomas Jefferson, Orestes A. Brownson, Social Darwinism in American Thought) one might have predicted that they would become the Parringtons of the postwar years. Instead, they have merged their interest in ideas into political or topical histories (Boorstin, *The Genius of American Politics* and *The Americans*; Schlesinger, *The Age of Jackson* and *Age of Roosevelt*; Hofstadter, *The American Political Tradition*, and *Age of Reform*).

The final theme suggested is that of interdisciplinary influences, least significantly from the social sciences and a concern with quantification, more significantly from the American Studies movement and a concern mainly with literary analysis. These interdisciplinary influences have also contributed to specialized studies.

INDEX

Index

Calhoun, John, 142-43, 227-30, 241
Callender, John, 10
Calvin, John, 235-36, 241
Carnegie, Andrew, 221:86n, 223
Cartwright, William, 302
Caruthers, William Alexander, 146
Casady, Thomas Edgar, 32:-57n
Caughey, John W., 148:46n, 291:3n
causal power and autonomy of ideas, in Beard, 95-98, 100-103, 105-108; in Becker, 121-22; in Buckle, 27-29; in Commager, 258-59; in Curti, 151-52, 165-69; in Draper, 25; in Eggleston, 59; in Gabriel, 222-24, 228-30, 235-37, 242-43; in Lovejoy, 254-55; in Miller, 187-92, 196-97, 210-11, 253-54; in Morison, 175-77, 181, 185-86; in Parrington, 135-39; in Persons, 269, 276; in Robinson, 79-80; in Tyler, 33-36, 43-46
Channing, Edward, 296
Channing, William Ellery, 127, 240
Charter for the Social Sciences in the Schools, A (Beard), 89
Chase, John W., 188:34n
Chauncy, Charles, 269
Christianity and Modern Thought (Gabriel), 213:-73n
Civil War, 127, 128:7n, 153, 215
Clark, John Bates, 221: 86n
Clay, Henry, 138, 142
Cochran, Thomas, 287:42n, 291
Cohen, Morris, 146:41n

Columbia Teachers College, 151
Columbia University, 69, 87, 88, 110
Colwell, James L., 124:1n
Commager, Henry Steele, 155:59n; 256-64, 310; on American diplomacy and the two world wars, 257-58; on Beard, 260-62; on causal power and autonomy of ideas, 258-59, 275-76; on civil liberties, 257-58; environmental interpretation of ideas, 260-62; ideas as instruments, 259-61; on James (William), 262-64; on Parrington, 257-59; on Persons, 274-76, 281; reaction to totalitarianism, 258, 262-64; sympathy for progressive education, 257; theoretical relativism, 261-62
Constitution, United States, 91-92, 102-103, 261-62
Cooper, James Fenimore, 146
Cornell College (Iowa), 110
Cornell University, 33, 110
Cotton, John, 37, 132, 144, 199, 268
Counts, George, 8:28n
Course of American Democratic Thought, The (Gabriel), 213, 218-42, 265, 271
Cowley, Malcolm, 148:46n, 245, 246:103n
Crafts, William, 146
creative thought, 78. *See also* causal power and autonomy of ideas
Croce, Benedetto, 99
Croly, Herbert, 89
Cromwell, Oliver, 198
Cross, Barbara, 250:110n
Cross, Robert, 250:110n
"Currents of Thought in His-

315